The Hedonics of Taste

THE
HEDONICS OF TASTE

Edited by
ROBERT C. BOLLES
University of Washington

LEA LAWRENCE ERLBAUM ASSOCIATES, PUBLISHERS
1991   Hillsdale, New Jersey   Hove and London

Lawrence Erlbaum Associates, Inc., Publishers
365 Broadway
Hillsdale, New Jersey 07642

Library of Congress Cataloging in Publication Data

The Hedonics of taste / edited by Robert C. Bolles.
    p. cm.
Includes bibliographical references and index.
ISBN 0-8058-0366-1
1. Taste.   2. Food habits—Psychological aspects.   3. Hedonism.
I. Bolles, Robert C.
BF261.H43   1991
152.1′67—dc20   90-22079
                                                         CIP

Printed in the United States of America
10 9 8 7 6 5 4 3 2 1

Contents

Preface

Promoting a cause is a tricky business. How does one sell a concept, especially one as old as hedonism? Does one push it as a revival, or as a brand new idea? Or should one take the middle road that it has been with us all along; it never left us. Down underneath we are all hedonists, and always have been. Without answering that one here, I will move on to another tactical question, which is whether one should push for the cause in a quiet, unthreatening way, or go for it in a grand manner, as Watson did with behaviorism. Let us begin by considering Watson's declaration-of-war approach.

You start with a broad theory, a general motivational theory based on hedonic principles. Then you argue how such a hedonic theory might be usefully applied in different areas of psychology. One might start with social psychology, an area that is notorious for studying phenomena that are theoretically curious but empirically unimportant, in the sense of accounting for very little variance. Consider cognitive dissonance, which is surely an interesting effect, but an effect that no one pretends accounts for more than 1% of the variance in behavior in any social situation. To get social psychology on the right track, it needs a hedonic theory, because the one thing we know for sure about people is that we like some folks a lot more than we like others. That is a robust phenomenon—a good starting point.

Cognitive psychology could use a dose of hedonic theory too. Remember that Charles Osgood once got into the question of meaning, and to get at this tough old nut he had a great number of subjects rate a great number of words on a great number of scales and then took his truckloads of punched cards off to the first great computer, the Illiac, to get the data factor analyzed. What the computer found was that there was one very large prime factor, which obviously had to be labeled good-bad. Then there were a couple of minor, hard to interpret factors, and everything else was noise. So it seems that Osgood long ago demonstrated to his cognitive colleagues the overwhelming importance of hedonics in the overall meaning of things. Unfortunately, no one was paying any attention, so it will probably have to be demonstrated all over again.

I am saying that one could go into hedonism on a massive scale, build a broad, general new theory of behavior, and try to sell the concept to everybody all at once. It is a tempting prospect; I can foresee wonderful consequences. But I am going to abstain, because I can also see troublesome consequences. So what I am going to do here is leave social and cognitive and all the other troubled areas of psychology to their own fates. Instead, I focus in on a narrow, relatively unpopular and unimportant corner of experimental psychology that is involved with the chemical senses. I will limit myself to the hedonics of taste.

There are good reasons for following such a restricted path. One is purely historical; in his chapter Booth observes that the word "hedonism" comes from the old Greek word for honey, the same word they used to describe a sweet taste. It seems appropriate somehow to begin the promotion of hedonic thinking in the realm where the word began, i.e., in the hedonics of taste. Second, this is a realm where a handful of experimenters survived and did research during the bad times when we might have lost hedonism altogether. And thanks to their noble commitment and effort, we have a substantial data base, and a bit of theory. Third, in the past decade or so quite a number of researchers have turned their attention to taste preferences, and so it seems appropriate to celebrate the fact that these new findings can be stuck into a very old conceptual framework that includes the ancient concept of hedonism.

The scientists who have contributed to this book have approached the hedonics of taste from many different angles. We start with a historical chapter, and a couple of chapters that discuss basic conceptual and methodological issues. Then different writers worry about developmental aspects, physiological substrates, and the social aspects of hedonics. We look at it functionally, comparatively, and clinically. A number of us look at the hedonics of taste from a learning point of view. Learning is vital because you and I and many animals must learn what, where, when, and how much to eat.

A lot of different types will be found here, dataphiles and theorists, mechanists and cognitivists, unifiers and disrupters; a lot of different folks are here. And sure enough, each of us has our own perspective. I seriously believe that the greatest glory of psychology is its tremendous diversity. The divergence of approaches and attitudes and issues and phenomena we work on obviously exerts strong centrifugal forces that tend to pull us apart. But even while that is true, our diversity somehow gives us great power to accomplish good things when we can all get together on something. And here we have all gotten together on something we share in spite of our differences, and that is an involvement for one reason or another with the hedonics of taste.

Robert C. Bolles

*Dedicated
to the memory of
Paul Thomas Young*

1 Hedonism

Robert C. Bolles
University of Washington

Hedonism is a very old concept; it has been around for about 25 centuries. Over the centuries its popularity and respectability have waxed and waned somewhat, and one thing I want to do in this chapter is document some of this coming and going. Perspective on these ups and downs seems desirable to help us all understand why, at the present time, the concept of hedonism seems to be on a healthy rise. These days it appears to be gaining in popularity and acceptability in the psychological community, and it would be nice if we could comprehend why this is happening. I think a bit of history is called for. Let me begin by anticipating the conclusion of my historical review. My conclusion is that everyone believes in some sort of hedonistic principle—unless there are compelling reasons at the moment for believing in some other set of principles. Hedonism is always true, but from time to time other doctrines are seen as more important.

THE BEGINNINGS OF HEDONISTIC THINKING

The origins of the idea are lost in antiquity. But we do know something about Democritus, who died about 370 BC, and who was an outspoken advocate. Unfortunately, only a few fragments of Democritus's writing survive, so our understanding of what he said about hedonism rests with reading his critics, such as Aristotle, who was not very sympathetic to the idea. Then there was Epicurus, who lived about a century later, and who formed a rather popular philosophical school in Athens. Some of his work has survived, and it shows him endorsing the mechanistic philosophy of atomism as well as the ethical doctrine of hedonism, both of which had come mainly from Democritus. Now there is no logical reason

1

why one could not be a cognitive hedonist, or, for that matter, a mechanistic stoic, but by and large that does not happen. For obscure reasons, almost all the early hedonists were mechanistic, in the style of Democritus, and almost all the stoics were cognitive, or spiritualistic, like Plotinus. The two sets of doctrines seem empirically to go together, as we will see.

Epicurus put it simply: Pleasure is good. Not only does it feel good, it is morally, ethically, and spiritually good. Pleasure is right and proper. The curse on mankind is pain, not just physical pain but also the sort of psychological pain that results from worrying about things. We tend to pain ourselves with anxiety about acquiring material things, and about our own ambitions. It is our concern with power and fame that makes us miserable. It is our fear of death and whatever else the gods may do to us that makes us tremble. And this pain, and anxiety, and misery, and trembling is ethically bad and morally wrong. Epicurus's proposal for fixing all our human troubles is that we should lead our lives in such a way as to maximize pleasure and minimize pain. In practice this means foregoing momentary pleasures and committing oneself to a modest and meaningful life of work and friendship. Pleasures of the body soon pass away; those of the mind endure. The desired contentment or peace of mind was called ataraxia.

It was a viable and rather popular ethical doctrine, according to the classic authority (Bailey, 1928), and it was promoted by several influential writers (see also Watson, 1895). However, it was roundly opposed by the Platonists, the neoplatonists, the stoics, Plotinus, and the early Church philosophers. And when it came to a contest between the hedonists and the Church, it is obvious after the fact who would win out. We who have grown up in the western world know that it all went to the Church; we have all learned that if something we do is pleasurable, it is probably sinful. We are supposed to suffer, and pleasure is bad. And as the Church took charge of human thought for a dozen centuries or so, hedonism virtually disappeared. The works of the hedonists were lost.

Then when the infidels were driven out of Europe in the 1500s their libraries were looted, and original Greek writings became available again. The works of Epicurus ultimately fell into the hands of one Pierre Gassendi, a French philosopher, who then devoted his life to the translation and promotion of Epicurus's ideas. His major publication (Gassendi, 1649) introduced the old Greek atomism as well as the venerable hedonism concept to a new age of intellectuals. The well established Aristotelian philosophy, and science, were crumbling. Galileo had turned his primitive telescope to Jupiter and seen its moons circling about. He had measured the speed of falling objects. Harvey had discovered how the blood circulates. The official, Aristotelian view of science was falling apart, and some alternative was desperately needed, according to Gassendi, and he was right there to provide it.

Gassendi's greatest importance, however, came from his friends: Mersenne the mathematician who kept in touch with all his friends, Descartes the brilliant if unbalanced philosopher, Hobbes the eccentric Englishman. These were the people who would initiate a new era of scientific and materialistic thought. Atomism would be a consistent part of the new approach, and it would be reflected in the work of Boyle, friend of both Hobbes and Locke, in the work of Newton, and in the work of most of the new innovative thinkers. Hedonism was another regular part of it. For example, John Locke took hedonism for granted. He said (Locke, 1690) that the immediate source of all our actions is some idea we have of pleasure (or pain). But here Locke was introducing a new kind of hedonism for us to think about, something different from what the Greeks had concerned themselves with.

PSYCHOLOGICAL HEDONISM

With Locke the concept of hedonism took a curious and important twist. In earlier times, it had been an ethical matter. Pleasure was ethically good. But for Locke it was a psychological principle. We *necessarily* act so as to maximize anticipated pleasure. Whether it is good or bad is of no consequence, it is the principle according to which we act, for better or for worse. Locke tells the story of a man in a tavern, a man we might think of as a drunkard. The man sits there and sees the glass of liquor and anticipates the pleasure of intoxication. Down it goes. Sitting next to the drunkard is a ''man of virtue.'' This gentleman sits there and sees the glass of liquor and he too anticipates the pleasure of intoxication. However, he also anticipates the pain of tomorrow's hangover. He abstains. It looks like a matter of virtue, something to do with human character.   But, no, Locke tells us, each man is just following the same simple hedonistic principle; both men are maximizing their pleasure. They differ only in what they see and can anticipate as future pleasures and pains. Morally, they are the same. Thus, hedonism after Locke was no longer an ethical doctrine, it had become a psycho-logical principle. It was no longer an issue of good or bad, but a proposition about why we act the way we do.

This new hedonism, which we may call *psychological hedonism,* was widely accepted. It was endorsed by Hume and Hartley and all the other associationists (whom we will get back to shortly). It was also endorsed, perhaps not as a universal explanatory principle, but at least as a rather general principle, by the likes of Thomas Reid (1764), who was too conservative to endorse any universal psychological rule. We should recall that Reid was a Christian, a Presbyterian minister, in fact. Reid's common sense position was that the human mind could not be bound by any rigid set of rules. But even so, everyone seemed to accept the psychological reality of the new hedonism, even if they were not yet willing to accept it as general law of psychology. We find many of the early psychol-ogists, or proto-psychologists, of the 19th century talking about the pleasure–pain principle. And we find many of their conservative, unpsychological con-temporaries talking about it too.

Hedonism was extended in several ways. Thus, Jeremy Bentham believed in the psychological principle, but he wanted to extend it to society, the law, and economic considerations. The just society, he said, is one that provides the greatest good (pleasure) to the greatest number of its citizens (Bentham, 1828). Like Hobbes (1651), his purpose was to show how to reform society, starting with simple psychological principles such as hedonism. One of Bentham's closest friends was James Mill, who had been schooled at Edinburgh in the common sense tradition of Reid, but who broke away from that tradition to be a rigid associationist (Mill, 1829). For Mill there were two psychological rules, associationism and the pleasure–pain principle. And that was all there was; Mill made it very simple.

Mill's son, John Stuart Mill, made it a little more complicated, and his close friend Alexander Bain, made it much more so, and a lot better (Bain, 1864). Bain saw behavior as determined in many different ways, but fundamentally, it is the idea of pleasure that controls our voluntary acts. Bain and the younger Mill collaborated in reviving and revising the older Mill's psychological treatise (Mill, 1869), which then had considerably more impact than it did back in 1829. Thus, by the 1860s psychological hedonism was back, and alive and well, and definitely in the public eye.

Here I have to digress to deal with another vital development. When Darwin (1859) began to argue for the continuity of man and beast (at that time woman was rather over on the beast side of the dichotomy so I better not say anything further about that), he had a young colleague named Romanes who believed wholeheartedly in continuity, and who sought to support his belief by gathering stories about the human qualities of thought and motivation demonstrated by animals (Romanes, 1882). He had a remarkable set of accounts, mostly of household pets, who, according to his stories, showed various human-like emotions, such as remorse, revenge, jealousy, and so on. They also demonstrated all sorts of intellectual abilities. In this latter regard he cited the case of a dog that, by his account, had sufficient "mechanical understanding" to be able to operate the latch of the front gate so that it could go out on the street. A lot of good people believed his stories and his conclusions. But there soon appeared one Lloyd Morgan (1894) to blow it all away.

Morgan's own dog was also able to open his front gate, but Morgan was more impressed with the stupidity, the rigidity and stereotypy of the behavior than by its evidence of intelligence. It seems that Morgan had been there to witness the dog "accidentally" opening the gate the first time. It had tried to stuff its face through the small hole surrounding the latch, thus evidencing very little mechanical understanding. After doing it hundreds of times the animal still displayed the same awkward behavior. Morgan saw little indication of what he could call intelligence in his dog's gate-opening behavior.

Morgan's conclusion from analyzing this and many other of Romanes' stories, as well as his own abundant observations, was that animals are not as human-like as one might suppose. Instead, he said, the evidence shows that animals are capable of simple associative learning, which gives them a lot of flexibility, and apparent intelligence. Morgan's simple associative learning was a very different kind of conceptual entity from Romanes' human-like intellectual faculties.

Morgan (1894) went on to examine the associative process more directly by means of an experiment, and it is, as far as I know, the first real experiment having anything to do with the hedonics of taste. Baby chicks, never before given food, were offered cinnibar caterpillars. The chicks began to eat them, but evidently cinnibars taste terrible. After beginning to eat, the chicks' reaction was head-shaking, bill-wiping, and backing away. The next day when offered cinnibars again, the young birds would not eat them, but showed head-shaking, bill-wiping, and so on. It is all just associative learning, Morgan said. The visual stimulus, which initially evokes eating, becomes associated with the taste of the cinnibar, and with the painfulness of the taste. So, upon being tested the next day the reaction was controlled by the associative learning occurring the day before, The visual impression had evidently gotten linked with the subsequent taste, and more importantly with the painful nature of the taste. Thus, for Morgan the hedonic consequence, the pain of the taste, became part of the learned associative structure. The painful expectation is part of what is learned. His account of the behavior was basically hedonistic: If the caterpillars had tasted better, the baby birds would have liked them and would have eaten them. The little birds' behavior was being controlled by their idea of pleasure and pain. Thus we see Morgan right where Bain was, and about where Locke had been! Just before the turn of the century we had in the pleasure–pain principle a popular and workable motivation concept. It was supported by a noble old philosophical tradition as well as by Morgan's experimental analysis. But we soon lost the hedonic concept.

THE DEMISE OF HEDONISM

The person who was most prominent in following up Morgan's animal learning ideas was E. L. Thorndike, whose work on cats in the puzzlebox appeared in 1898, but without any theory to go with the data. But when the theory appeared, in 1911, it was dazzling, a major coup. Thorndike said that hedonism was too mentalistic and should be replaced. He believed that the whole business of learning was very mechanistic (Thorndike could not resist commenting on what he assumed was going on in the neurones—neither could Freud, his contemporary, for whatever that is worth). He said that there was no evidence that his cats had learned anything intellectual, anything involving ideas. What the steady, gradual improvement over trials looked like to Thorndike was the operation of some sort of automatic, machine-like, stamping-in process that made a direct connection between the situational stimuli and the reinforced response. Thorndike (1911) argued that the hedonistic idea was no good, and that what was needed to explain animal learning was some sort of what he called the law of effect (the effect or consequence of the response is what matters) or what we would later call a reinforcement mechanism.

Thus, it is apparent that Thorndike sought to do away with hedonism as an explanatory device, and to replace it with a principle of reinforcement. It is not the pleasures of the future, or their anticipation, that control our behavior, he said, but the pleasures of the past (it was actually Troland, 1928, who made that neat distinction). The goodies of life do not pull us forward toward them, but rather guide us by having, in the past, built the strength of this or that behavior. Hedonism as an explanatory mechanism was about to be eclipsed by a reasonable alternative.

Next comes along John Watson, the Behaviorist, who thought that even Thorndike was too mentalistic. He understood that the reinforcement concept was fundamentally just a restatement of the hedonism concept; it was basically just a translation from the anticipation of future goodies to the remembrance of past goodies. Watson was too mechanistic to accept either alternative, so he just wiped out the whole thing, and introduced a contiguity model of learning (Watson, 1914). The stimulus and the response occurring together suffices, and no special event to follow, either a hedonic event or a reinforcer, is necessary to generate a learned association.

For a while Watson's view of the situation prevailed, but then for a number of reasons the reinforcement position began to regain currency. Thanks to Hull and Skinner becoming converts to the reinforcement position in the 1930s, and thanks to their enormous contributions to learning theory, the consensus shifted so that by 1950 or so reinforcement theory had come to prevail. By 1950 or so we were all reinforcement theorists (well, almost all of us were). At that point hedonism was virtually dead.

Hedonism had prospered 2500 years ago, and then was wiped out. It had disappeared because there appeared a large number of Christians, who believed in something else that was more important. Christians want to live forever, and the only way to do that is to forego worldly pleasures (Anon, 1611). For centuries there were all those Christians, who evidently wanted to be immortal, and who were willing to live in the most gruesome circumstances here and now to achieve that end. Then as serious, literal Christianity began to fade, reasonable, interesting alternative philosophies began to emerge. Hedonism popped up again with Gassendi, as we have seen, because it is a reasonable alternative. It gradually gained currency until the early 1900s, when something else emerged. The new thing was linked to the growing faith in the mechanistic philosophy. We began to believe that we did not need to think about psychological matters, things like pleasure and pain, and ideas like motivation, because the mechanism was now understood. And the mechanism was reinforcement, the automatic strengthening of S–R associations.

Hull was the scientist, and he was ready (Hull, 1943) to explain all behavior with a neat set of deductive principles, one of which was a law of reinforcement. Skinner was the engineer who was ready to build a better world, a utopia in fact, with a bunch of M & Ms. Everything would be put in order by appropriately reinforcing all the behaviors he wanted. The point is that by the 1960s hedonism was dead. Nobody believed in it because we had this more important alternative, the alternative of Thorndike and Hull and Skinner.

THE ECLIPSE OF REINFORCEMENT

It all looked very rosy for the reinforcement people by the middle of the 1960s. Operant conditioners were reaching out into the schools, the psychological clinic, the home, and everywhere that one person might wish to alter the behavior of someone else (which means everywhere). That was a healthy and important development. It also looked pretty good on the theory side of things. Numerous details of Hull's theory had not stood up very well, but the main lines of his theory were still intact. For some time, all through the 1960s, it looked like we had the right kind of theory; it was S–R, it explained almost all behavior in terms of learned S–R associations, and it all happened through reinforcement. Moreover the theory had been extended from its original domain, the rat laboratory, to the diverse areas of psychology. The S–R reinforcement theory reigned supreme in social, developmental, clinical, and human experimental psychology. Reinforcement theory had come to prevail in all of psychology. We had a paradigm, or something like it.

But then, going into 1970 or thereabouts, the wheels started falling off reinforcement theory. At this point I must take the reader aside and confess that I really enjoy telling this part of the story. However, I have told it a few times already (e.g., Bolles, 1975, 1979), so it does not seem right to tell it again. I could, and I would like to, but I won't. I will just give some citations to myself and some of my friends who just happened to be hanging around when the wheels came off. John Garcia (Garcia & Koelling, 1966) found that learning was not homogeneous; an animal will learn some things enormously easier than it learns other things, so reinforcement principles have to be augmented by other principles that have to do with the appropriateness, or the biological importance, of what is to be learned. Rescorla (1968) began to demonstrate convincingly that Pavlovian conditioning was not the mindless, mechanical kind of process that everyone had thought it to be. It seemed instead to involve curiously cognitive matters, such as the prediction and the expectation of forthcoming events. Jenkins (Brown & Jenkins, 1968) hinted at the notion that much of the pigeons' key-pecking behavior (the fundamental data base for operant conditioners) occurred for Pavlovian rather than operant reasons. Williams and Williams (1969) showed that this was indeed the case, and Jenkins has subsequently supported this conclusion in a number of studies. Bolles (1970) was able to make a case that reinforcement had little or nothing to do with avoidance learning in rats. Staddon (Staddon & Simmelhag, 1971) was able to show that reinforcement might have nothing to do with pigeons working in Skinner boxes, and that the whole business of schedules was probably misguided.

The reinforcement concept was suddenly in so much trouble that a few radicals (Bindra, 1972; Bolles, 1972) seriously proposed that there was no such thing as reinforcement. There was the widely used reinforcement *procedure,* to be sure, with which one might be able to change the behavior of one's charges, but the idea of a corresponding reinforcement *process* that caused behavior to change was a myth, we contended. It is interesting that the evidence that would ultimately take the whole enterprise apart came from a variety of people, several experimental procedures, and diverse considerations. But all these different lines of evidence appeared almost all at once right around 1970. While it is taking some more years to make the demise of reinforcement theory convincing and to win converts to the idea that reinforcement is dead (a basic part of a paradigm-shift), the beginning of the end of the reinforcement concept can be pinpointed rather sharply at 1970.

Part of the trouble with the reinforcement concept was that from the outset it was too mechanistic to deal adequately with psychological matters. It dated from the time of John B. Watson, a time when behaviorism was very serious business. By 1970 psychology had begun to show a much more cognitive face. That was part of the reason for the demise. Another part was that some of us began to free ourselves from the structuralistic constraints of pure associationism, and began to think about behavior in functional and evolutionary ways. In short, one of the things that made it possible to accept the loss of the reinforcement idea in particular, and the Hullian type of theory in general, was that we had some alternative ways of thinking about things.

How about hedonism, that grand old idea that was once wiped out by the Christians, only to arise again. What about hedonism, in opposition to which Thorndike had first offered us the reinforcement mechanism. What is the score on hedonism, which was wiped out again because at one time psychologists so much wanted to become mechanistic and "scientific." Is hedonism due to rise once more? Yes, I believe it is. I think we will see it become once again a reasonable proposition.

HEDONISM DURING THE DARK AGES

Here I want to fold back the history of the concept, partly to explore more fully how it got eclipsed, and partly to celebrate the remarkable fact that even when hedonism was out of style and quite unpopular there was a curious tradition of taste (and odor) research carried out by workers who held stubbornly to the outmoded hedonic perspective. Even when the Behaviorists were running rampant across psychology, trying to forbid such nonsense, there was a handful of free-spirited souls who were talking about hedonism. The opposition was formidable. Let us look back to examine it.

Watson (1914) admonished psychologists that it was his intention "to combat the idea that pleasure or pain had anything to do with habit formation." His warning was directed mainly at the introspectionists, particularly those in the tradition of the first psychologist, Wundt, who studied the contents of the mind. The self-appointed Wundtian spokesman who sought vigorously to lead American psychology in the introspectionist tradition was, of course, E. B. Titchener at Cornell. Titchener simplified Wundt's elaborate analysis of "feelings," which included pleasure and pain, in two ways. First, Titchener made it one dimensional; all feelings represented various degrees of good or bad. Anything else that might distinguish different feelings could be broken down into different sensory contents. It was mostly a matter of content. Then came a further simplification; Titchener (1924) said that good and bad feelings themselves could be broken down into different sensations arising from the body. Thus, it became *all* a matter of content. Surely there was nothing left of a motivational principle. Wundt had left that option open because he viewed his own system as "voluntaristic," even though he was little concerned with behavior itself. But Titchener gave up that option; he was exclusively concerned with the organization, or structure, or content of the mind. He was certainly not the least interested in behavior. Watson's admonition was not directed toward the structuralistic character of Titchener's psychology, indeed, he was a structuralist himself. What he went to war about was the subjective, introspective bent of Titchener's analysis. He rejected the mind, and with it went pleasure and pain. With it too went all motivational concepts. The mechanist, by and large, views things nonmotivationally, because that is all too mentalistic.

Reinforcement people also regard everything nonmotivationally. They have no use for hedonistic principles. Thus, Thorndike would have nothing to say about motivation until the 1930s. Watson never did say anything about it. Neither did Guthrie; he approached motivation much as Titchener had, reducing it all to a special class of stimuli that he called maintaining stimuli because they persisted to guide behavior until some behavior, such as eating, put an end to them. For his part, Pavlov (1927) admitted that his dogs had to be hungry before they would evidence any conditioning, but otherwise he attached no importance to motivation. It was a peculiarly structuralistic period, during which there was no place for such an old fashioned idea as that motivation had anything to do with behavior. Such a notion was much too mentalistic to be tolerated.

I want to emphasize that the same historical forces that produced the eclipse of hedonistic ways of thinking were also having a much bigger and broader effect on behavior theory: They led to the obliteration of all motivational thinking. It was not just hedonism; all kinds of motivational concepts were taboo during the dark ages. There was, however, a handful of heretics who talked openly about these tabooed subjects. Curiously, most of these people were at Harvard at one time or another. McDougall, the greatest of the heretics, was there for some years. James's student Holt was there early on, and Holt's student Tolman started from there. Tolman was vitally important, of course, in getting psychologists thinking about drive and incentive, and a variety of cognitive matters. Troland was also there until around 1930. Thus, there was this curious tradition of Harvard scholars who insisted on thinking about motivation at a time when almost no one else was. There was also, as we see next, a genuine hedonist there!

Harvard's hedonist was a rather shadowy character named J. G. Beebe-Center, who was there around 1930. (He is shadowy because it is so difficult to find out anything about him, like what years he was at Harvard.) He had subjects judge the attractiveness of odors or tones. He wrote a few papers and a book (Beebe-Center, 1932) that describes a mass of his own research plus a great variety of odds and ends of other work coming from the English-speaking world and Europe. The book is quite useful because it covers the hedonistic literature up to that time quite thoroughly. But Beebe-Center had no students of any consequence and his research was never followed up. He also produced nothing of theoretical importance for hedonism. And so when he was gone hedonism looked to be gone. It looked very much as though the whole enterprise begun by Epicurus twenty-something centuries ago had finally come to an end. It was surely on the brink of extinction. But no, there remained one hedonist, the man to whose memory this book is dedicated.

THE SOLITARY HEDONIST

The solitary hedonist came from what seems like a rather unlikely background. P. T. Young liked to refer to himself as Titchener's last student. His degree with the ultimate, antimotivational structuralist was 1918, and while Titchener lived another 9 years and had many later students, Young may have been the last believer. For a decade or so after getting his degree Young did Titchener-type research. Human subjects would smell different odorants, assess their pleasantness or unpleasantness, and also report on a variety of body sensations or other bits of consciousness. Young was also looking for physiological correlates of pleasant and unpleasant stimuli. All of this was legitimate work in the introspective tradition. But none of it was turning out very well. Pleasant feelings could arise in too many different ways, for purely sensory reasons or for quite psychological reasons (Young, 1936). These internal feelings did not lend themselves to the same sort of structural analysis that was possible with the perception of external stimuli. Then Young set out on a new tack, something new that his mentor, the old structuralist, would surely not have approved of; Young started studying hedonism in animals.

Later on (1961) Young could tell us that he rejected Titchener's purely structuralistic view of what was proper in psychology because of his deep conviction that in addition to having stimulus information value, stimuli also have emotional value. And that was the aspect he wanted to study. So he rebelled against his venerable teacher. A curious coincidence perhaps is that Titchener's *first* student, M. F. Washburn, was also a rebel who initially stuck with the faith (thus she translated Wundt's Ethics), but then strayed. Her most significant research was also with animals and she also became very interested in the motivation of their behavior. She was one of the first psychologists to study incentive motivation in animals, a concept closely allied to hedonics. Curious.

Young saw a number of advantages in studying emotional reactions to stimuli in animals. He could step aside from the old introspective question of whether his subjects were aware of their pleasure or how they perceived it. Rats either accepted a tasty solution or they rejected it. Consumatory behavior was so much simpler and more objective than the sort of data he had been obtaining from human introspectors. And he no longer had to try to tie it to physiological measures, or to anything else. Even so, he would no doubt have been delighted to know of the recent work of Grill (e.g., Grill & Norgren, 1978) showing that the rat makes faces to express its pleasure or displeasure at what it is consuming. Even Titchener would have liked that.

Young discovered that the acceptability of different tastes depends on the animal's history, whether, for example, a given taste has been associated with recovery from a deficiency. Thus, there is a learning factor. He also discovered that the acceptability of a solution depends on how the acceptance is measured. Thus, in a brief preference test rats like very concentrated sugar solutions, while on an overnight or 24-hr test they drink much more of sugars that are isotonic, about 8%. So there is a postingestive physiological factor.

These learning and physiological factors have to be worked out and understood before we can assess how much the rat likes a particular taste. The animal's emotional reaction to what it consumes is a wonderfully complex matter. Although the acceptance or rejection of a substance is the basic datum, we must have multiple measures under different conditions if we are to understand the basic mechanisms. And so Young had a research program. It kept him and his students busy for more than 30 years, from the late 1920s on into the 1960s. At the beginning of this period no one else was interested in these questions. By the end of it a lot of people were running rats on sugar solutions, or on recently invented saccharine, or on salt solutions. At the start of the Young era, almost no one was thinking about any sort of motivation principles, but by the time Young retired, a lot of people were thinking about incentive motivation (i.e., motivation that depends on the stimulus properties of things in the environment such as how good something tastes). By the end of his research career there were even a few other hedonists (e.g., Pfaffman, 1960). He gave us much of the original normative data on what rats like and dislike. Some of his old conclusions have been wrinkled somewhat by more recent investigations, but that is just the way Young knew it would be. That is perhaps why he did not take his own conclusions very seriously; he was more serious about the methods and procedures for studying hedonics.[1]

The big picture shows that hedonism is coming back because motivation came back some years ago (it was needed to explain behavior) and because reinforcement has succumbed more recently (it failed to provide the promised explanatory mechanism). On a smaller scale, it appears that all of us who write these chapters are much indebted to P. T., the solitary hedonist.

REFERENCES

Anon. (1611). *Holy Bible.*

Bailey, C. (1928). *The Greek atomists and Epicurus.* Oxford: Clarendon.

Bain, A. (1864). *The senses and the intellect,* 2nd edition.

Beebe-Center, J. G. (1932). *The psychology of pleasantness and unpleasantness.* New York: Van Nostrand.

Bentham, J. (1828). *The utilitarian world.*

Bindra, D. (1972). A unified account of classical conditioning and operant training. In A. H. Black & W. F. Prokasy (Eds.), *Classical conditioning II: Current research and theory.* New York: Appleton.

Bolles, R. C. (1970). Species-specific defense reactions and avoidance learning. *Psychological Review, 77,* 32–48.

Bolles, R. C. (1972). Reinforcement, expectancy and learning. *Psychological Review, 79,* 494–409.

Bolles, R. C. (1975). Learning, motivation, and cognition. In W. K. Estes (Ed.), *Handbook of learning and cognitive processes.* Hillsdale, NJ: Lawrence Erlbaum Associates.

Bolles, R. C. (1979). *Learning theory.* New York: Holt.

Brown, P. L., & Jenkins, H. M. (1968). Auto-shaping of the pigeon's key-peck. *Journal of the Experimental Analysis of Behavior, 11,* 1–8.

Darwin, C. (1859). *The origin of species.*

Garcia, J., & Koelling, R. A. (1966). Relation of cue to consequence in avoidance learning. *Psychonomic Science, 4,* 123–124.

Gassendi, P. (1649). *The life and death of Epicurus.*

Grill, H. J., & Norgren, R. (1978). The taste-reactivity test. I. Mimetic responses to gustatory stimuli in neurologically normal rats. *Brain Research, 143,* 263–269.

Hobbes, T. (1651). *The leviathan.*

Hull, C. L. (1943). *Principles of behavior.* New York: Appleton.

Locke, J. (1690). *An essay concerning human understanding.*

---

[1]One of the most interesting and challenging of the many conceptual issues that Young dealt with is whether the acceptability of a foodstuff, the mere fact that the animal consumed it avidly, could be taken as evidence that the animal liked it, that it aroused some affective reaction, and that it had hedonic value. As we have seen, Young settled this question affirmatively 60 years ago; acceptability meant affect. But his simple resolution of the question has not stuck. Some of the present writers appear to go along with Young's approach, but other writers balk at this easy way out. These skeptics want some further evidence of an emotional reaction, some indication that the animal really likes the stuff, before they will accept consumption as a matter of hedonics. Young's old question is still a very interesting one.

Mill, J. (1829). *Analysis of the phenomena of the human mind.* Annotated 2nd edition, 1869.

Morgan, C. L. (1894). *Introduction to comparative psychology.*

Pavlov, I. P. (1927). *Conditioned reflexes.* Translated by G. V. Anrep. London: Oxford University Press.

Pfaffman, C. (1960). The pleasures of sensation. *Psychological Review, 67,* 253–268.

Reid, T. (1764). *Inquiry into the human mind.*

Rescorla, R. A. (1968). Probability of shock in the presence and absence of CS in fear conditioning. *Journal of Comparative and Physiological Psychology, 66,* 1–5.

Romanes, G. J. (1882). *Animal intelligence.*

Staddon, J. E. R., & Simmelhag, V. L. (1971). The "superstition" experiment: A reexamination of its implications for the principles of adaptive behavior. *Psychological Review, 78,* 3–43.

Thorndike, E. L. (1898). Animal intelligence: An experimental study of the associative process in animals. *Psychological Review Monograph Supplement, 2* (No. 8).

Thorndike, E. L. (1911). *Animal intelligence.* New York: Macmillan.

Titchener, E. B. (1924). *A text-book of psychology.* New York: Macmillan.

Troland, L. T. (1928). *Fundamentals of human motivation.* New York: Van Nostrand.

Watson, J. (1895). *Hedonistic theories from Aristippus to Spencer.*

Watson, J. B. (1914). *Behavior: An introduction to comparative psychology.* New York: Holt.

Williams, D. R., & Williams, H. (1969). Auto-maintenance in the pigeon: Sustained pecking despite contingent non-reinforcement. *Journal of the Experimental Analysis of Behavior, 12,* 511–520.

Young, P. T. (1936). *Motivation of behavior.* New York: Wiley.

Young, P. T. (1961). *Motivation and emotion.* New York: Wiley.

2 Taste, Smell, and Pleasure

Linda M. Bartoshuk
Yale University School of Medicine

Taste and smell are often considered to be closely related. We have a term to describe the combination of the two: flavor. In many areas of experimental psychology as well as in ordinary life, we treat flavor as if it were a single sensory attribute. We see flavor used as a cue in experiments on learning and we speak of good and bad flavors in cuisine. Yet taste and smell have different characteristics. An appreciation of the differences provides insight into what must be one of the major functions of the chemical senses: the selection of appropriate nutrients.

Taste identifies a few specific nutrients in a variety of foods while olfaction is tuned to identify food objects, not nutrients per se. Both taste and smell sensations produce affect as well as information. The affect of taste is present at birth and can be modulated by body state. The affect of smell is not present at birth but can be acquired through pairing of odors with affective experiences. The evidence for these statements follows.

LOCATION OF RECEPTORS AND THE LOCALIZATION OF SENSATION

Taste receptor cells form clusters much like the segments of an orange. These orange-like structures are the taste buds. Taste buds are buried in the tissue of three different kinds of visible structures on the tongue called papillae. The fungiform papillae look like tiny button mushrooms and are located on the tip and the front edges of the tongue. The foliate papillae look like a series of parallel lines on the rear edges of the tongue. The circumvallate papillae are large circular structures located in an inverted V on the rear of the tongue. These three papillae types are laid out in the shape of an oval on the tongue. The density of taste buds is greatest on the edges and diminishes toward the center. The center of the tongue is virtually devoid of taste. In addition to the taste buds buried in papillae on the tongue, there are taste buds on the roof of the mouth (at the boundary between the hard and soft palates) that are not in papillae.

We are subjectively unaware of the location of these receptors. This failure to localize taste seems to occur because the brain uses touch to obtain localization information. That is, when taste sensations occur along with touch sensations in the mouth, the brain localizes the taste to the areas touched. Stroking from the tip of the tongue to the center with a Q-tip saturated in a strong taste solution will demonstrate this. The taste will seem to fill the path of the Q-tip (Bartoshuk et al., 1987).

Olfactory sensations during eating or drinking seem to come from the mouth even though the olfactory receptors are at the top of the nasal cavity, just under the eyes. The only time olfactory sensations are localized in the nasal cavity is when we inhale a pungent agent like horseradish. In this case we feel the path the volatiles take on their way to the olfactory receptors because tactile receptors in the lining of the nose are stimulated. During normal eating, odors go from the mouth into the nasal cavity and up to the olfactory receptors. Since there are no localization cues, the entire experience is localized to the mouth where the touch is experienced. Rozin (unpublished data) demonstrates this with a flavorless gum chewed while chocolate odor was pumped into the mouth intermittently. For at least some subjects, the gum seemed to taste chocolate whenever the odor was present.

PATHOLOGIES

Olfaction.   The olfactory nerve divides into small nerve bundles that pass through small holes in a fragile bone (the cribiform plate) on their way to the brain. Head injuries that fracture this bone can sever the olfactory neurons. Although the neurons are capable of regeneration from the periphery, scar tissue that forms over the holes in the cribiform plate appears to block their progress back to the brain. In addition to trauma, the olfactory nerve can be damaged by viruses and toxins (possibly by direct invasion of the nerve). Finally, polyps growing inside the nose can block the olfactory cleft through which odorants must pass to reach the receptors. The vulnerability of the olfactory system results in both anosmia (total inability to smell) and hyposmia (reduced ability to smell).

Taste.   The taste system is more robust than the olfactory system as measured by real-world performance. However, this stability does not mean that the taste system does not suffer damage. If damage is localized, then patients often fail to notice any losses.

The failure to experience taste loss from localized damage results from two factors. First, when taste is abolished on one area, taste intensities appear to increase on the remaining areas. This was shown first by anesthesia experiments. Halpern and Nelson (1965) showed that in the rat neural responses from the back of the tongue actually increased when the nerve innervating the front of the tongue was anesthetized. They interpreted this as a release of inhibition. A similar result was obtained by Ostrum, Catalanotto, Gent, and Bartoshuk (1985) with human subjects and dental anesthesia. When taste was abolished on the front of one side of the tongue with dental anesthesia, taste intensities of a variety of stimuli were either unchanged or increased. Nerves innervating various areas of the tongue appear to exert inhibition on one another (possibly in the CNS). When one nerve is temporarily anesthetized, it no longer contributes to the overall taste experience but it also no longer inhibits the other nerves.

A case of Ramsey-Hunt's Syndrome provided additional evidence for this interpretation. This disorder is caused when the chicken pox virus reactivates and damages a variety of cranial nerves on one side of the body. In one individual (Bartoshuk, Pfaffmann, & Catalanotto, 1989; Pfaffmann & Bartoshuk, 1989) taste was completely lost on the side affected although the patient had no subjective awareness of any taste loss. Localized testing (Bartoshuk, 1989) showed that tastes were perceived to be unusually intense on the unaffected side. When the damaged taste nerves began to regenerate, the unaffected side showed decrements in taste. We suggest that as the affected nerves regenerated, they regained their ability to inhibit the other side.

The second factor preventing patients from experiencing localized taste losses is the localization illusion (noted above). The illusion was demonstrated in the patient with Ramsey-Hunt's Syndrome by "painting" a taste solution across the front of the tongue from the unaffected to the affected side. The taste sensation invaded the damaged area (Bartoshuk, Pfaffmann & Catalanotto, 1989).

GENETIC VARIATION

Taste. Some individuals are taste blind for certain bitter compounds including PTC (phenylthiocarbamide) and PROP (6-n-propylthiouracil), as well as relatively insensitive to other bitter compounds like caffeine (Bartoshuk, 1979; Fischer, 1967; Fox, 1932; Harris & Kalmus, 1949; Lawless, 1980). These nontasters carry two recessive genes for this trait. Tasters may be either heterozygous or homozygous for the dominant gene. Nontasters show reduced sensitivity to some sweet compounds (including sucrose) as well as for the bitter compounds (Gent & Bartoshuk, 1983).

Olfaction.   Androstenone does not smell the same to everyone. Some do not perceive it at all, others perceive a floral odor, and still others perceive a urinous odor (Gilbert & Wysocki, 1987). A variety of other odorants show variation in the intensity of the perceived odor. The genetic contribution to this variation is not known.

THE TUNING OF TASTE AND SMELL

Taste.   Taste quality names (sweet, salty, sour, and bitter) are abstract terms that can be used as metaphors because of their value connotations. For example, the value expressed by ''she is a sweet person'' or ''he has a bitter outlook on life'' is unambiguous.

The idea of four basic tastes emerged in the 19th century. Two great psychophysicists in Europe battled over the relation among the four taste qualities. One of them, Kiesow (1896), believed that the taste qualities were analogous to colors in vision. His views persuaded a variety of American psychologists who later wrote influential texts. These Americans had access to Kiesow's views because they, as well as Kiesow, were students of Wilhelm Wundt in Leipzig. Öhrwall, a Swedish psychophysicist believed that the four taste qualities were independent enough of one another to be considered four separate senses. Öhrwall (1901) argued that the four taste qualities together make up taste much as touch, temperature, and pain make up the skin senses.

Modern research supports Öhrwall's position on the independence of the four taste qualities. For example, the four tastes can be independently manipulated via cross adaptation (McBurney & Bartoshuk, 1973). That is, adaptation to a substance of one taste quality has little effect on the taste of a substance with a different taste quality. In addition, phenomena that might seem most likely to show relations among the qualities instead show that taste qualities retain their integrity. For example, the taste modifiers once believed to transmute one quality into another, can now be seen to have their effects by modifying only one quality. Exposing the tongue to *Gymnema sylvestre* (Bartoshuk et al., 1969) reduces or abolishes sweetness. Exposing the tongue to Miracle fruit or *Synsepalum dulcificum* (Bartoshuk et al., 1969, 1974) adds a sweet taste to acids.

Mixture interactions do not involve qualitative changes either. Mixing substances of two different qualities usually results in the reduction of both qualities but both still retain their qualitative identity.

The debate between Kiesow and Öhrwall has a parallel in the debate over fiber types in the neurophysiology of taste. Pfaffmann (1955) working on the cat and the rat, initially believed that there were no fiber types but later work on a greater variety of species showed considerable evidence for fiber types (Frank, 1973; Pfaffmann, 1974; Scott & Chang, 1984). These may mediate the four basic tastes experienced by human subjects.

Olfaction.   Olfactory quality names are concrete. Olfactory quality terms derive from the name of the object that emits the odor (e.g., smoky, chocolate, vanilla, lemon, minty). Perhaps the most dramatic difference between taste and olfactory qualities concerns the number of qualitatively different sensations possible. Taste qualities in addition to sweet, salty, sour, and bitter have been proposed (e.g., metallic, alkaline) but even these modest additions are controversial. Olfactory qualities, on the other hand, are so numerous that virtually no two experts agree on a list.

The relations among various olfactory qualities is less clear in olfaction than in taste. Is there some fundamental set of elemental qualities from which all others can be derived as combinations of the elements? Cain (1987) argues for olfactory "templates in memory" which represent specific mixtures experienced. This is discussed further shortly.

Olfactory neurophysiology offers no clues about the mediation of possible elementary odors. Olfactory fibers do not fall into simple categories that suggest elemental odors.

PROCESSING OF MIXTURES: THE KEY
TO THE FUNCTIONS OF TASTE AND SMELL

Taste.   Few stimuli in the real world are simple. Thus the way in which we process complex stimuli determines the usefulness of the senses. Early approaches to the perception of complex stimuli identified two types of sensory mixtures: analytic and synthetic. In analytic mixtures, the identity of the components is retained in the mixture. Playing a high, medium, and a low note on a piano provides an example of an analytic auditory mixture. All three frequencies can be identified. In synthetic mixtures, the identity of the components fuse into a qualitatively new sensation. Mixing colors with a color wheel (or by mixing lights) provides an example of a synthetic mixture. The identity of the components is lost and the color of the resulting mixture is qualitatively distinct from the component colors.

Taste mixtures have been treated as analytic by most psychophysicists. Von Skramlik (1922) even studied the duplication of complex tastes with mixtures of substances that tasted sweet, salty, sour, and bitter. It is easy to demonstrate that subjects can identify the components of mixtures of substances with simple tastes (Bartoshuk, 1975). However, Erickson and Covey (1980) argued that taste was nonetheless synthetic. They asked subjects to taste a variety of pure compounds as well as mixtures constructed from pairs of the compounds. Subjects were asked to classify each taste as unitary or not unitary; they described some of the mixtures as unitary. Although this might seem to suggest that the subjects perceived a new fused taste, this is not the case. The subjects were not asked to describe the unitary taste. If they had been, other studies suggest (Szczesiul,

Grill, & Bartoshuk, 1987) that they would have named the typical quality of the stronger component in the mixture. The components in the Erickson and Covey study were not equated for perceived intensity. This permitted the weaker component to disappear through mixture suppression (Bartoshuk, 1975; Lawless, 1979; Pangborn, 1960).

The analytic nature of taste is important in any consideration of the function of the taste sense. The following discussion considers evidence that taste serves to identify specific beneficial nutrients in foods. Those nutrients are sodium and sugar and these are labeled by the salty and sweet taste qualities. Further, taste serves to identify potential poisons. These are labeled by the bitter quality.

Olfaction.   Olfactory mixtures show some similarity to those of taste but also show fascinating differences. For example, some two-component olfactory mixtures have been shown to be analytic (Laing, Panhuber, Wilcox, & Pittman, 1984). However, of paramount importance, the olfactory domain contains many more qualitatively distinct sensations than that of taste. For any given individual there may be many odors that have not been encountered. Even relatively familiar odors may be hard to name (Cain, 1984). Further, our real-world experience is usually with complex olfactory mixtures. Although we have at least some analytic ability (and the master perfumer may have many occasions to use it), we also have the ability to process olfactory stimuli holistically (Cain, 1987). Cain has suggested that we build up a library of templates for salient odor mixtures. When we encounter a particular mixture that fits one of the templates, we can identify it. This serves to identify the object that produced it. In the case of food, olfaction permits us to identify food objects. Note that olfaction is not tuned to the identification of nutrients per se but rather to the foods that contain the nutrients.

THE AFFECT OF TASTE AND SMELL

Affect seems to be an intrinsic part of taste and smell experience. However, contrast the universality of the liking for sweet and the dislike for bitter with the variability of liking for some odorants like butterscotch. The affect of taste is present at birth but the affect of smell is not.

Taste.   Some of the most elegant evidence that the affect of taste is present at birth comes from studies of facial expressions in human neonates (Jacobs, Smutz, & DuBose, 1977; Rosenstein & Oster, 1988; Steiner, 1977) As well as the newborn of other species (Ganchrow, Oppenheimer & Steiner, 1979; Jacobs, Smutz, & DuBose, 1977). The evidence is the clearest for sweet and bitter. If a drop of sugar is placed on the tip of the newborn's tongue, the facial expression is described as "resembling an expression of 'satisfaction' " accompanied by a "slight smile" and "eager licking of the upper lip." If a drop of quinine is placed on the tip of the tongue, the facial expression is described as "a typical arch form opening of the mouth with the upper lip elevated, the mouth angles depressed, and the tongue protruded in a flat position" often "followed by spitting or even by the preparatory movements of vomiting" (Steiner, 1977).

Neonatal responses to NaCl are ambiguous. However, developmental work with sheep (Mistretta, 1981) led to the insight that in some species the ability to taste NaCl develops after birth. Work with rats shows that the affect for NaCl is present at the rat's first encounter with salt (Nachman & Cole, 1971). The classic paper of Wilkins and Richter (1940) showed a salt craving in a young boy who needed sodium as the result of adrenal insufficiency. The parent's description of the boy's behavior toward salty foods, suggests that he liked them on initial exposure to the salty taste.

Olfaction.   Olfactory affect is not present at birth. Lipsitt, Engen and their colleagues (cited in Engen, 1979, 1982) performed a delightful experiment with 1- and 2-year-old children that demonstrated the children's affective indifference to odors. The children were seated in front of a table containing several toys. Odorants were delivered through holes in a screen located behind the toys. The mother as well as observers behind a one-way mirror classified the reactions of the children as expressing pleasure, displeasure, or neutrality. The odors tested included two that were pleasant and two that were unpleasant by adult evaluation. Forty percent of the children failed to show affect to any of the odorants. Even excluding these children, analyzing the remaining data did not produce significant differences among the odorants. But by the age of three, children have begun to acquire affect similar to that of adults (Schmidt & Beauchamp, 1988).

Liability of the Learned Affect of Olfaction.   The affect associated with taste and that associated with smell are modifiable by experience but olfactory affect is more labile. Simple exposure is sufficient to change the affect associated with odors (Cain, 1979; Cain & Johnson, 1978). For example, exposure to citral (lemon smell) reduced its pleasantness while exposure to isobutyric acid (rancid smell) reduced its unpleasantness (Cain & Johnson, 1978). Social factors can also change the affect of odors (Birch, 1980, 1987; Galef, 1979; Kirk-Smith & Booth, 1987).

Conditioned preferences have been experimentally produced by pairing odors with pleasurable experiences like sweet taste or calories (e.g., Booth, Lee, & McAleavey, 1976; Zellner, Rozin, Aron, & Kulish, 1983). Conditioned aversions have been studied extensively by learning theorists. This negative affect is produced when a flavor is experienced in association with nausea (Pelchat, Grill, Rozin, & Jacobs, 1983). In rats, taste aversions are believed to be easier to condition than smell aversions (Palmerino, Rusiniak, & Garcia, 1980).

Conditioned aversions in humans have a longer history. Clinicians interested in finding methods of helping alcoholics utilized conditioned aversions as early as the 1930s (Lemere & Voegtlin, 1940; Voegtlin, 1940). Individuals form conditioned aversions to many foods and beverages under the normal conditions of life (Bernstein & Webster, 1980; Garb & Stunkard, 1974; Logue, Ophir, & Strauss, 1981). Just as with other species, the key element in the conditioning is the association of a flavor with nausea (Pelchat & Rozin, 1982). An analysis of the foods to which aversions generalize suggests that the aversions are more likely to be formed to the olfactory components than to the taste components of the flavor (Bartoshuk & Wolfe, unpublished data). If the purpose of a conditioned aversion is to prevent ingestion of a food previously associated with illness, then conditioning an aversion to an odor which labels the food makes good sense.

Dependence of Taste Affect on Metabolic State.   Cabanac (1971) coined the term "alliesthesia" to describe hedonic changes produced by changing the state of the body. For example, the palatability of sweetness diminishes after consumption of sugar (Cabanac, Minaire, & Adair, 1969), while it increases after the injection of insulin (Jacobs, 1958; Mayer-Gross & Walker, 1946; Rodin, Wack, Ferrannini, 1985). The palatability of saltiness is also related to body state. Deprivation of NaCl increases the palatability of saltiness while consumption of NaCl decreases it (Beauchamp & Cowart, 1985; Pfaffman, 1959).

Surprisingly little information is available about changes in odor affect associated with changes in metabolic state. When affect is acquired by an odorant does the affect retain the properties of the previous situation? Cabanac (1971) showed that the pleasantness of orange odor was reduced after consumption of sucrose. Thus the affect of orange behaved the way the affect of sweetness behaves. Orange odor is paired with sweetness in our culture. If the pleasantness of the orange had been acquired in some other way (e.g., pairing with a positive emotional experience), would the affect depend on metabolic state?

WISDOM OF THE BODY

Origin of the Idea.   The body has automatic mechanisms that allow us to adapt to a variety of circumstances (e.g., the heart beats faster when we increase voluntary activity). Starling (1923) used the phrase "wisdom of the body" to title a Harvey lecture on these mechanisms. Cannon (1939) used the phrase as the title for his famous book on homeostasis out of respect for Starling. Richter (1942–43) extended this idea to the behavioral realm and suggested that bodily needs requiring resources that had to be sought in the environment might produce cravings for the needed substance that would motivate the search.

The Clara Davis studies of the 1930s showing that human infants will select an array of foods that provide the essential nutrients, seemed to support Richter's idea. Further, Richter (1936, 1942–43) did a series of studies on "specific hungers" that provided evidence for the existence of specific hungers for certain nutrients. This very reasonable, even elegant formulation ultimately proved to be wrong. Looking back at this literature, the distinctions between taste and smell prove important.

A specific hunger mechanism requires that the nutrient of interest produce a sensation that can be detected by the organism that needs it. An examination of the tastes and smells of the macro and micronutrients as well as poisons is thus important.

Micronutrients. Micronutrients consist of vitamins and minerals. Some vitamins have tastes (sour or bitter for the most part) and some have characteristic odors but only in high concentrations. At the concentrations in which they occur in foods, vitamins are essentially tasteless and odorless.

Minerals have tastes when they are in the form of salts. The tastes of salts are easily described. Small cations like lithium and sodium taste salty. Cations larger than sodium (e.g., potassium, calcium, etc.) taste bitter as well as salty. The bitterness of some of these cations is greater for tasters of PTC/PROP (Bartoshuk, Rifkin, Marks, & Hooper, 1988). For large, complex cations (e.g., saccharin) the charge matters less and the structure, more. The complex cation may taste either bitter or sweet depending on the structure. These bitter and sweet tastes may also be more intense to tasters of PTC/PROP (Bartoshuk, 1979; Bartoshuk et al., 1988).

Small anions have little taste themselves and have little effect on the tastes of cations. As the size of the anion increases, it becomes capable of exerting inhibition on the tastes of the cation (Bartoshuk, Rifkin, & Speers, 1980; Beidler, 1953). Like the cation, when the anion is large and complex, its charge is no longer the critical factor and it may taste either bitter or sweet depending on its structure.

Macronutrients. Macronutrients consist of proteins, carbohydrates, and fats. Proteins are usually tasteless and odorless. The apparent odor of the proteins we consume (e.g., bacon, beef, fish) is produced by small amounts of volatiles mixed with the protein (often present in the fat). Fats have essentially no taste and no smell. Carbohydrates include starch and sugars. Starch has no taste and no smell to humans but may have a taste to rats (Sclafani & Mann, 1987).

There are many sugars but only a few are sweet. Sucrose, glucose, and fructose are the sweetest sugars. Sweetness has been the subject of a great deal of research (e.g., Dobbing, 1987). Sweetness appears to be mediated through more than one type of receptor site (see Bartoshuk, 1987, for a review of this issue). This permits the genetic variation in the perceived intensities of sweeteners noted earlier. The artificial sweeteners so important in our current food world are not all sweet to other species. Of particular interest, aspartame is sweet only to higher primates (Hellekant, Glaser, Brouwer, & Van der Wel, 1981). The existence of multiple receptor sites for sweetness permits the fine-tuning of the sweet sense. A general receptor site that would be responsive to all sugars would be biologically unwise since we can metabolize only a few sugars. The system we have, renders sweet only those sugars that are biologically valuable.

Antinutrients.   One final class of nutrients should be considered. Poisons are substances that interact with our physiologies in a deleterious fashion. Although there are many exceptions, poisons tend to taste bitter. This suggests that the bitter sense may have evolved as a primitive poison detector. Bitterness, like sweetness, is mediated by multiple receptor site types (McBurney & Bartoshuk, 1973; McBurney, Smith, & Shick, 1972). The existence of multiple bitter sites permits us to taste as bitter many chemically different compounds. Because poisons have a variety of chemical structures, a poison detection system would have to have the capacity to respond to this chemical diversity.

Role of Taste and Smell in Nutrition.   The only nutrients that have tastes that could be used to identify them are sodium (salty), sugar (sweet) and poison (bitter). No nutrients have smells that could be used to identify them. However, *foods* have smells that can be used to identify them.

Incidentally. the present formulation draws attention to the taste quality sour. If the taste system evolved to be the sensory system that mediates true wisdom of the body, then what is the function of sourness? Posing this question to colleagues has produced a variety of possibilities. The ability to taste sour might have evolved to protect the mouth from acids or to label unripe fruit, or to label the presence of vitamin C; however, none of these possibilities are as compelling as the obvious functions associated with salty, sweet, and bitter. Sourness may simply be the result of acid sensitivity built into early membranes.

NUTRITIONAL FUNCTIONS OF TASTE AND SMELL

The chemical senses provide both the information and the affect to direct our selection of appropriate nutrients. Taste allows us to analyze our foods for the presence of sodium, sugar, or poison. The pleasantness of salty and sweet is present at or near birth and is affected by body need. This is true wisdom of the body as Richter originally envisioned it. Smell allows us to holistically identify foods. Odors take on affect by pairing with affective experiences. This is a kind of wisdom of the body also but it operates through learning.

Neither of these two wisdoms of the body are foolproof but their flaws are not the same. The taste-mediated body wisdom goes awry with certain disease states. For example, individuals with hypertension should limit salt intake and individuals who are obese may find that they must limit sugar intake. These body needs do not diminish the innate pleasantness of salty and sweet.

The olfaction-mediated wisdom of the body can go awry because the learned affect may not necessarily lead to beneficial food choices. For example, perhaps because chocolate is paired with fat, starch, and sugar in desserts, it becomes highly preferred, yet chocolate can produce migraine headaches in susceptible individuals (Blau & Diamond, 1984; Hanington & Harper, 1968). Conditioned aversions may form to healthy foods eaten before or during a gastro-intestinal illness. Odors associated with calories become pleasant whether an individual needs the calories or needs to lose weight.

Note that most of the problems associated with liking foods that are not solved by our body's wisdom (innate or learned) involve overconsumption. Mechanisms that evolved in times when nutrients were scarce might not include shut off mechanisms to prevent overconsumption. In addition to this, we must note that the nutritional diseases of overconsumption are chronic diseases. Evolution is not likely to provide mechanisms to prevent chronic diseases because they occur after the reproductive years. The innate, taste-mediated wisdom of the body solves acute problems like the need for NaCl to correct sodium-water balance, the need for glucose fuel, and the need to avoid poisons. The learned olfaction-mediated wisdom of the body solves moderately acute problems like getting vitamins, minerals and calories.

In spite of the failure of these mechanisms to provide long term nutritional guidance, both wisdoms of the body contribute to the remarkable ability of the omnivore to select a beneficial diet.

REFERENCES

Bartoshuk, L. M. (1975). Taste mixtures: Is mixture suppression related to compression? *Physiology and Behavior, 14*, 643–649.

Bartoshuk, L. M. (1979). Bitter taste of saccharin: Related to the genetic ability to taste the bitter substance 6-*n*-propylthiouracil (PROP). *Science, 205*, 934–935.

Bartoshuk, L. M. (1987). Is sweetness unitary? An evaluation of the evidence for multiple sweets. In *Sweetness* (pp. 33–46) (ILSI Human Nutrition Reviews). London: Springer-Verlag.

Bartoshuk, L. M. (1989). Clinical psychophysics of taste. *Gerodontics, 4*, 249–255.

Bartoshuk, L. M., Dateo, G. P., Vandenbelt, D. J., Buttrick, R. D., & Long, L. (1969). Effects of *Gymnema sylvestre* and *Synsepalum dulcificum* on taste in man. In C. Pfaffman (Ed.), *Olfaction and taste, III* (pp. 436–444). New York: Rockefeller University Press.

Bartoshuk, L. M., Desnoyers, S., Hudson, C., Marks, L., O'Brien, M., Catalanotto, F. C., Gent, J., Williams, D., Ostrum, K. M. (1987). Tasting on localized areas. In S. Roper & J. Atema (Eds.), *Olfaction and taste IX. Annals of the New York Academy of Sciences, 510*, 166–168.

Bartoshuk, L. M., Gentile, R. L., Moskowitz, H. R., & Meiselman, H. L. (1974). Sweet taste induced by miracle fruit (*Synsepalum dulcificum*). *Physiology and Behavior, 12*, 449–456.

Bartoshuk, L. M., Pfaffmann, C., & Catalanotto, F. (1989, June). *Why is taste loss so often unnoticed?* Poster presented at the 1st Annual Meeting of the American Psychological Society, Washington, D.C.

Bartoshuk, L. M., Rifkin, B., Marks, L. E., & Hooper, J. E. (1988). Bitterness of KCl and benzoate: Related to PTC/PROP. *Chemical Senses, 13,* 517–528.

Bartoshuk, L. M., Rifkin, B., & Speers, M. (1980). Tastes of salts. In H. van der Starre (Ed.) *Olfaction and taste VII* (pp. 367–370). IRL Press, Ltd.: Washington, D.C.

Beauchamp, G. K., & Cowart, B. J. (1985). Congenital and experiential factors in the development of human flavor preferences. *Appetite, 6,* 357–372.

Beidler, L. M. (1953). Properties of chemoreceptors of tongue of rat. *Journal of Neurophysiology, 16,* 595–607.

Bernstein, I. L., & Webster, M. M. (1980). Learned taste aversions in humans. *Physiology & Behavior, 25,* 363–366.

Birch, L. (1980). Effects of peer models' food choices and eating behaviors on preschoolers' food preferences. *Child Development, 51,* 489–496.

Birch, L. (1987). The acquisition of food acceptance patterns in children. In R. A. Boakes, D. A. Popplewell, & M. J. Burton (Eds.), *Eating habits: Food, physiology, and learned behavior* (pp. 107–130). Chichester, England: Wiley.

Blau, J. N., & Diamond, S. (1984). Dietary factors in migraine precipitation: The physicians' view. *Headache, 25,* 184–187.

Booth, D. A., Lee, M., & McAleavey, C. (1976). Acquired sensory control of satiation in man. *British Journal of Psychology, 67,*

Cabanac, M. (1971). Physiological role of pleasure. *Science, 173,* 1103–1107.

Cabanac, M., Minaire, Y., & Adair, E. R. (1969). Influence of internal factors on the pleasantness of a gustative sweet sensation. *Communications in Behavioral Biology, Part A, 1,* 77–82.

Cain, W. S. (1979). Labiality of odor pleasantness. In J. H. A. Kroeze (Ed.), *Preference behaviour and chemoreception,* (pp. 303–315). London: IRL.

Cain, W. S. (1984). What we remember about odors. *Perfumer & Flavorist, 9,* 17–21.

Cain, W. S. (1987). Taste vs. smell in the organization of perceptual experience. In J. Solms, D. A. Booth, R. M. Pangborn, & O. Raunhardt (Eds.), *Food acceptance and nutrition* (pp. 63–77). New York: Academic Press.

Cain, W. S., & Johnson, F. (1978). Lability of odor pleasantness: Influence of mere exposure. *Perception, 7,* 459–465.

Cannon, W. B. (1939). The wisdom of the body. New York: W. W. Norton.

Dobbing, J. (Ed.). (1987). *Sweetness* (ILSI Human Nutrition Reviews). London: Springer-Verlag.

Engen, T. (1979). The origin of preferences in taste and smell. In J. H. A. Kroeze (Ed.), *Preference behaviour and chemoreception* (pp. 263–273). London: IRL.

Engen, T. (1982). The perception of odors. Orlando, FL: Academic Press.

Erickson, R. E., & Covey, E. (1980). On the singularity of taste sensations: What is a taste primary? *Physiology and Behavior, 25,* 79–110.

Fischer, R. (1967). Genetics and gustatory chemoreception in man and other primates. In M. R. Kare & O. Maller (Eds.), *The chemical senses and nutrition* (pp. 61–81). Baltimore: The Johns Hopkins University Press.

Fox, A. L. (1932). The relation between chemical constitution and taste. *Proceedings of the National Academy of Sciences, 18,* 115–120.

Frank, M. (1973). An analysis of hamster afferent taste nerve response functions. *Journal of General Physiology, 61,* 588–618.

Galef, B. G. (1979). Social transmission of learned diet preferences in wild rats. In J. H. A. Kroeze (Ed.), *Preference behaviour and chemoreception,* (pp. 219–231). London: IRL.

Ganchrow, J. R., Oppenheimer, M., & Steiner, J. E. (1979). Behavioral displays to gustatory stimuli in newborn rabbit pups. *Chemical Senses and Flavour, 4,* 49–61.

Garb, J. L., & Stunkard, A. J. (1974). Taste aversions in man. *American Journal of Psychiatry, 131,* 1204–1207.

Gent, J. F., & Bartoshuk, L. M. (1983). Sweetness of sucrose, neohesperidin dihydrochalcone, and saccharin is related to genetic ability to taste the bitter substance of 6-n-propylthiouracil. *Chemical Senses, 7,* 265–272.

Gilbert, A. N., & Wysocki, C. J. (1987). The smell survey results. *National Geographic, 172,* 515–525.

Halpern, B. P., & Nelson, L. M. (1965). Bulbar gustatory responses to anterior and to posterior tongue stimulation in the rat. *American Journal of Physiology, 209,* 105–110.

Hanington, E., & Harper, A. M. (1968). The role of tyramine in the aetiology of migraine, and related studies on the cerebral and extracerebral circulation. *Headache, 8,* 84–97.

Harris, H., & Kalmus, H. (1949). The measurement of taste sensitivity to phenylthiourea (PTC). *Annals of Eugenics, 15,* 24–31.

Hellekant, G., Glaser, D., Brouwer, J., & Van der Wel, H. (1981). Gustatory responses in three prosimian and two simian primate species (*Tupapia glis, Nycticebus, Galago senegalensis, Callithrix jacchus jacchus,* and *Saguinus midas niger*) to six sweeteners and miraculin and their phylogenetic implications. *Chemical Senses, 6,* 165–173.

Jacobs, H. L. (1958). Studies on sugar preference: I. The preference for glucose solutions and its modification by injections of insulin. *Journal of Comparative and Physiological Psychology, 51,* 304–310.

Jacobs, H. L., Smutz, E. R., & DuBose, C. N. (1977). Comparative observations on the ontogeny of taste preference. In J. M. Weiffenbach, (Ed.), *Taste and development: The genesis of sweet preference* (pp. 99–107). Bethesda, MD: U.S. Dept. of HEW.

Kiesow, F. (1896). Beiträge zur physiologischen Psychologie des Geschmackssinnes, *Philosophische Studien, 12,* 225–278.

Kirk-Smith, M. D., & Booth, D. A. (1987). Chemoreception in human behavior: Experimental analysis of the social effects of fragrances. *Chemical Senses, 12,* 159–166.

Laing, D. G., Panhuber, H., Willcox, M. E., & Pittman, E. A. (1984). Quality and intensity of binary odor mixtures. *Physiology and Behavior, 33,* 309–319.

Lawless, H. T. (1979). Evidence for neural inhibition in bittersweet taste mixtures. *Journal of Comparative and Physiological Psychology, 93,* 538–547.

Lawless, H. (1980). A comparison of different methods used to assess sensitivity to the taste of phenylthiocarbamide (PTC). *Chemical Senses, 5,* 247–256.

Lemere, F., & Voegtlin, W. L. (1940). Conditioned reflex therapy of alcoholic addiction: Specificity of conditioning against chronic alcoholism. *California and Western Medicine, 53,* 268–269.

Logue, A. W., Ophir, I., & Strauss, K. E. (1981). The acquisition of taste aversions in humans. *Behavior Research & Therapy, 19,* 319–333.

Mayer-Gross, W., & Walker, J. W. (1946). Taste and selection of food in hypoglycaemia. *British Journal of Experimental Pathology, 27,* 297–305.

McBurney, D. H., & Bartoshuk, L. M. (1973). Interactions across stimuli with different taste qualities. *Physiology and Behavior, 10,* 1101–1106.

McBurney, D. H., Smith, D. V., & Shick, T. R. (1972). Gustatory cross adaptation: sourness and bitterness. *Perception and Psychophysics, 11,* 228–232.

Mistretta, C. M. (1981). Neurophysiological and anatomical aspects of taste development. In *Development of perception* (pp. 433–455). New York: Academic Press.

Nachman, M., & Cole, L. P. (1971). Role of taste in specific hungers. In L. M. Beidler (Ed.), *Handbook of sensory physiology, Volume IV, Chemical Senses, Part 2, Taste* (pp. 337–362). New York: Springer-Verlag.

Öhrwall, H. (1901). Die Modalitäts- und Qualitatsbegriffe in der Sinnesphysiologie und deren Bedeutung. *Skandinavian Archiv für Physiologie, 11,* 245–272.

Ostrum, K. M., Catalanotto, F. A., Gent, J. F., & Bartoshuk, L. M. (1985). Effects of oral sensory field loss of taste scaling ability. *Chemical Senses, 10,* 459.

Palmerino, C. C., Rusiniak, K. W., & Garcia, J. (1980). Flavor-illness aversions: The peculiar roles of odor and taste in memory for poison. *Science, 208,* 753–755.

Pangborn, R. M. (1960). Taste interrelationships. *Food Research, 25,* 245–256.

Pelchat, M. L., Grill, H. J., Rozin, P., & Jacobs, J. (1983). Quality of acquired responses to tastes by *Rattus norvegicus* depends on type of associated discomfort. *Journal of Comparative Psychology, 97,* 140–153.

Pelchat, M. L., & Rozin, P. (1982). The special role of nausea in the acquisition of food dislikes by humans. *Appetite, 3,* 341–351.

Pfaffmann, C. (1955). Gustatory nerve impulses in rat, cat and rabbit. *Journal of Neurophysiology, 18,* 429–440.

Pfaffmann, C. (1959). The sense of taste. In J. Field, H. W. Magoun, & V. E. Hall (Eds.), *Handbook of physiology, section I. Neurophysiology* (pp. 507–533). Washington, D.C.: American Physiological Society.

Pfaffmann, C. (1974). Specificity of the sweet receptors of the squirrel monkey. *Chemical Senses and Flavor, 1,* 61–67.

Pfaffmann, C. P., & Bartoshuk, L. M. (1989, April). *A case of unilateral taste loss.* Paper presented at the 11th Annual Meeting of the Association for Chemoreception Sciences, Sarasota, Florida.

Richter, C. P. (1936). Increased salt appetite in adrenalectomized rats. *American Journal of Physiology, 115,* 155–161.

Richter, C. P. (1942–43). Total self regulatory functions in animals and human beings. *Harvey Lecture Series, 38,* 63–103.

Rodin, J., Wack, J., Ferrannini, E., & DeFronzo, R. A. (1985). Effect of insulin and glucose on feeding behavior. *Metabolism, 34,* 826–831.

Rosenstein, D., & Oster, H. (1988). Differential facial responses to four basic tastes in newborns. *Child Development, 59,* 1555–1568.

Schmidt, H. J., & Beauchamp, G. K. (1988). Adult-like odor preferences and aversions in three-year-old children. *Child Development, 59,* 1136–1143.

Sclafani, A., & Mann, S. (1987). Carbohydrate taste preferences in rats: glucose, sucrose, maltose, fructose and polycose compared. *Physiology and Behavior, 40,* 563–568.

Scott, T. R., & Chang, F. (1984). The state of gustatory neural coding. *Chemical Senses, 8,* 297–314.

Skramlik, E. von. (1922). Mischungsgleichungen im Gebiete des Geschmackssinnes. *Zeitschrift für Psychologie und Physiology des Sinnesorgane, 53,* 36–78.

Starling, E. H. (1923). The wisdom of the body (Harveian Oration). London: H.K. Lewis & Co.

Steiner, J. (1977). Facial expressions of the neonate infant indicating the hedonics of food-related chemical stimuli. In J. M. Weiffenbach (Ed), *Taste and development: The genesis of sweet preference* (pp. 173–188). Bethesda, MD: U.S. Dept. of HEW.

Szczesiul, R., Grill, H., & Bartoshuk, L. M. (1987, August–Sept.). Recognition of components in taste mixtures: Analytic or synthetic? 95th Annual Meeting of the American Psychological Association, New York (Poster).

Voegtlin, W. L. (1940). The treatment of alcoholism by establishing a conditioned reflex. *American Journal of the Medical Sciences, 199,* 802–810.

Wilkins, L., & Richter, C. P. (1940). A great craving for salt by a child with cortico-adrenal insufficiency. *Journal of the American Medical Association, 114,* 866–868.

Zellner, D. A., Rozin, P., Aron, M., & Kulish, C. (1983). Conditioned enhancement of human's liking for flavor by pairing with sweetness. *Learning and Motivation, 14,* 338–350.

3 Learned Ingestive Motivation and the Pleasures of the Palate

David A. Booth
University of Birmingham

GETTING A KICK OUT OF EATING

Hedonic experience is the occurrence of a pleasure (Gk. *hedone,* pleasure), i.e., the person has bodily sensations accompanied by a sensual thrill. In our culture at least, sexual climax has the reputation of providing one of the most intense pleasures. The Greek word, though, derives from the pleasures of eating, and specifically the delights generated by the taste of honey and of ripe fruit (Gk. *hedys,* sweet). Thus, the ancients considered the sweet taste on the tongue to be a paradigm of pleasurable experiences, consonant with a literal reading of the title of this book, "hedonics" of taste, i.e., hedonic reactions to gustatory stimulation.

However, there is the looser sense of a person's "taste" or "palate," as in the proverb *de gustibus non disputandum est*—there's no accounting for taste. Delight to the palate does not derive just from tastes in the strict gustatory sense. Classic approbations such as *nectar* or *ambrosia* refer to far more than mere sweetness or any combination of purely gustatory stimuli. Tactile stimulation (the food's texture), food aroma sensed retronasally during chewing and swallowing (integrated with tastes into the food's flavor), and even, in the right context, mild chemical discomfort (e.g., astringency and pepperiness), all contribute to positive appreciation of food in the mouth. Indeed, in a halo effect, by metaphor or by full metonymy, "taste" in food embraces all facets of the sensory complex, including evaluation of the served appearance and extending to the culinary concept and conventional appropriateness to the occasion as well.

Hence, the ineluctable meld of ordinary language and everyday experience provides a strong basis for the broad assumption that real pleasure can be evoked by culinary luxuries and no doubt by many foods and drinks regarded as high in quality that do not have to be sweet at all.

Scientific Study of Pleasures of the Palate

Scientists who talk about and investigate hedonic responses to food and drink must therefore have due respect for real, rich and not uncommon phenomena (Booth, 1987a). Here though lies an empirical and conceptual minefield.

Presumably, no one really doubts that pleasures are experienced, if no more than occasionally by the lucky ones of us. Nevertheless, those set in a physical reductionist mould, and ignorant of or unconvinced by experimental cognitive psychology, believe that private experience such as of a sensual thrill is not open to scientific investigation. Experimental psychologists on the whole have acted as though the pleasures of eating are far too evanescent and ill-specified to be studied by their science or are somehow the biologist's province or, contrariwise, too mundane or even commercially important for academic dignity. Those behavioral and social scientists who have tried to study the pleasures of the palate have characteristically ended up far away, such as in the pharmacology of rats or in statistics from the food market.

A constructive scepticism would be more appropriate than blind optimism in the scientific study of hedonic reactions. It is much more difficult than most psychologists have acknowledged to measure affective experience in a causal role within the thinking and behavior of an organism. We each know what it is to have fun eating or drinking and it seems so obvious when others enjoy their food and drink. Yet what of the distinction between eating just because I want to and getting a real kick out of it? To study our pleasures empirically, we have to grapple with distinctions between motivation and emotion, between behavioral disposition and subjective experience, and in particular between a glad participation and the seeking of sensual thrills.

Beyond the human adult are even greater problems. What does the smile of a human infant or the ingestive fixed action pattern of a rat tell us of the pleasure they might be feeling? The pathetic fallacy would be especially pathetic in a scientific discipline whose developmental specialists have increasingly discovered how crucial, even vital, to the health and education of the young is a natural tendency of adults to overattribute intention and experience on the basis of the infant's prelinguistic reactions (Booth, 1978a). Maybe, as we shall see by the end of this chapter, some dissociation between the gustofacial reflex and ingestive motivation could give us a handle on oral pleasures but the movements by themselves hopelessly confound dispositional response with hedonic quality.

Eating What You Like

Interpretation of data on the motivation to eat is riddled with conceptual muddles of this sort. A key example is what philosophers have dubbed the hedonistic fallacy. This is the argument that all behavior must be motivated by pleasure (or pain) because if we do something it must in some sense be pleasing to us and whatever we do not want to do is in that sense necessarily unpleasing. Such confusion between physical pleasures and pleasing activity has wrecked more than one line of research on eating motivation, as is illustrated later.

Another example is the term "reward." In psychology, its proper meaning is reinforcement of instrumental learning. Yet, all too conveniently, it connotes pleasure. The term has consequently been misused in many analyses of behavioral or neural processes of ingestion, misinterpreting as operant behavior the unarguably unconditioned and conditioned elicitative components of food preference and of the maintenance of ingestion throughout a meal.

Much research on human food perception, preferences and intakes is weakened by a more general fallacy, that of introspectionism (Booth, 1987a, 1987d). This arises from a longstanding and still highly seductive misunderstanding of the language for expressing purely subjective viewpoints ("it seems to me that . . ."). Grammatically, such expressions refer to the contents of states of consciousness. The physiological reductionists naively regard what people say about their private experiences as direct insight into a Mind mysteriously "secreted" by the Brain. This dualism finds ready alliance with the tradition in both psychophysics and psychometrics that takes rating scores to be measurement scales, directly quantitating experiences such as sensations and affect (cf. "magnitude estimation").

The study of subjective experience is undoubtedly a proper part of psychology. Yet it is a part only and one of the most complicated and least understood parts, not the simplest and clearest. The key point that so many have neglected is that the verbal profession or nonverbal expression of private experience does not provide access to another world beyond observable behavior. The language we use to express a viewpoint can do that because it disavows all claims to objective realism. Hence, experiential language is totally misunderstood if taken as the somehow irrefutable description of something real that becomes unmistakably visible when we turn metaphorical eyeballs inward and "report" what we "see" (Lyons, 1986; Wittgenstein, 1953). Pleasures are expressed, not reported.

Ratings should instead be used objectively, to identify influences on eating motivation and to measure how strong they are. This chapter shows how such study of these influences yields a methodology by which genuine expressions of pleasure can be analyzed out of linguistic communications and other kinds of behavioral performance in eating situations.

How Not to Build a Science of Oral Pleasure

Hedonics has become a fashionable jargon word recently among psychologists of animal behavior. The intention seems to be to lay claim to be studying something more than the intake of fluids or solids or the tongue movements stimulated by taste. Invariably, however, the only observations that are being referred to are the relative vigor of ingestion.

People's ratings of preferences or likings for foods and beverages have long been termed hedonic by practitioners of sensory evaluation of foods. Yet all that can be obtained from these verbal expressions is an estimate of the behavioral disposition to choose among the items rated. To date, there has been nothing in verbal or nonverbal data from people or other animals that distinguishes the directedness in behavior from the subjective experiencing of emotional affect of pleasurable thrills. So there is no empirical justification for these hedonic imputations.

This loose talk is not benign. It both reflects and promotes poor scientific thinking about sensory preferences and ingestive motivation. Cabanac (1971), for example, speculated about extraordinarily specific and precise biological functions for oral pleasures, on the basis of what people say about plain sweet solutions after they have been nauseated. The widespread pursuit of this approach has served only to obscure the importance of some elementary facts. It is entirely obvious that eating inhibits the motivation to eat (ingestion satiates). There has never been any doubt either that satiety functions to limit intake to some extent and thus makes some contribution to control of body weight. Plain saccharin solutions and concentrated glucose loads have no part in normal eating and so their effects should not be expected to bear on the role of everyday satiety (or palatability) in obesity.

To study hedonic reactions to tastes, then, we need to make observations that succeed in distinguishing pleasure from pleasantness and experienced emotion from behavioral motivation in the phenomena of ordinary ingestive behavior. The prospect of such a methodology has recently opened up as a result of extending studies of the learned basis of wanting to eat (Baker, Booth, Duggan, & Gibson, 1987; Booth, 1972e, 1985; Booth, Lovett, & McSherry, 1972) into efforts to measure the determinants of consumer choices among foods (Booth, Thompson, & Shahedian, 1983; Booth & Blair, 1989; Conner et al., 1988a, 1988b).

NORMAL INGESTIVE MOTIVATION

The control of normal food intake is almost entirely learned. The basic observations establishing this were reported nearly 20 years ago in rats (Booth, 1972e; Booth & Davis, 1973; Booth et al., 1972; Booth & Simson, 1971; Booth, Stoloff, & Nicholls, 1974) and people (Booth, Lee, & McAleavey, 1976). This theory and the evidence, with others' relevant data and views, have been fully reviewed every 5 years or so since (Booth, 1976, 1980a, 1985; Booth, Toates, & Platt, 1976). The present account therefore concentrates on further recent support for the original theory and new divergent accounts.

The general mechanism of appetite that was identified is the associative conditioning of ingestive facilitation and inhibition to configurations of salient dietary, somatic and environmental stimuli by various normal nutritional after-effects of eating. Much subsequent research into the disposition to eat or drink has unfortunately been based on concepts and experimental paradigms that ignore this theoretical construct and the evidence for nutritional conditioning of multisensory and often highly contextualized food preferences. In recent years, however, nutritional conditioning of preferences or intakes has begun to attract wider interest. Some research has been done with somatic or environmental stimuli as well as with dietary cues. Yet no other laboratory has run an experiment capable of elucidating learned dependence of sensory preferences on internal stimuli. The phenomenon nevertheless appears to have been replicated by several other groups, although they do not invoke the two-dimensional interpretation (Birch & Deysher, 1985; Mook et al., 1986; Van Vort & Smith, 1987) and some much more complex and incompletely operationalized concepts have been adduced (Deutsch, 1978, 1983; Mook, 1988).

Failures to mention the original reports of caloric preference conditioning have been allied with some possibly minor misconceptions of the phenomena (Bolles, Hayward, & Crandall, 1981; Deutsch, Molina, & Puerto, 1976; Holman, 1975). There is potential for more serious confusion behind denial of the existence of the prior observations (Arbour & Wilkie, 1988) and from invalid interpretations of the original evidence for contextualization of the preferences (Deutsch, 1983; Van Vort & Smith, 1987), especially when those data are reproduced alongside (Smith & Gibbs, 1979)! Our scientific understanding is most put at risk, however, by the study of dietary intake and selection and of food preference conditioning without full control of the oral stimuli (Booth, 1972c, 1972d, 1987b), without attention to the known physiology of food's postingestional actions (Booth, 1981a, Booth & Davis, 1973), and without a workable theoretical network of behavioral and physiological mechanisms that gives the learning processes realistic roles in the control of ingestion (Booth, 1980b, 1988).

Question-begging assumptions might be expected in the study of such an everyday phenomenon as eating behavior. Culture-bound culinary prejudices would not be surprising either (Booth, 1987c). More arbitrary is an ideology of neurological reductionism that is rampant among behavioral scientists in this field (Booth, 1990b, 1990c). Worst, though, is the mutually reinforcing neglect of the literatures and methodologies of behavioral plasticity by physiologists and of basic physiology by experimenters on learning (Booth, 1987e).

Toxiphobia

Major examples of these deficiencies in research strategy arise from the interest in conditioned taste aversions. Toxiphobia has been used to bolster several ideas about learned ingestive motivation that were refuted by the original demonstrations of nutritional conditioning. These false doctrines include the feebleness of conditioned preferences or even their nonexistence, the conditionability of taste only, and attribution of several features to conditioned taste aversions—that they are uncontextualized and respondent and hence hedonic (or, better, algesic, since a pain not a pleasure) and, most extraordinary of all, constitute a major mechanism of homeostasis. These issues are picked up in the following update on learned eating.

The idea that eating motivation is based on aversions is patently unrealistic. Food poisoning is so rare compared with the pervasiveness of positive enthusiasm for food and drink that people and other animals show in their behavior, even without any imposed deprivation (Booth, 1972d). Also, literally under the very nose of every experimenter several times each day, there is overwhelming anecdotal evidence for learned contextualized olfactory and visual preferences for foods.

Toxin-Conditioned Odor Aversions.   Contrary to claims that it is restricted to taste (Garcia & Ervin, 1968), toxiphobia to untastably low concentrations of insoluble odorants was demonstrated shortly after the first reports of poison-conditioned taste aversion, using the same method (Pain & Booth, 1968). The olfactory nature of the cues has been fully confirmed using damaged (Domjan, 1973; Supak, Macrides, & Chorover, 1971) and intact (Baker & Booth, 1989b; Ruddy, 1980) anosmic rats. Curiously enough, the first observations of learned suppression of saccharin drinking depended on olfactory cues, generated by irradiation (Garcia, Kimeldorf, & Hunt, 1961).

Malnutrition-Conditioned Food Aversions

One reason that aversion conditioning has been so influential was the evidence for nutritional conditioning of aversions that emerged concurrently with the toxiphobic paradigm (Rozin & Kalat, 1971). This encouraged a subsequent focus in human studies on the relatively infrequent (though not unimportant) phenomenon of aversion to a foodstuff. In the laboratory paradigms at least, the learning process involved in the "specific appetite" for thiamine and some other micronutrients was clearly shown to be the conditioning of aversion to the sensory characteristics of the deficient diet. One issue still outstanding is whether such aversive conditioning can be contextualized to the more common mild degree of nutrient deficiency, as appetitive conditioning can be (Baker et al., 1987; Gibson & Booth, 1986).

Unfortunately, the myth got about and persists to this day that preferences are harder to condition than aversions. This was because the only paradigm used in attempts to condition preferences was so-called recovery from chronic nutrient deficiency or from illness; an unknown degree of malaise remained and so it would be remarkable if any preference at all was observed.

Rozin and Kalat (1971) had some difficulty designing conclusive demonstrations of the acquisition of genuine preferences. It entirely begs this issue when the relative preference/aversion actually observed is called *hedonic*. The need for such designs was lessened, however, by the enormous intakes of tastes or odors that were conditioned by dilute calories (Booth, 1972e; Booth et al., 1972). Also, it could be argued that the onus of proof shifts once the strength of everyday food preference motivation is taken into account. Indeed, how strong an aversion is demonstrated by a thirsty rat's avoidance of drinking from a tube expected to contain water with a sweet taste?

Nutrient-Conditioned Food Preferences

The first clear demonstrations of caloric conditioning of flavor preferences were published in 1972 by Booth, Lovett, and McSherry. Likely true-positive preferences for various arbitrary levels of sweetness were conditioned in freely fed rats by the effects of dilute glucose or of dilute or concentrated gluco-oligosaccharides (low-glucose maltodextrin, a partial hydrolysate of starch, one US brand name for which is Polycose). The conditioning effect of concentrated maltodextrin also on preferences for other tastants, but specifically from the start of a meal, was shown by a discrete trials procedure in briefly food-deprived rats by Booth and Davis (1973). Van Vort and Smith (1983) confirmed the conditioning of a relative preference from the start of a meal for the flavor paired with absorption of the whole of a nutrient mixture over a flavor paired with the small part that misses an open gastric fistula.

From the strength of such acquired preferences and also from their specificity to the state of the gut during training (Booth, 1972e; Booth & Davis, 1973; Gibson & Booth, 1989), it was predicted (Booth, 1976, 1980a) that pairing cues with nutrition rather than with deprivation would condition the cues to initiate meals, as Weingarten (1985) found. Indeed, because the learning was strong enough to reverse the innate preference for greater sweetness, Booth et al. (1972) proposed that all eating motivation was based on the caloric conditioning of preferences. They dubbed this learned response "trophophilia," to point the contrast with toxiphobia. In support of this, Booth, Stoloff, and Nicholls (1974) showed that rat pups' increasing intake of solids away from the dam outside the nest could be largely accounted for by nutritional conditioning of food preferences. Social interaction facilitates such acquisition and differentiation of eating motivation in rats (Galef, 1989) and people (Birch, Zimmerman, & Hind, 1980) but such effects of conspecifics may well depend on the ingested materials delivering nutritional reinforcement.

Nutritional Conditioning of All Sensory Modalities.   The caloric conditioning also of odor preference has been shown using almond flavoring, which the rat perceives as the untastable aroma of benzaldehyde, as we do (Marie, Land, & Booth, 1987); this study (Booth, 1985) was an extension of the taste-potentiated toxic conditioning of odor aversion (Rusiniak, Hankins, Garcia, & Brett, 1979), run in that laboratory in 1980 using our standard paradigm of including malt-odextrin in a flavored diet presented to mildly deprived rats. No potentiation was seen and the odor preference was conditioned in a few trials, confirming earlier observations of virtually one-trial conditioning with nutritional reinforcers (Booth, 1972e; Booth & Simson, 1971). It now seems that this lack of a potentiation effect was because of the strength of the conditioning when the carbohydrate was ingested and the flavor was sensed at the same time; when the association is weakened by delaying carbohydrate ingestion by 10 minutes, saccharin does have a potentiating effect on caloric conditioning of odor preference (D. Robertson, G. V. Thomas, & D. A. Booth, unpublished data).

Many so-called flavors currently used in nutritional conditioning in fact have no taste and therefore must function as odors. Considering the theoretical weight that has been put on the distinction between taste and odor, use of the equivocal term flavor is unfortunate except in case of definite odor–taste mixtures.

The emphasis on taste also leads to scientific neglect of tactile cues within the mouth. These may well be more salient than taste in many ordinary foods like vegetables and meats. Texture preferences and aversions are also readily conditioned by nutritional effects (Booth, 1972e; Booth & Baker, 1990).

Tastes are indeed poor distinguishers of food materials compared with aroma and appearance (Le Magnen, 1967). Furthermore, like the texture as well as the taste of food, its aroma is most strongly sensed from within the mouth, by passage of vapor up the back of the nose during chewing and swallowing (Marie et al., 1987). So it should not be surprising if modalities other than taste are important in food preferences. Taste does not have an overwhelming role among the sensory characteristics that motivate mature ingestion, not even the taste of sweetness to which rats and human beings have such a strong congenital in-gestive reflex.

Rather, likings for foods and drinks, and indeed their contextualization to social occasions and physiological states, are highly specific acquisitions from exposure to eating situations. Habituation, caloric and other nutritional condi-tioning, socio-affective reinforcement and quite possibly more complex learning processes establish dispositions to accept and refuse to ingest particular mate-rials, identified by their distinctive characteristics in whatever modality.

Metabolic Conditioning.   The appetitive conditioning effect of glucose and its starch-related polymers in fed rats is likely to depend on its oxidation, i.e., to be truly caloric, because the effect was repeated using intravenous infusion of glucose (Mather, Nicolaidis, & Booth, 1978; Tordoff & Friedman, 1986). Major oral effects have in any case been excluded by replication using intragastric administration (Baker & Booth, 1989a; Booth et al., 1972; Deutsch, 1978; Elizalde & Sclafani, 1988).

Rapid absorption and metabolism of glucose or fructose also induce satiety

(Booth, 1972a, 1972b; Booth & Jarman, 1976). Indeed, the conditioning of preferences, not just failure to condition aversion at physiological doses, has been proposed as a criterion of a satiety signal (Booth, 1980b, 1985). However, while admitting the reality of metabolic satiety, some have placed much greater emphasis on cholecystokinin (CCK) as a candidate satiety signal (Smith & Gibbs, 1979). Peripheral secretion of CCK has been suggested as a mediator of caloric conditioning (Mehiel & Bolles, 1988). This cannot be correct since the unconditioned stimulus would not then be arising from energy metabolism; in any case, carbohydrates do not stimulate CCK secretion from the gut (Liddle et al., 1986). Indeed, it has been reported that CCK-conditioned preferences occur only in the young rat pup (Hall, 1988)—a result casting in doubt the status of CCK as a normal satiety signal.

Further evidence that energy metabolism conditions preferences comes from use of nonglucogenic substrates such as fats (Deutsch, 1978) and ethanol, which also satiates (Booth, 1981a). Deutsch and Walton (1977) first reported preference-conditioning by alcohol, although without emphasizing its metabolic mediation. Sherman et al. (1983) reported unpotentiated ethanol-conditioned odor preferences not long after maltodextrin-conditioned odor preference without potentiation had been demonstrated there (see above). Mehiel and Bolles (1984, 1988) have exploited the phenomenon further, gaining evidence of contextualization to drive.

Sensory Conditioning of Aversions.   Many claims to have conditioned caloric preferences are confounded by sensorily conditioned aversions to the control cues or even to the calorically richer diet (then sometimes misinterpreted as satiation; see Booth, 1972e). Bulking agents such as kaolin and chalk generate nasty oral sensations by turning to cement on wetting in the mouth (Bolles et al., 1981; Booth, 1972b; Le Magnen, 1957). Caloric conditioning is also overwhelmed by the use of nauseating (Booth 1972a; Cabanac & Fantino, 1979; McCleary, 1953) and throat-rasping hypertonic solutions of free sugars (Booth et al., 1972; Deutsch et al., 1976), or of fats not exposed to digestion by salivary lipase (Deutsch et al., 1976). Any preference conditioning is made more difficult by the use of highly astringent concentrations of alcohol, the burn of peppers (Booth, 1982), tastants such as citric acid and quinine (Booth & Davis, 1973) and aversive odorants such higher concentrations of the terpenes (C. Eastman & D. A. Booth, unpublished data).

Sensory rather than caloric conditioning of preferences and aversions (Bolles et al., 1981; Fanselow & Birk, 1982) is also more likely when the rats are too deprived to detect satiating calories (Booth, 1972b; Booth & Jarman, 1976) and/or when foods are presented simultaneously that have insufficient differences in caloric density. Neither meal sizes (Booth, 1972e) nor preferences (Booth, 1980a) are conditioned reliably unless the difference in caloric densities is much greater than the 2:1 ratio used by Bolles et al. (1981), for example, even when the diets are presented separately to only mildly deprived rats. It is obviously crucial to distinguish sensory conditioning of aversion from caloric conditioning of preference.

Noncaloric Nutritional Reinforcers in Rats and People.   The first examples of nutritional conditioning of preferences did not come from energy metabolism but from essential amino acids. Gastric intubation of a mixture of amino acids like that in high-quality protein conditioned an odor preference in one trial in young rats deprived of protein (Booth & Simson, 1971). Preferences could also be conditioned to taste cues (Booth & Simson, 1974) or to textures (Booth & Baker, 1990). In addition, it turned out that substantial deficiency in protein intake was not necessary; deprivation of the protein from only one meal was sufficient for the protein amino acids to have conditioning power (Baker et al., 1987; Simson & Booth, 1974; Booth, 1974b).

It is therefore important now to investigate the ability of a number of vitamins and essential minerals to condition preferences after only slight deprivation (or some decline in release from stores). Such preference acquisition would be more functional than the aversions resulting from extreme deficiency. Nevertheless, on a normally variegated diet, caloric preference conditioning is sufficient to ensure adequate intake of most or all micronutrients.

THE CONDITIONED STIMULUS
AND THE PREFERENCE PEAK

The calorically and osmotically conditioned "reversal of the sweetness preference gradient" (Booth et al., 1972) demonstrated that the conditioned stimulus (CS) was not the quality of sweetness but a particular intensity of sweetness. That is, the concept of an intradimensional stimulus generalization gradient applied. When the lesser sweetness was the more calorific and/or the greater sweetness was more hypertonic, then the conditioned preference declined from the lesser sweetness to the greater, reversing the innate gradient over that range. Booth et al. (1972) did not test sweetnesses outside the range between the pair of conditioned intensities, but generalisation decrements would be expected to have replaced both the innate decline in preference by a learned decline below the preferred lesser sweetness and also the innate rise in preference by a decline of conditioned aversion above the greater sweetness intensity. Similarly, when the greater sweetness level had been calorically conditioned, the learned peak of preference would have been at that level, with declines in preference not only at lower sweetnesses but also, contrary to the innate gradient, at higher sweetnesses. Richardson, Williams, and Riccio (1984) have also clearly distinguished between such two-sided stimulus generalization decrements and stimulus intensity dynamism in the case of lithium-conditioned aversion to 10% sucrose.

Preference Psychophysics

Booth, Thompson, and Shahedian (1983) proposed that a discrimination mechanism operated between the most preferred level of a CS dimension and higher or lower levels, just as it did in judgments of intensity of that sensory quality, at least in Fechner's view. The theory is that the decline in learned preference is proportional to the discriminable difference from the peak-preferred intensity, both to lower intensities and to higher intensities equally. That is, if the stimulus concentrations were scaled in units of equal discriminability, the preference peak should be symmetrical and indeed pointed, i.e., an isosceles triangle; this inverted V shape "unfolds" into a straight line when the sign of the slope above the most preferred intensity is reversed (Booth, Conner, & Marie, 1987; Conner, Haddon, Pickering, & Booth, 1988b).

Because all tests of this theory of individual perception of familiar characteristics have so far supported it (Booth, 1987d), we can say "toodle-doo" to the skewed U of the traditional hedonic curve. The usual peak is rounded and rather flat because individuals having a wide range of peak preferences are grouped together, to produce at best a normal curve. Also, the upper limb is typically less steep than the lower limb; this is because raw concentrations have been plotted, whereas at moderate intensities it usually is ratios of concentration that are equally discriminable, not differences in concentration (Booth et al., 1983).

This straight-line relationship between strength of preference and perceptual distance from peak preference in discriminability units has been confirmed in many adult people for sweetness of foods and drinks (Conner, Haddon, & Booth, 1986; Conner, Land, & Booth, 1987; Conner et al., 1988b; Conner & Booth, 1988). It has also been shown for saltiness (Conner, 1988; Conner, Booth, Clifton, & Griffiths, 1988a), for which there is no innate preference but a process of acquisition of preference for salt levels to which infants are exposed from about 4 months (Harris & Booth, 1987). The isosceles triangle has been shown even for the innately aversive taste of bitterness, preferred at some stronger or milder level in coffee (Booth, Conner, & Gibson, 1989). Indeed, linear unfolded preferences have been found for every modality tested in familiar foods and drinks, including aroma (Marie, 1986), thickener (Conner, 1988), and coffee whitener color and mouthfeel (N.J. Richardson & D.A. Booth, unpublished). This in turn supports the interpretation of preference peaks as pairs of generalisation gradients around the CSs and hence the theory that all food preferences are learned, including that for sweetness in familiar foods.

These linear functions provide unprecendently powerful diagnostics for the cognitive processes within a person that integrate multiple inputs into single or multiple outputs (Booth et al., 1987; Booth & Blair, 1989). In particular, the distinction between stimulus intensity and stimulus preference can be used to diagnose the occurrence of subjective experiences such as sensations and pleasures (Booth, 1987a; Booth et al., 1987). We shall come to pleasures later but to illustrate the measurement of sensations by discrimination data, consider an instance of a single sensory characteristic of a food, namely the taste of caffeine in a drink of coffee. We found that everybody's taste preferences were sensitive to caffeine level but that only about half the respondent's bitterness ratings discriminated different ratios of caffeine concentration against the background of the roasted coffee bean flavor (Booth et al., 1989). That is, gustatory stimulation by caffeine sometimes influenced coffee preference without consciousness of its bitterness.

CONTEXT-DEPENDENCE OF CONDITIONED
FOOD PREFERENCES

Despite claims that toxins condition aversions to tastes as such, the contextual dependence of toxiphobia has been repeatedly demonstrated, both to internal cues generated by drugs (e.g., Revusky, Pohl, & Coombes, 1980) and to cues in the external environment (e.g., Sjöden & Archer, 1981). In the case of facilitation of ingestion, it proved remarkably easy to condition eating jointly to a food cue and to a nutritionally relevant internal cue such as the degree of distension of the stomach, in either rats (Booth, 1972e; Booth & Davis, 1973; Gibson & Booth, 1989) or people (Booth et al., 1976a; Booth, Mather, & Fuller, 1982; Booth & Toase, 1983). Because the acquired facilitation was most clearly seen in dramatic increases in meal size in the rat fed dilute diets, this phenomenon has been dubbed conditioned desatiation. Nevertheless, by definition the phenomenon also involves a food-specific internal control of ingestion at the start of a meal and so it is equally a form of learned appetite.

There is evidence that the absence of either element in this dietary-visceral compound cue eliminates the learned desatiation response (Booth & Toase, 1983; Gibson & Booth, 1989). So the learning appears to have involved spontaneous configuring, the control of the conditioned ingestion by a *Gestalt*. This phenomenon has also been shown recently among flavor elements in toxiphobia (Forbes & Holland, 1985).

Need Cues

Revusky (1968) proposed that the need for water provided a drive cue that could be conditioned in compound with flavors. Subsequent discussion of satiation conditioning with him encouraged the development of the configural account of the conditioning of meal sizes by food's energy density (Booth, 1977a, 1977b, 1980a). However, Revusky et al. (1980) were unable to support such a theory using toxic conditioning of hunger and thirst; probably the 48-hour periods of deprivation of food or water that they used induced mixtures of caloric and water deficits that would be very difficult to discriminate. The classic maze-running approach to analysis of drive cues has been revived with somewhat more success (Capaldi & Davidson, 1979; Capaldi & Friedman, 1976) but, as noted earlier, the overnight deprivation conventional in such experiments probably reduces the strength of the appetitive reinforcement from caloric loads. Using nutritional flavor preference conditioning, Capaldi and Myers (1982) were able to extend Revusky's thirst effect to hunger. Similarly, Fedorchak and Bolles (1987) have found that hunger enhances flavor preferences conditioned during food deprivation by caloric ingestion but not those conditioned by noncaloric sweetener. However, these effects of drive state are additive and so are not configural. Indeed, those designs were not counterbalanced by preference-conditioning during repletion. So the observed effects could have arisen from drive acting nonassociatively during performance (Fedorchak & Bolles, 1987) rather than from the operation of learned drive cues, unlike the satiation/appetite conditioning effects (Booth, 1972e, 1977b, 1980a; Booth & Davis, 1973; Gibson & Booth, 1989).

Considerable confusion can arise unless a distinction is kept between drive effects and drive cue effects and also a dispositional or reaction-tendency view of motivation is sustained against notions of satiety as a physiological signal or even an autonomic response. Only a truly behavioral analysis makes sense of the definition of the learning of satiety as the conditioning of sensory control of meal size disconfounded from uncontextualized aversion/preference (Booth, 1972e, 1985). The dissociation of facilitatory and inhibitory effects of the same oral cue between beginning and end of the test meal is crucial. Once the habituation of ingestive responding to the oral cue has been excluded (Booth, 1977b; Gibson & Booth, 1989), the simplest account is that some internal change occurs during the meal that serves to cue the direction of the reaction to the dietary stimulus.

Learned ingestive dispositions tied to a nutritional state are appetites and satieties for that state. The interoceptive cuing might be calories (a signal generated by oxidation of any metabolic fuel) or a specific nutrient (Baker et al., 1987; Booth, 1974a, 1987b; Gibson & Booth, 1986). It might be some nutritionally less specific gut state, however, such as a moderate degree of fullness of the stomach (Booth, 1977b; Gibson & Booth, 1989).

The contextual cue could equally well be a cognitive representation of the external environment. In people, this might be awareness of an habitual mealtime. Equally, a food preference could be tied to a cultural convention such as breakfast menus (Birch, Billman, & Richards, 1984) or to participating in some ritual or being an appreciative guest and hence wanting to eat something one would never eat at home.

Multidimensional Motivational Psychophysics

This learned facilitation or inhibition of ingestion by a configural conditioned stimulus or *Gestalt* of dietary, somatic and environmental stimuli is susceptible to psychophysical discrimination analysis, just as simple cuing is as explained earlier. Since the conditioned response is not the summation of the effects of separate sensory elements, the intensity generalization gradients for the configured elements have to be integrated. This requires a rule for interactive mental combination of the physical dimensions. Among the simplest possibilities for integration rules are the averaging or the adding of values on discrete perceptual dimensions (Anderson, 1981), objectively measured in units of their discriminabilities (Booth, 1987d; Booth & Blair, 1989). Such rules of "mixture psychophysics" are equivalent to those proposed for integration of features generally in object recognition (Ashby & Perrin, 1988) and sensory difference testing (Ennis & Mullen, 1986).

Unlike the animal data in this area to date, human data already at hand force the postulation of more than a single point of integration in at least some eating motivation (Booth & Blair, 1989; Lewis & Booth, 1986). The elaborate series of cognitive processes usually postulated for human thinking may not actually be required in order to explain habitual behavior, even habits as complicated as the human selection and consumption of foods. Nonetheless, the theoretical network of integration mechanisms that is minimally required to account for the control of eating, even in the rat, has to include not only visceral physiology but also the perceptual, cognitive and motor-control stages of neural processing and of the information processing that transforms inputs into outputs across the whole organism (Booth, 1979, 1987a, 1988b). A minimal sketch of these transforms is given in Fig. 3.1.

This diagram is not another of the familiar unoperationalized maps of fuzzy verbal concepts. It is a mechanistic psychobiosocial theory that precisely specifies the experimental designs required to test it and then to elaborate or simplify it in the light of the results. Each node with more than one input can be represented by a hypothetical formula and the correctness of that equation tested by multiple regression of individual performance in a set of similar well-specified situations (Booth & Blair, 1989).

Phenomena of sufficient complexity to provide data supporting a cognitive path analysis as minimally rich as this are required in order to open up the possibility of determining whether pleasures of the palate accompany eating, as we shall now see.

Approach and Consum(m)atory Behavior

First, though, we should clarify the possible role of tastes in evoking pleasures during eating.

Instrumental versus Reactive Learning.   The term *hedonic* and the notion of a reaction to the taste as such, regardless of context, have been used to insist on the involuntary nature of conditioned taste aversions. Part of this view is the dismiss-

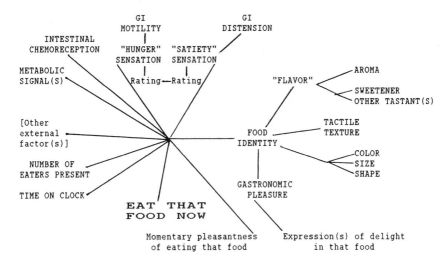

FIG. 3.1. Path analysis within an individual's repeated behavior to distinguish pleasure from motivation. Each line represents a partial regression between measured variables; the absence of a line indicates no linear association between variables. This diagram is a causal theory that can be tested against data on the values of the variables collected from adequately designed observations of the individual faced repeatedly with variants of a particular type of situation (Booth, 1987a, 1987d; Booth & Blair, 1988).

al of olfactory, visual, and even gustatory preferences as mere discriminative instrumental behavior, guiding the organism to food sources rather than giving it the pleasure of ingesting them (Garcia & Ervin, 1968; Garcia et al., 1985). Yet the originally observed preferences conditioned to olfactory as well as gustatory cues, even when contextualized, were clearly capable of driving intake up to enormous volumes (Booth, 1972e; Booth et al., 1972). In fact, the boot is on the other foot. It seems far more necessary to invoke discriminative avoidance of contextual cues in the so-called aversions to taste, as the actually observed refusal to sample cannot be an elicited response to current tasting of the averted drink. The stronger the "aversion," i.e. the less saccharin the rat drinks, the less taste "algesics" there can be.

Fractionation of Eating Motivation.   Palatability cannot be defined as the ingestive reflex evoked particularly by tastants, be the motor pattern unconditioned or conditioned (Grill & Berridge, 1985). These taste reflexes just happen to be readily visible. The orotactile reflexes of mastication are just as strong in facilitating ingestion but not so easy to observe. Furthermore, olfactory stimuli are not only used in approach but their retronasal delivery also helps to maintain ingestion, sometimes most vigorously as just pointed out. Approach and consumption can be differentially conditioned (Weingarten & Martin, 1989), and so eating motivation is not always unitary. We might wish to restrict a concept like palatability to the maintenance of ingestion. Nevertheless, the fact would remain that the hunt can also be a big thrill—sometimes, to travel is better than to arrive. So behavioral fractionation does not settle any issues of hedonic measurement.

HEDONIC REACTIONS TO SWEETNESS IN AND OUT OF FOODS

Just as the word the Greeks had for sweet was the same in root as their word for pleasure, so also in English, as in other languages, *sweet* is a metaphor or almost a synonym for all that is attractive, pleasurable and emotionally satisfying (Booth et al., 1972; Chiva, 1985).

The psychological realities of this affinity of the sweet taste to hedonic reactions generally are much misunderstood. Ill-founded functional assumptions have often been made in consequence.

A major difficulty that must be faced is that no source of sweet delight operates with mechanical invariance. Sensual pleasures are subject to considerable cultivation, the thrill arising from an acquired taste. All pleasures can cloy, including that of sweetness itself as the poets have so wrily observed (Booth et al., 1972). This satiety for sweetness (Wooley, Wooley, & Dunham, 1972) may be no different from any other stimulus-specific satiety (Rolls et al., 1981a, 1981b) but it could sometimes also involve satiation (repletion-dependent aversion) conditioned by osmotic effects of sugar (Booth et al., 1972).

This leads us to a crucial distinction between the inborn liking for sweetness as such and the actual roles of sweetness in mature eating motivation.

Function of the Innate Sweetness Reflex

Mother's milk is rich in free and combined amino acids and amino sugars that are essential to the survival, growth and immunity to infection of newborn mammals. Yet these vital nitrogenous compounds are liable to stimulate the gustatory receptors that are essential for omnivorous mammals to detect toxic plant alkaloids. For such detection to be any use, it must prevent any of the material being swallowed (preferably by conspecifics as well as by the taster) and so stimulation of these bitter receptors triggers innately reflex movements. (The same expulsive movements can be conditioned to other oral stimuli and in turn support avoidance of visual and olfactory warnings.)

Cultures vary in their attitude to milk as a food for adults but, for many, mother's milk or the ungulate's substitute remains an epitome of delight in literature if not in actual habit (although for a different evaluation, see Rozin &

Pelchat, 1988). Weaning practices also vary widely between and within cultures (sometimes to dire effect), but the young baby's need for wet nursing is never doubted. Indeed, honey and other sweeteners are placed on the nipple to encourage "weak" sucklers (Weiffenbach, 1975); this suggests strong similarity between the sweetener and the milk, else licking off the honey might encourage behavior other than sucking!

Omnivorous mammals have the problem, however, that the nitrogen in milk is vital but the nitrogen in plant alkaloids is lethal. The foraging child and indeed adult therefore needs as fully effective a way as possible of detecting these potent poisons and spitting them out. Giving such an inborn reflex to bitterness, what the survival of the suckling then requires is a class of receptors that distinguishes the aliphatic hydroxyl and perhaps carbonyl groups of amino acids from the aromatic context of the nitrogen atoms in alkaloids. Also, the stimulation of these aliphatic hydroxyl receptors must either gate out the bitter receptors or trigger a reflex that counters the expulsive reflexes to bitterness (Booth, 1990a; Booth et al., 1987). Then the tactile reflexes can ensure that the newborn baby suckles vigorously. However, this adaptation also makes aliphatic polyols (especially those with an aldehyde group, i.e., sugars) innately liable to facilitate eating through life, at least in unfamiliar contexts.

From such considerations it seems improbable that the liking for sweetness has anything to do with attracting mammals to plant sugars as sources of calories. On the contrary, some plants may have evolved sugar-rich coverings for their mature seeds as a superreleaser for the infantile protein preference, in order to exploit animal mobility to colonise new growing sites. So, although the promise was that Canaan flowed with the animal sweets, milk and honey, the Israelite scouts came back from it with bunches of fruit.

Learned Sweet Food Preferences

Whatever function it had, the innate ingestive reflex to gustatory stimuli similar to some sugars and amino acids now guarantees the acceptability of a sweetened new food. As a result, where there is the technology to mass-produce sucrose and other sugars, sweetness becomes a major dietary principle (Booth, 1987c; Conner & Booth, 1988) and hence a powerful food marketing tool, despite moralistic outrage (Fischler, 1987).

Nevertheless, within a familiar cuisine, no taste—not even the sweet taste— is any more important than any other salient characteristic to the choices between foods or beverages. This is because the observable strength of motivation to consume familiar foods and drinks is entirely learned, for their sweetness no less than other tastes, aromas, textures, colors, etc.

To obtain sound evidence whether or not sweetness or other taste sensations do give greater pleasure than other food attributes, therefore, we have to get objective evidence, not just work from our culture-bound intuitions. Furthermore, we have to distinguish affect from the powerful motivation to eat foods that often have obvious tastes. However, the cognitive theory and the measurement technique needed to find out about such mediating processes have yet to be applied to the problem.

MEASUREMENT OF EATING MOTIVATION

Pleasures versus Pleasantness

Not only physiologists but even psychologists have neglected to consider the variety of cognitive processes that could be involved in sweet water pleasantness rating, let alone to attempt to work out how people were caused to give the ratings they did. Being pleased must not be confused with having pleasure; a pleasing activity is different from a pleasurable experience.

This conceptual sloppiness has contributed to the popularity in the field of food preferences and obesity of a theory of the biological function of pleasure (Cabanac, 1971). The data on which this theory was based were obtained by the very odd procedure of asking people to rate the pleasantness of plain sweetened water and the even odder interpretation (especially for the French palate) of high pleasantness ratings as an expression of the full emotional quality of pleasure. Maybe the raters tried to think of still lemonade, or were expressing their attitudes to sugar or to artificial sweeteners. No less likely, perhaps they regressed to infancy subconsciously and showed in their pleasantness ratings the inborn continuous increase in preference with increasing sweetness.

"Negative alliesthesia" (literally, the suppression of a sensation by some other effect) was defined as the rated un/pleasantness of a sweetness sensation (not, as the word implies, its intensity) becoming less pleasant as the result of a glucose load (Cabanac, 1971). This is an inappropriate neologism for nothing other than satiety, albeit induced by an abnormal nutrient preparation and tested artificially and insensitively on a nonfood and, when the sugar load is drunk, confoundedly with sensory boredom (Wooley et al., 1972).

In contrast, if typical foods (physically sampled or merely named) are rated for how pleasing it would be to eat them at that moment, one of the most sensitive measures of the general level of hunger/satiety can be obtained (Booth, 1972d, 1981b; Booth et al., 1982). We shall consider this measure of our eating motivation in some detail because its logic has generally been poorly comprehended and yet is crucial to the understanding of measures of pleasures.

Appetite/Satiety: How Pleasing It Is to Eat Foods

Because saying how pleased one is has the function of a general expression of motivation, pleasantness ratings of foods can be used to assess all aspects of appetite. In the case of appetite for food, this includes palatability, appropriateness to the situation, the behavioral meaning attributed to abdominal sensations, or the overall level of desire for food (hunger) and its inverse, the level of satiety. However, the use of ratings to study the physiology and pharmacology of human eating and drinking has been plagued by the nonsensical introspectionist assumption (Ryle, 1949; Wittgenstein, 1953) that attaching numbers to experiential and wish-expressing language measures subjective experiences and hence that the mere wording of a rating succeeds in differentiating its use from other ratings (Booth, 1987a, 1987d).

Ratings are really the more or less skillful linguistic transmission of what the person recognizes in the objective situation and/or in the manner in which the situation would actually be dealt with. The empirical content of a verbal score is therefore whatever measurements of aspects of the situation and/or of responses to it that can demonstrably be extracted from the rating. It has yet to be shown that ratings referring to different aspects of the eating situation, such as bodily sensations of hunger and satiety, attractiveness of food, known time to or from eating, or the strength of the desire to eat, can in fact be used to pick out actually different variables and hence could even possibly be measures of different experiences. In fact, these ratings are all highly correlated with each other and correlated with the amount in calories that would be eaten (Booth, 1987a; Hill, Blundell, & Leathwood, 1987). Hence all that the different ratings are known to measure is the one and the same disposition to eat in the rated situation. Even if people were asked to rate specifically sensual thrills, there would likely be no evidence from the intercorrelations that these ratings picked out anything different.

Some confusion has arisen from the presumption of some stability over time behind ordinary usage of the concepts of preference, aversion and palatability. Unfortunately, many workers on food intake control have tried to "define" this invariance into the phenomena. The truth is that the facilitation or inhibition of the ingestion of a material having particular sensory characteristics, relative to the ingestive disposition towards other foods, can vary qualitatively as well as quantitatively over times as short as a few minutes: for example, as already cited, the relative preference for a food can reverse from the beginning to the end of a meal (Booth, 1972e; Booth & Davis, 1973; Booth et al., 1982; Van Vort & Smith, 1987).

The ordinary ideas of satiety and of appetite, hunger and thirst are those of, by contrast, potentially transient states of mind. Again, however, all that we observe is the relative facilitation/inhibition of ingestion of particular materials at any given point or period of time, or ratings of the foods and drinks that, despite a wide variety of wordings, all correlate with actual energy intake from a menu (Booth, 1987a; Booth et al., 1982).

Furthermore, unless qualified by reference to an object of desire such as a nutrient or a foodstuff, appetite and satiety are concepts of a facilitation or (eating-induced) inhibition of ingestion that is general to food and perhaps drink, also in contrast to palatability and preference. (We have the words hunger and thirst because we sometimes need to distinguish between the appetite for foods and the appetite for fluids, rather than the usual appetite for a meal where drink comes with the food.)

It is foolish to use one aspect of ordinary usage of words like palatability and satiety to limit the scientific interpretation of data, however. It is entirely an empirical matter how general or specific the facilitation or inhibition of ingestion is in a particular sort of situation. The best-known example of specificity is the transient inhibition of the tendency to eat more of specifically that food which has just been eaten (Booth, 2976; Le Magnen, 1956; Rolls et al., 1981b; Treit, Spetch, & Deutsch, 1983). Hence, an offering of new food can start up eating again. Shakespeare (*Othello*) saw no paradox in saying that the Coolidge effect on sexual desire will "give to satiety a fresh appetite." In that sense, specific satieties may be more abundant than specific appetites (Booth, 1985; Mook, 1988).

It must be emphasized, though, that these satieties and appetites are situationally specific dispositions to ingest (Baker et al., 1987; Booth, 1972e), not necessarily related to particular bodily mechanisms as Mook (1988) seems to presuppose. Indeed, the above account also shows that satiety is a phenomenon that cannot be confined to postingestionally arising inhibition, as many seem to think.

Equally, hunger cannot refer only to eating induced by physiological signals, nor appetite only to eating evoked by diet; this is a persisting muddle arising from reductionist misconceptions about behavioral phenomena (Booth, 1987a); on that definition, the difference in words would have very little use, for most eating is controlled by both internal and external environments jointly (Booth, 1972e, 1978b, 1985; Weingarten, 1985). Similarly against reduction, pleasure is not definable as a sort of autonomic activation, even if stimuli to the skin or viscera and a degree of physical excitation are normally necessary to experiencing a thrill.

It is not surprising from these logical considerations, then, that it has proved unproductive and confusing to take what someone says about how things seem or rates as what is desired as a description of an inner world on which drugs and nutrients act, somehow just as they do on cells. We know that nutrients really act on cells in the wall of the intestine, the liver, and parts of the brain; indeed, there is also electrophysiological evidence that they generate neuronal signals in all those places. Similarly we know that drugs act on neurotransmission in the GI tract, liver, pancreas, and all parts of the brain. It is therefore impossible to come to any mechanistic conclusion from observing the effects of administering a nutrient or a drug simply on overall ingestive behavior, on some parameter of intake or on a verbal communication (Booth, 1990b). The proper scientific job is to relate the cellular actions of the administered chemical to the cerebral processes that those cells participate in and then relate the operation of that neural network to the organization of behavior. Behavioral analysis is an objective mechanistic interpretation of observable responses (intakes, choices, ratings) in specified situations.

That is, appetite and satiety or the pleasures of eating do not float like ghosts in the brain. They are aspects of the overall performance of the organism. To progress in a genuinely physiological psychology, we have to isolate causal processes both within the brain and perhaps the viscera and also the causal transformations within behavior between environmental inputs and outputs (Booth, 1990b). To understand the psychology of motivation and hedonics, we must have a fully operationalized theory of the mentation within that behavior.

HOW TO MEASURE A THRILL

We can now come in conclusion to the experimental problem of distinguishing a gastronomic thrill from mere palatability. Evidence for pleasure over and above motivation has two essentials. First, it requires some output indicative of pleasure and not just motivation. Secondly, there must be observable some dissociation between that output and measures of motivation that do not necessarily imply pleasure.

The Hedonic Measure

In sensory evaluation, scores anchored on various qualifications of the word "like" (and dislike") have been called the "hedonic scale." Ratings of pleasantness, preference and propensity to choose are often nowadays also termed "hedonic scaling."

In fact, the psychometric properties of the multiple liking categories are not good (it is not a linear scale). Moreover, no mere layout for scoring should be called a scale. More importantly, though, expressing a liking for a food item or rating the tasting of a drink as pleasant is no evidence that a pleasure has been evoked. Given the demand characteristics implicit in presenting a range of stimuli with a range of possible responses (Poulton, 1979, 1989; Conner et al., 1987), even "like extremely" or "very pleasant" ratings may mean no more than that the test item is the least bad of a mediocre bunch. At best, hedonic ratings may be taken to express relative preferences—or indeed perhaps relative aversions, whether or not the ratings move down among the *unpleasant* and *dislike* categories.

The most fundamental issue, though, however precise or imprecise the scores, is their empirical meaning. Whether the scores measure anything at all is entirely a matter of the rater's objective performance in using the scoring procedure to make judgments about the stimuli. What response would be a valid index of pleasure?

The construct of affect or emotionality includes diffuse excitation and lack of direct functionality in the specific behavior that is appropriate. Thus the index might be some movement that is not part of the processes of ingestion itself (whether or not the movement can interfere with ingestion). The smile is an obvious candidate, but grinning may not always go well with sipping, biting or chewing! Autonomic and brain activity measures are classic but have serious problems of validation. It can even be a problem whether the excitation relates to pain or pleasure, although if the motivational measures show that the eating situations have been kept attractive to the individual respondent, this ambiguity in the physical indices of affect does not matter.

Soothing and even analgesic effects of the sweet taste in human and rodent infants (Blass, 1987) might be considered as a hedonic measure. However, the quieting effect is tonic and so the necessary tests of an individual's habitual response pattern with multiple variants of a situation would be extremely laborious, if possible at all because of learning during testing. Also, the occurrence of a quieting effect is no indication in itself of an infantile version of the experience of pleasure, especially while so many issues remain unresolved about subjective experience in human infants, let alone in other species (Booth, 1978a).

The linear network design for diagnosing pleasure could be explored much more economically with verbal responses in human adults. A vocabulary would have to be found and used in a way by each person that expressed sensual thrill quite distinctly from interest in eating. Pleasantness ratings fail to do that and *liking* is no better. Rating the liking for the sweetness, crispness, or whatever, as distinct from for the food overall, is intended to assess attitude to specifically the sensory characteristics of the food on offer, or even the affect that they evoke. Yet liking ratings are well correlated with overall ratings of food choice (Booth, 1987d) or reported actual behavior (Tuorila, 1988). Not only should the vocabulary make a clear distinction between wish to eat the food and the pleasure evoked by eating it but the two ratings have to be shown to be dissociated in the conditions under test. If the ratings covary to an extent approaching their reliabilities, then there is no evidence that they reflect more than one underlying variable (Booth, 1987a).

Dissociation between Motivation and Pleasure

The methodologically essential dissociation between liking a food and getting a kick out of it is unlikely psychologically or even logically to be qualitative or categorical, i.e., to include occurrences of pleasure in the absence of positive motivation. That is, the dissociation would almost inevitably have to be quantitative.

Thus, to get evidence that pleasures exist, we need situations in which strong positive motivation is not accompanied by as much pleasure as usual and/or where substantial pleasure accompanies a weak or negative motivation which is often not appreciably pleasurable. Then the measures of pleasure and motivation will be decorrelated, disconfounding the thrill from the disposition. When dissociated from measures of motivation in this way, the graded output that is a construct-valid expression of pleasure can be used to identify the occurrence of the sensual experience and to estimate its magnitude, as the subjectivists merely assume that a "direct scaling" procedure does.

Finding Some Thrilling Food

The test food must of course be eaten in circumstances where it might really give sensual pleasure. So, having specified the formal methodological requirements for getting evidence that a pleasure has actually been experienced (and how strong it was), we must return to our intuitive and scientific knowledge of the realities of human (or animal) life to see if we can make observations that meet these conditions.

An important relaxation of the requirements is that these observations do not have to be made in experimentally fully controlled conditions. A deterministic theoretical model must still be applied to measurements made of the effective variations in influences on the responses, but these observations can come from spontaneously occurring situations. That is, we can try to think of differences between monitorable natural situations that might provide a big thrill with only modest interest or, on the other hand, a strong attraction but little pleasure in it.

A conceptually simple structure of such differences would be a pair of aspects of the situation which each began to invoke increasing pleasure only at the levels at which they evoked relatively strong motivation. Depending on how the individual integrated those two influences, both of them present at just above the "pleasure threshold" might induce strong pleasure at moderate motivation, whereas a combination of a strongly motivating level of one and a poorly motivating level of the other might produce substantial motivation with no pleasure. "Balance" in the flavoring of food and drinks may be an example. Lightly salted and faintly smelling onion soup might be more weakly flavored than perfect but still delicious, whereas the right taste with no aroma or a powerful onion aroma with no taste are just soups to be eaten. Such designing from the armchair is no use; we are dealing with real-life experiences. We need expert cooks on the investigating team and genuinely discriminating gastronomic enthusiasts to provide the data.

Other sorts of dissociation between motivation and pleasure might rely on changes over time in the respondent. An example is the difference between relative novelty and habitual indulgence, such as in a high-quality ice cream flavor.

For sure, any experiment or even controlled observations on hedonic reactions to foods must be thoroughly naturalistic. Otherwise the normal phenomena will not be observed. This is not because they are beyond scientific investigation, or are weak or even nonexistent. The brute fact is that crass artificiality, personal dislikes and boring repetition are all killers of pleasure.

ENVOI

To sum up, then, the hedonic element is much harder to measure than has been traditionally assumed, in and out of psychology. Nothing is gained, and much is lost, by careless extension of the idea of hedonic experience to the observed behavioral dispositions of conditioned preference and appetite.

Nevertheless, we now have strong enough methodology to diagnose perceptual, cognitive and motivational processes in individuals. By the use of such causal analysis of individual mentation, it is becoming scientifically feasible to show whether pleasures occur that influence expressive behavior and whether they amplify the cooler contributions to motivation.

As it happened, perhaps not entirely coincidentally, this individual cognitive method was developed from a discrimination model of the generalization decrements around multidimensional conditioned food-preference stimuli. It would therefore be appropriate to give more research attention to the neglected phenomena of normal animal and human learning to recognize foods and related experience-based changes in their acceptability.

REFERENCES

Anderson, N. H. (1981). *Foundations of information integration theory.* New York: Academic Press.

Arbour, K. J., & Wilkie, D. M. (1988). Rodents' (*Rattus, Mesocricetus,* and *Meriones*) use of learned caloric information in diet selection. *Journal of Comparative Psychology, 102,* 177–181.

Ashby, F., & Perrin, N. (1988). Towards a unified theory of similarity and recognition. *Psychological Review, 95,* 124–150.

Baker, B. J., & Booth, D. A. (1989a). Preference conditioning by concurrent diets with delayed proportional reinforcement. *Physiology and Behavior, 46*(4), 585–59.

Baker, B. J., & Booth, D. A. (1989b). Genuinely olfactory preferences conditioned by protein repletion. *Appetite, 13,* 223–227.

Baker, B. J., Booth, D. A., Duggan, J. P., & Gibson, E. L. (1987). Protein appetite demonstrated: learned specificity of protein-cue preference to protein need in adult rats. *Nutrition Research, 7,* 481–487.

Birch, L. L., & Deysher, M. (1985). Conditioned and unconditioned caloric compensation: Evidence for self regulation of food intake by young children. *Learning and Motivation, 16,* 341–355.

Birch, L. L., Billman, J., & Richards, S. S. (1984). Time of day influences food acceptability. *Appetite, 5,* 109–116.

Birch, L. L., Zimmerman, S. I., & Hind, H. (1980). The influence of social-affective context on the formation of children's food preferences. *Child Development, 51,* 856–861.

Blass, E. M. (1987). Opioids, sweets and a mechanism for positive affect. In J. Dobbing (Ed.), *Sweetness* (pp. 115–140). London: Springer-Verlag.

Bolles, R. C., Hayward, L., & Crandall, C. (1981). Conditioned taste preferences based on caloric density. *Journal of Experimental Psychology: Animal Behavior Processes, 7,* 59–69.

Booth, D. A. (1972a). Satiety and behavioral caloric compensation following intragastric glucose loads in the rat. *Journal of Comparative and Physiological Psychology, 78,* 412–432.

Booth, D. A. (1972b). Feeding inhibition by glucose loads, compared between normal and diabetic rats. *Physiology and Behavior, 8,* 801–805.

Booth, D. A. (1972c). Caloric compensation in rats with continuous or intermittent access to food. *Physiology and Behavior, 8,* 891–899.

Booth, D. A. (1972d). Taste reactivity in satiated, ready to eat and starved rats. *Physiology and Behavior, 8,* 901–908.

Booth, D. A. (1972e). Conditioned satiety in the rat. *Journal of Comparative and Physiological Psychology, 81,* 457–471.

Booth, D. A. (1974a). Food intake compensation for increase or decrease in the protein content of the diet. *Behavioral Biology, 12,* 31–40.

Booth, D. A. (1974b). Acquired sensory preferences for protein in diabetic and normal rats. *Physiological Psychology, 2,* 344–348.

Booth, D. A. (1976). Approaches to feeding control. In T. Silverstone (Ed.), *Appetite and food intake* (pp. 417–478). West Berlin: Abakon Verlagsgesellschaft/Dahlem Konferenzen.

Booth, D. A. (1977a). Satiety and appetite are conditioned reactions. *Psychosomatic Medicine, 39,* 76–81.

Booth, D. A. (1977b). Appetite and satiety as metabolic expectancies In Y. Katsuki, M. Sato, S. F. Takagi & Y. Oomura (Eds.), *Food intake and chemical senses* (pp. 317–330). Tokyo: University of Tokyo Press.

Booth, D. A. (1978a). Language acquisition as the addition of verbal routines. In R. N. Campbell & P. T. Smith (Eds.), *Recent advances in the psychology of language. Formal and experimental approaches* (pp. 219–241). New York: Plenum Press.

Booth, D. A. (1978b). Prediction of feeding behavior from energy flows in the rat. In D. A. Booth (Ed.), *Hunger models: Computable theory of feeding control* (pp. 227–278). London: Academic Press.

Booth, D. A. (1979). Preference as a motive. In J. H. A. Kroeze (Ed.), *Preference behaviour and chemoreception* (pp. 317–334). London: IRL.

Booth, D. A. (1980a). Conditioned reactions in motivation. In F. M. Toates & T. R. Halliday (Eds.), *Analysis of motivational processes* (pp. 77–102). London: Academic Press.

Booth, D. A. (1980b). Glucose-induced satiety assessed by state-dependent conditioned preference/aversion. *Abstracts: Seventh International Conference on the Physiology of Food and Fluid Intake (IUPS), Warsaw.*

Booth, D. A. (1981a). The physiology of appetite. *British Medical Bulletin, 37,* 135–140.

Booth, D. A. (1981b). How should questions about satiation be asked? *Appetite, 2,* 237–244.

Booth, D. A. (1982). Normal control of omnivore intakes by taste and smell. In J. E. Steiner & J. R. Ganchrow (Eds.), *Determination of behaviour by chemical stimuli* (pp. 233–243). London: IRL Press.

Booth, D. A. (1985). Food-conditioned eating preferences and aversions with interoceptive elements: Learned appetites and satieties. *Annals of New York Academy of Sciences, 443,* 22–37.

Booth, D. A. (1987a). Cognitive experimental psychology of appetite. In R. A. Boakes, M. J. Burton & D. A. Popplewell (Eds.), *Eating habits* (pp. 175–209). Chichester: Wiley.

Booth, D. A. (1987b). Central dietary "feedback onto nutrient selection": not even a scientific hypothesis. *Appetite, 8,* 195–201.

Booth, D. A. (1987c). Evaluation of the usefulness of low-calorie sweeteners in weight control. In T. H. Grenby (Ed.), *Developments in sweeteners—3* (pp. 287–316). London: Elsevier Applied Science.

Booth, D. A. (1987d). Objective measurement of determinants of food acceptance: sensory, physiological and psychosocial. In J. Solms, D. A. Booth, R. M. Pangborn, & O. Raunhardt (Eds.), *Food acceptance and nutrition* (pp. 1–27). London: Academic Press.

Booth, D. A. (1987e). How to measure learned control of food or water intake. In F. M. Toates & N. E. Rowland (Eds.), *Feeding and drinking. Techniques in the behavioral and neural sciences, Volume 1* (pp. 111–149). Amsterdam: Elsevier.

Booth, D. A. (1988). A simulation model of psychobiosocial theory of human food-intake controls. *International Journal of Vitamin and Nutrition Research, 58,* 55–69.

Booth, D. A. (1990a). Learned role of tastes in eating motivation. in E. D. Capaldi & T. L. Powley (Eds.), *Taste, experience and feeding.* Washington, DC: American Psychological Association.

Booth, D. A. (1990b). The behavioral and neural sciences of ingestion. In E. M. Stricker (Ed.), *Handbook of behavioral neurobiology, Volume 10: Food and water intake.* New York: Plenum Press.

Booth, D. A. (1990c). Protein- and carbohydrate-specific craving: neuroscience and sociology. In M. I. Friedman & M. R. Kare (Eds.), *Chemical senses: Appetite and nutrition.* New York: Marcel Dekker.

Booth, D. A., & Baker, B. J. (1990). dl-Fenfluramine challenge to nutrient-specific textural preference conditioned by concurrent presentation of two diets. *Behavioral Neuroscience, 104,* 226–229.

Booth, D. A., & Blair, A. J. (1989). Objective factors in the appeal of a brand during use by the individual consumer. In D. M. H. Thomson (Ed.), *Food acceptability* (pp. 329–346) London: Elsevier Applied Science.

Booth, D. A., & Davis, J. D. (1973). Gastrointestinal factors in the acquisition of oral sensory control of satiation. *Physiology and Behavior, 11,* 23–29.

Booth, D. A., & Jarman, S. P. (1976). Inhibition of food intake in the rat following complete absorption of glucose delivered into the stomach, intestine or liver. *Journal of Physiology, 259,* 501–522.

Booth, D. A., & Miller, N. E. (1969). Lateral hypothalamus mediated effects of a food signal on blood glucose concentration. *Physiology and Behavior, 4,* 1003–1009.

Booth, D. A., & Simson, P. C. (1971). Food preferences acquired by association with variations in amino acid nutrition. *Quarterly Journal of Experimental Psychology, 23,* 135–145.

Booth, D. A., & Simson, P. C. (1974). Taste aversion induced by an histidine-free amino acid load. *Physiological Psychology, 2,* 349–351.

Booth, D. A., & Toase, A. M. (1983). Conditioning of hunger/satiety signals as well as flavour cues in dieters. *Appetite, 4,* 235–236.

Booth, D. A., Conner, M. T., & Gibson, E. L. (1989). Measurement of food perception, food preference, and nutrient selection. *Annals of the New York Academy of Sciences, 561,* 226–242.

Booth, D. A., Conner, M. T., & Marie, S. (1987). Sweetness and food selection: measurement of sweeteners' effects on acceptance. In J. Dobbing (Ed.), *Sweetness* (pp. 143–160). London: Springer-Verlag.

Booth, D. A., Lee, M., & McAleavey, C. (1976a). Acquired sensory control of satiation in man. *British Journal of Psychology, 67,* 137–147.

Booth, D. A., Lovett, D., & McSherry, G. M. (1972). Postingestive modulation of the sweetness preference gradient in the rat. *Journal of Comparative and Physiological Psychology, 78,* 485–512.

Booth, D. A., Mather, P., & Fuller, J. (1982). Starch content of ordinary foods associatively conditions human appetite and satiation, indexed by intake and eating pleasantness of starch-paired flavours. *Appetite, 3,* 163–184.

Booth, D. A., Stoloff, R., & Nicholls, J. (1974). Dietary flavor acceptance in infant rats established by association with effects of nutrient composition. *Physiological Psychology, 2,* 313–319.

Booth, D. A., Thompson, A. L., & Shahedian, B. (1983). A robust, brief measure of an individual's most preferred level of salt in an ordinary foodstuff. *Appetite, 4,* 301–312.

Booth, D. A., Toates, F. M., & Platt, S. V. (1976b). Control system for hunger and its implications in animals and man. In D. Novin, W. Wyrwickà, & G. A. Bray (Eds.), *Hunger: Basic mechanisms and clinical implications* (pp. 127–142). New York: Raven Press.

Cabanac, M. (1971). Physiological role of pleasure. *Science, 173,* 1103–1107.

Cabanac, M., & Fantino, M. (1979). Origin of olfacto-gustatory alliesthesia: intestinal sensitivity to carbohydrate concentration? *Physiology and Behavior, 18,* 1039–1045.

Capaldi, E. D., & Davidson, T. L. (1979). Control of instrumental behavior by deprivation stimuli. *Journal of Experimental Psychology: Animal Behavior Processes, 5,* 355–367.

Capaldi, E. D., & Friedman, F. (1976). Deprivation and reward as compound stimuli. *Learning and Motivation, 7,* 17–30.

Capaldi, E. D., & Myers, D. E. (1982). Taste preferences as a function of food deprivation during original taste exposure. *Animal Learning and Behaviour, 10,* 211–219.

Chiva, M. (1985). *Le doux et l'amer. Sensation gustative, emotion et communication chez le jeune enfant.* Paris: Presses Universitaires de France.

Conner, M. T. (1988). *Measurement of the sensory determinants of food acceptance.* Unpublished doctoral thesis, University of Birmingham.

Conner, M. T., & Booth, D. A. (1988). Preferred sweetness of a lime drink and preference for sweet over non-sweet foods, related to sex and reported age and body weight. *Appetite,* 10, 25–35.

Conner, M. T., Booth, D. A., Clifton, V. J., & Griffiths, R. P. (1988a). Individualized optimization of the salt content of white bread for acceptability. *Journal of Food Science, 53,* 549–554.

Conner, M. T., Haddon, A. V., & Booth, D. A. (1986). Very rapid, precise measurement of effects of constituent variation on product acceptability: consumer sweetness preferences in a lime drink. *Lebensmittel-Wissenschaft und -Technologie, 19,* 486–490.

Conner, M. T., Haddon, A. V., Pickering, E. S., & Booth, D. A. (1988b). Sweet tooth demonstrated: individual differences in preference for both sweet foods and foods highly sweetened. *Journal of Applied Psychology, 73,* 275–280.

Conner, M. T., Land, D. G., & Booth, D. A. (1987). Effects of stimulus range on judgments of sweetness intensity in a lime drink. *British Journal of Psychology, 78,* 357–364.

Deutsch, J. A. (1978). The stomach in food satiation and the regulation of appetite. *Progress in Neurobiology, 10,* 135–153.

Deutsch, J. A. (1983). Dietary control and the stomach. *Progress in Neurobiology, 20,* 313–332.

Deutsch, J. A., & Walton, N. Y. (1977). Rat alcoholism model in a free cgoice situation. *Behavioral Biology, 19,* 349–360.

Deutsch, J. A., Molina, F., & Puerto, A. (1976). Conditioned taste aversion caused by palatable nutrients. *Behavioral Biology, 16,* 161–174.

Domjan, M. (1973). The role of ingestion in odor-toxicosis learning in the rat. *Journal of Comparative and Physiological Psychology, 84,* 507–521.

Elizalde, G., & Sclafani, A. (1988). Starch-based conditioned flavor preferences in rats: influence of taste, calories and CS-US delay. *Appetite,* 11, 179–200.

Ennis, D. M., & Mullen, K. (1986). Theoretical aspects of sensory discrimination. *Chemical Senses, 11,* 513–522.

Fanselow, M. S., & Birk, J. (1982). Flavor-flavor associations induce hedonic shifts in taste preference. *Animal Learning and Behavior, 10,* 223–228.

Fedorchak, P. M., & Bolles, R. C. (1987). Hunger enhances the expression of calorie- but not taste-mediated conditioned flavor preferences. *Journal of Experimental Psychology: Animal Behavior Processes, 13,* 73–79.

Fischler, C. (1987). Attitudes towards sugar and sweetness in historical and social perspective. In J. Dobbing (Ed.), *Sweetness* (pp. 83–98). Heidelberg: Spring-Verlag.

Forbes, D. T., & Holland, P. C. (1985). Spontaneous configuring in conditioned flavor aversion. *Journal of Experimental Psychology: Animal Behavior Processes, 11,* 224–240.

Galef, B. G. (1989). Enduring social enhancement of rats' preferences for the palatable and the piquant. *Appetite, 13,* 81–92.

Garcia, J., & Ervin, F. R. (1968). Gustatory-visceral and telereceptor-cutaneous conditioning. Adaptation in the internal and external milieus. *Communications in Behavioral Biology, 1,* 389–415.

Garcia, J., Kimeldorf, D. J., & Hunt, E. L. (1961). The use of ionizing radiation as a motivating stimulus. *Psychological Review, 68,* 383–395.

Garcia, J., Lasiter, P. S., Bermudez-Rattoni, F., & Deems, D. A. (1985). A general theory of aversion learning. *Annals of New York Academy of Sciences, 443,* 8–21.

Gibson, E. L., & Booth, D. A. (1986). Acquired protein appetite in rats: dependence on a protein-specific need state. *Experientia, 42,* 1003–1004.

Gibson, E. L., & Booth, D. A. (1989). Dependence of carbohydrate-conditioned flavor preference on internal state in rats. *Learning and Motivation, 20,* 36–47.

Grill, H. J., & Berridge, K. C. (1985). Taste reactivity as a measure of the neural control of palatability. *Progress in Psychobiology and Physiological Psychology, 11,* 1–61.

Hall, W. G. (1988). Preferences conditioned by CCK in rat pups. *Society for Neuroscience Abstracts*

Harris, G., & Booth, D. A. (1987). Infants' preference for salt in food: its dependence upon recent dietary experience. *Journal of Reproductive and Infant Psychology, 5,* 97–104.

Hill, A., Blundell, J. E., & Leathwood, P. D. (1987). Effects of meal composition on appetite, satiety and food preferences. *Human Nutrition, 41*A, 224–257.

Holman, E. W. (1975). Immediate and delayed reinforcers for flavor preferences in rats. *Learning and Motivation, 6,* 91–100.

Le Magnen, J. (1956). Hyperphagie provoquée chez le rat blanc per alteration du mécanisme de satiété peripherique. *Comptes Rendues de la Société de Biologie, Paris, 150,* 32–34.

Le Magnen, J. (1957). Le mécanisme d'établissement d'un appétit différentiel pour des régimes de diverse densitiés caloriques. *Journal de Physiologie, 49,* 1105–1117.

Le Magnen, J. (1967). Food habits. In C. F. Code (Ed.), *Handbook of physiology. Alimentary canal, Vol. 1* (pp. 11–30). Washington DC: American Physiological Society.

Lewis, V. J., & Booth, D. A. (1986). Causal influences within an individual's dieting thoughts, feelings and behaviour. In J. M. Diehl & C. Leitzman (Eds.), *Measurement and determinants of food habits and food preferences* (pp. 187–208). Wageningen: Department of Human Nutrition, Agricultural University.

Liddle, R. A., Green, G. M., Conrad, C. R., & Williams, J. A. (1986). Proteins but not amino acids, carbohydrates, or fats stimulate cholecystokinin secretion in the rat. *American Journal of Physiology, 251,* G243–G248.

Lyons, W. (1986). *The disappearance of introspection.* Oxford: Oxford University Press.

Marie, S. (1986). *Perception of aroma from food in the mouth.* Unpublished doctoral Thesis, University of Birmingham.

Marie, S., Land D. G., & Booth D. A. (1987). Comparison of flavour perception by smell and by mouth. In M. Martens, G. A. Dalen & H. Russwurm (Eds.), *Flavour science and technology* (pp. 301–308). Chichester: Wiley.

Mather, P., Nicolaidis, S., & Booth, D. A. (1978). Compensatory and conditioned feeding responses to scheduled glucose infusions in the rat. *Nature, 273,* 461–463.

McCleary, R. A. (1953). Taste and post-ingestion factors in specific-hunger behavior. *Journal of Comparative and Physiological Psychology, 46,* 411–421.

Mehiel, R., & Bolles, R. C. (1984). Learned flavor preferences based on caloric outcome. *Animal Learning and Behavior, 12,* 421–427.

Mehiel, R., & Bolles, R. C. (1988). Learned flavor preferences based on calories are independent of initial hedonic value. *Animal Learning and Behavior, 16,* 383–387.

Mook, D. G., Brane, J. A., Gonder-Frederick, L., & Whitt, J. A. (1986). Satieties and cross-satieties for three diets in the rat. *Physiology and Behavior, 36,* 887–895.

Mook, D. G. (1988). On the organization of satiety. *Appetite, 11,* 27–39.

Pain, J. F., & Booth, D. A. (1968). Toxiphobia to odors. *Psychonomic Science, 10,* 363–364.

Poulton, E. C. (1979). Models for biases in judging sensory magnitude. *Psychological Bulletin, 86,* 777–803.

Poulton, E. C. (1989). *Bias in quantifying judgments.* Hillsdale NJ: Lawrence Erlbaum Associates.

Revusky, S. H. (1968). Effects of thirst level during consumption of flavored water on subsequent preferences. *Journal of Comparative and Physiological Psychology, 66,* 777–779.

Revusky, S. H., Pohl, R. W., & Coombes, S. (1980). Flavor aversions and deprivation state. *Animal Learning and Behavior, 8,* 543–549.

Richardson, R., Williams, C., & Riccio, D. C. (1984). Stimulus generalization of conditioned taste aversion in rats. *Behavioral and Neural Biology, 41,* 41–53.

Rolls, B. J., Rolls, E. T., Rowe, E. A., & Sweeney, K. (1981a). Sensory specific satiety in Man. *Physiology and Behavior, 27,* 137–142.

Rolls, B. J., Rowe, E. A., Kingston, B., Megson, A., & Gunary, R. (1981b). Variety in a meal enhances food intake in Man. *Physiology and Behavior, 26,* 215–221.

Rozin, P., & Kalat, J. W. (1971). Specific hungers and poison avoidance as adaptive specialization of learning. *Psychological Review, 78,* 459–486.

Rozin, P., & Pelchat, M. L. (1988). Memories of mammaries: adaptations to weaning from milk. *Progress in Psychobiology and Physiological Psychology, 13,* 1–29.

Ruddy, L. L. (1980). Nasal intubation: a minimally obtrusive anosmia technique applied to rats. *Physiology and Behavior, 24,* 881–886.

Rusiniak, K. W., Hankins, W. G., Garcia, J., & Brett, L. P. (1979). Flavor-illness aversions: Potentiation of odor by taste in rats. *Behavioral and Neural Biology, 25,* 1–17.

Sherman, J. E., Hickis, C. F., Rice, A. G., Rusiniak, K. W., & Garcia, J. (1983). Preferences and aversions for stimuli paired with ethanol. *Animal Learning and Behavior, 11,* 101–106.

Simson, P. C., & Booth, D. A. (1974). The rejection of a diet which has been associated with a single administration of a histidine-free amino acid mixture. *British Journal of Nutrition, 31,* 285–296.

Sjöden, P. -O., & Archer, T. (1981). Associative and non-associative effects of exteroceptive context in taste-aversion conditioning with rats. *Behavioral and Neural Biology, 33,* 74–92.

Smith, G. P., & Gibbs, J. (1979). Postprandial satiety. *Progress in Psychobiology and Physiological Psychology, 10,* 179–242.

Supak, T., Macrides, F., & Chorover, S. (1971). The baitshyness effect extended to olfactory discrimination. *Communications in Behavioral Biology, 5,* 321–324.

Tordoff, M. G., & Friedman, M. I. (1986). Hepatic portal glucose infusions decrease food intake and increase food preference. *American Journal of Physiology, 251,* R192–R196.

Treit, D., Spetch, M. L., & Deutsch, J. A. (1983). Variety in the flavor of a food enhances eating in the rat: a controlled demonstration. *Physiology and Behavior, 30,* 207–211.

Tuorila, H. (1988). Hedonic responses and attitudes in the acceptance of sweetness, saltiness and fattiness of foods. In J. Solms, D. A. Booth, R. M. Pangborn, & O. Raunhardt (Eds.), *Food acceptance and nutrition* (pp. 337–351). London: Academic Press.

Van Vort, W., & Smith, G. P. (1983). The relationship between the positive reinforcing and satiating effects of a meal in the rat. *Physiology and Behavior, 30,* 279–284.

Van Vort, W., & Smith, G. P. (1987). Sham feeding experience produces a conditioned increase of meal size. *Appetite, 9,* 21–29.

Weiffenbach, J. M. (Ed.). (1975). *Taste and development. The genesis of sweet preference.* Washington DC: US Government Printing Office.

Weingarten, H. P. (1985). Stimulus control of eating: implications for a two-factor theory of hunger. *Appetite, 6,* 387–401.

Weingarten, H. P., & Martin, G. M. (1989). Mechanisms of conditioned meal initiation. *Physiology and Behavior, 45,* 735–740.

Wittgenstein, L. (1953). *Philosophical investigations.* Oxford: Blackwells.

Wooley, O. W., Wooley, S. C., & Dunham, R. B. (1972). Calories and sweet taste: effects on sucrose preference in the obese and nonobese. *Physiology and Behavior, 9,* 765–768.

4 The Hedonics of Sugar and Starch

Anthony Sclafani
Brooklyn College

The concepts of "palatability" and "hedonic response" have long been associated with the sweet taste of sugar. As noted by Young (1967), the term "hedonic" is derived from a Greek root (hedon) that has two basic meanings: (1) sweet tasting and (2) pleasant. Similarly, in contemporary English sweet has two meanings: (1) the taste sensation induced by sugar, and (2) pleasing to the taste or, more generally, "pleasing to the mind or feelings" (Webster, 1975). This second meaning of sweet is similar to that given for the word palatable, i.e., "agreeable to the palate or taste" (Webster, 1975). The synonymy among the terms sweet, hedonic, and palatable derives from human biology. That is, the taste of sugar is innately pleasurable to humans; this is demonstrated by the orofacial and sucking responses displayed by newborn infants on their first exposure to sugar water (Ganchrow, Steiner, & Daher, 1983). (Note that "hedonic response" may be used to refer to negative [unpleasurable or unpalatable] as well positive [pleasurable or palatable] responses. Hedonic response is used here in a positive sense unless specified otherwise.)

In addition to humans, many other animal species are attracted to the sweet taste of sugar (Kare, 1971). Although strictly speaking, *sweet taste* refers to a human sensation, it has become commonplace to use the term in describing the behavioral and physiological responses displayed by nonhuman animals to sugars and artificial sweeteners. Similarly, the concepts of palatability and hedonic response, although originally derived from human experience, are also applied to nonhuman animals (Young, 1967). Thus, based on the observations that nondeprived rats readily consume sugar solutions and will perform various operant tasks to obtain sugar, it is inferred that sugar has a palatable, i.e., pleasing taste to rats.

Recent studies indicate that sugars are not the only carbohydrates with a pleasant taste to animals. That is, unlike humans, laboratory rats are very attracted to the taste of starch and starch-derived polysaccharides (Sclafani, 1987). Thus, starch is *sweet* to rats in the sense that it has a pleasant taste (see definition 2). However, starch is *not* sweet to rats in the sense that it tastes like sucrose (definition 1); rather starch-derived polysaccharides appear to produce a taste sensation qualitatively different from that of sucrose (Nissenbaum & Sclafani, 1987b; see below).

The hedonic response to carbohydrates is determined not only by taste but by a variety of other factors including the postingestive effects of the carbohydrates, the physiological state of the animal, and the animal's previous experience with foods. This chapter reviews the various factors that determine the palatability of sugar and starch. The discussion focuses on the laboratory rat as it is the most extensively studied species. Before discussing carbohydrate palatability in detail, conceptual and methodological issues related to the study of palatability in animals are reviewed.

CONCEPT AND METHODOLOGY

Concept

The hedonic response to carbohydrates, and food in general, is determined by a number of factors in addition to the orosensory properties of the food. This view represents a change from earlier conceptualizations of food hedonics and palatability. That is, in the early literature palatability was defined as the "hedonic value" of a food that depends solely on "taste, aroma, texture, temperature, appearance, and other sensory properties" (Young, 1961). Although palatability is still often used in this way, many investigators now define palatability as a *response* to food rather than as a stimulus attribute of food (e.g., Grill & Berridge, 1985; LeMagnen, 1987; Young, 1977). According to this latter interpretation, palatability refers to the hedonic response to a foodstuff that depends not only on orosensory qualities (i.e., flavor: taste, aroma, texture, etc.) but also the animal's current physiological state and its previous experience with foods. Palatability, then, is not an invariant property of food but represents a dynamic interaction between the orosensory and nutritional properties of the food and the behavioral experience and physiological state of the animal. Nevertheless, if all other factors are held constant, the palatability of a food, i.e., the *palatability response* elicited by the food, will vary as a function of the food's orosensory qualities, i.e., its flavor. (In this chapter the terms hedonic response and palatability response are used interchangeably.)

The multifaceted nature of palatability is illustrated in Fig. 4.1, which presents a conceptual model that I use to describe the hedonic response of rodents to sugar and starch. In this model, the *initial* hedonic response to a food is deter-

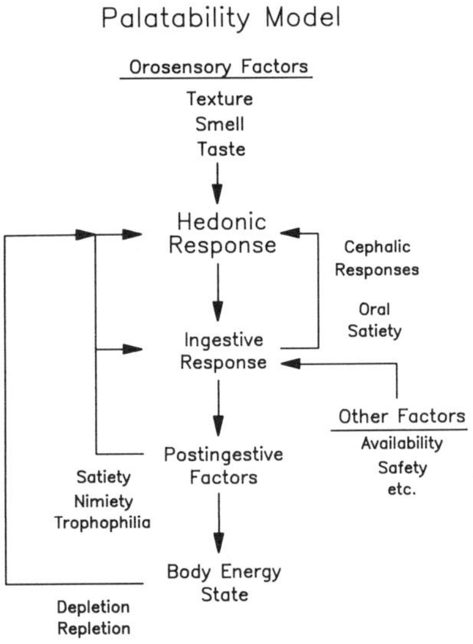

Palatability Model

FIG. 4.1. Conceptual model of carbohydrate palatability. See text for further description.

mined by the orosensory properties of the food and the animal's current physiological state. As the animal eats the food, the palatability response is modified as ingestive and postingestive factors come into play. These factors may have direct and immediate effects on food palatability via unconditioned reactions, as well as indirect and delayed effects via conditioning processes (Booth, 1985).

While the hedonic response to food is an important determinant of food intake, it clearly is not the only one. As indicated in Fig. 4.1, ingestive behavior is influenced by other factors, such as availability, i.e., how easy or difficult food is to obtain (Collier, Hirsch, & Hamlin, 1972), and safety, i.e., does the food expose the animal to pain or predation (Rozin & Zellner, 1985). For example, a sugar solution may elicit a strong hedonic response but the animal may consume only small amounts because of the work required to obtain the solution or because the drinking tube is electrified. Alternatively, a food that does not elicit a strong hedonic response may nevertheless be ingested because the animal anticipates some positive consequence, i.e., access to a preferred food or activity (see Rozin & Zellner, 1985). Some positive consequences (e.g., caloric repletion), however, may alter the animal's palatability response to the food (see the following).

Methodology

The hedonic response of animals to food cannot be directly measured but must be inferred from the animals' behavioral reaction to the food. The distinction between hedonic and nonhedonic determinants of the feeding response can be problematic. The *prima facie* evidence that carbohydrates elicit a hedonic response in rats is the willingess of nondeprived animals not only to consume readily available sugar or starch, but to press bars or run down alleyways to obtain small amounts of sugar or starch (Sclafani, 1987; Young; 1967).

As discussed in detail elsewhere, a number of techniques have been used to quantify the palatability response of animals to food stimuli (Grill & Berridge, 1985; LeMagnen, 1987; Sclafani, 1987; Young, 1967). These techniques involve measures of appetitive behavior (e.g., running or bar pressing for food) and consummatory behavior (e.g., orofacial reactivity, licking rates, sham-feeding behavior, intake measures) in choice or no-choice situations. There is no one optimal technique, but three in particular are widely used as measures of the palatability response. These include orofacial reactivity tests that analyze oromotor fixed action patterns elicited by intraoral infusions of taste solutions (Grill & Berridge, 1985), brief (1–3 min) consummatory response tests that measure integrated lick rates or consumption in one-choice or two-choice situations (Davis & Levine, 1977; Young, 1967), and sham-feeding tests which involve esophageal or gastric fistula preparations (Mook & Wagner, 1988; Weingarten & Watson, 1982a).

Using these techniques, it is possible to assess the contribution of the various factors that determine the palatability response. For example, by varying the orosensory properties of the food stimulus while keeping other factors (e.g., postingestive feedback, body energy state) relatively constant, the role of flavor in determining palatability can be determined. Similarly, the influence of postingestive factors on the palatability response can be assessed by varying postingestive feedback using, for example, sham-feeding or intragastric infusion procedures, while keeping other factors (e.g., orosensory stimuli) constant. To determine the impact of conditioning processes on the palatability response a variety of behavioral analysis techniques can be used (Booth, 1987).

CARBOHYDRATE TASTES

According to the palatability model depicted in Fig. 4.1, the hedonic response to food is initiated by orosensory stimuli which include taste, odor, texture, and temperature. With respect to carbohydrates, most attention has focused on taste and this is the subject of the present review. Recent studies indicate that rats have two separate tastes for sugars and starch-derived polysaccharides. The evidence to support this view is summarized in this section.

Sugar Taste

The sugar or *sweet* taste system has been extensively studied in rodents at both neural and behavioral levels (Jakinovich & Sugarman, 1988; Pfaffman, 1982). The three most common sugars, sucrose, fructose, and glucose, appear to produce qualitatively similar taste sensations in rodents. The three sugars evoke similar patterns of neural activity in peripheral gustatory nerves and in the nucleus tractus solitarius (NTS), the first gustatory relay nucleus in the brain (Jakinovich & Sugarman, 1988; Scott & Mark, 1986). In addition, rodents that acquire a conditioned taste aversion to one sugar when its consumption has been paired with toxicosis generalize this aversion to the other two sugars (Nissenbaum & Sclafani, 1987b; Nowlis, Frank, & Pfaffman, 1980). These and other findings suggest that sucrose, glucose, and fructose stimulate a common sweet-taste receptor which contains a glucose subsite and a fructose subsite (Jakinovich, 1984). Sucrose, being a glucose-fructose disaccharide, is the most potent naturally occurring stimulus for this receptor (Jakinovich, 1984).

There is now considerable evidence that rats as well as other animals have more than one type of sweet taste receptor (Beidler & Tonosaki, 1984; Jakinovich & Sugarman, 1988). Based on studies of single neuron responses, taste blockers, taste mixtures, and cross-adaptation among different sweeteners, it has been suggested that as many as six different sugar receptors and a saccharin receptor exist in mammals (Jakinovich & Sugarman, 1988). However, the degree to which activation of these different receptors produces similar sweet taste sensations is not certain. Furthermore, some tastants, in addition to stimulating sweet receptors, stimulate other taste receptors and thus produce complex taste sensations. The artificial sweetener saccharin, for example, in addition to its sweet taste, has a bitter taste to humans and is commonly thought to taste bitter to rats as well (see Morrison & Jessup, 1977), although recent data question this interpretation. Thus, Stewart and Krafczek (1988) reported that rats did not generalize conditioned saccharin aversions to bitter stimuli.

Note that while sweet taste sensitivity has been traditionally localized at the tip of the tongue, recent experiments indicate that the taste buds in the rat's palate (nasoincisor duct) are the most responsive to sugars (Travers, Pfaffman, & Norgren, 1986). This finding provides added meaning to the definition of *palatability* as pleasing to the palate.

Polysaccharide Taste

Starch consists of large glucose polymers in which the glucose molecules are arranged in long linear chains (amylose starch) or short, highly branched chains (amylopectin starch). When starch is hydrolyzed in the mouth and gut, shorter glucose polymers are produced which are ultimately hydrolyzed to maltose and then to glucose. Starch and starch-derived polysaccharides are relatively tasteless to humans and have long been assumed to be bland tasting to animals as well. Recent studies, however, demonstrate that rats and probably other species have a well-developed taste for starch-derived polysaccharides (Sclafani, 1987). (The term *polysaccharide* is used here to refer to starch-derived saccharides containing three or more glucose units).

The discovery of the rat's polysaccharide taste sensitivity emerged from experiments conducted with Polycose, a corn starch hydrolysate that contains approximately 91% polysaccharides, 7% maltose, and 2% glucose by weight (Ross Laboratories, 1977). Rats readily consume Polycose solutions and at low concentrations prefer Polycose to sucrose, glucose, fructose, and maltose solutions (Sclafani & Clyne, 1987; Sclafani & Mann, 1987). Furthermore, the preference threshold for Polycose is 26 times lower than that for sucrose and maltose (Sclafani & Nissenbaum, 1987a). These and other findings (Sclafani & Nissenbaum, 1987b) indicate that it is the taste of the polysaccharides and not the small amounts of sugar in Polycose that rats find attractive. Preference tests conducted with glucose polymers of different sizes further indicate that rats prefer polymers containing 4 to 8 glucose units (maltooliogsaccharides) to smaller polymers (maltotriose, maltose, and glucose) as well as to larger polysaccharides (maltopolysaccharides of 20 or more glucose units) (Sclafani, Hertwig, Vigorito, Sloan, & Kerzner, 1987). These behavioral findings suggested that rats have "polysaccharide" taste receptors which have several glucose subsites (Sclafani, 1987).

Additional findings indicate that the taste sensation evoked by polysaccharides differs from that produced by sucrose. That is, rats conditioned to avoid Polycose solutions by pairing Polycose ingestion with LiCl-induced malaise display little or no avoidance of sucrose solutions; likewise, rats conditioned to avoid sucrose show little avoidance of Polycose (Nissenbaum & Sclafani, 1987b). Rats also show little cross-generalization between maltose and sucrose taste aversions (Nissenbaum & Sclafani, 1987b; Spector & Grill, 1988), but do cross-generalize between Polycose and maltose aversions (Nissenbaum & Sclafani, 1987b). This latter finding suggests that maltose, a glucose-glucose disaccharide, stimulates polysaccharide taste receptors, which may account for previously unexplained observations concerning the rat's strong maltose preference (Pfaffman, 1982). Consistent with these behavioral findings, electrophysiological recordings from the NTS indicate that the pattern of neural activity evoked by Polycose is quite distinct from that evoked by sucrose (Giza, Antonucci, Sclafani, & Scott, 1988).

Based on this evidence, Sclafani (1987) has proposed that rats have two different taste systems for carbohydrates; a sweet taste system for the detection of sugar-rich foods (e.g., fruits) and a polysaccharide taste system for the detection of starch-rich foods (e.g., vegetables, grains). The polysaccharide taste system is presumably not stimulated by intact starch molecules, which are not soluble in water, but by smaller, soluble polysaccharide molecules cleaved from starch by the action of salivary amylase. Although rats have a particularly active form of salivary amylase (Kunstyr, Peters, & Gartner, 1976), the number of soluble polysaccharide molecules released in the mouth is presumably not very large and this may explain why the preference threshold of the polysaccharide taste system is so low (Sclafani & Nissenbaum, 1987a). Much remains to be learned about the organization and function of the two carbohydrate taste systems in rats and in other species. (In addition to rats, hamsters, gerbils, spiny mice, and bonnet macaques display strong preferences for Polycose solutions (Feigin, Sclafani, & Sunday, 1987; Sunderland & Sclafani, 1988).) Furthermore, the role of other orosensory systems, particularly the trigeminal system, in the behavioral response to carbohydrates requires much further study (see Berridge & Fentress, 1985; Sclafani, Nissenbaum, & Vigorito, 1987).

CARBOHYDRATE PALATABILITY

Taste Factors

Neonatal Rats.   In order to assess the palatability of sweet and starchy tastes in animals with minimal or no prior experience with carbohydrates, several studies have examined the ingestive responses of neonatal rats to intraoral infusions of tastants. These studies have revealed that rat pups as young as 6 days of age are attracted to sweet taste as evidenced by the consummatory responses elicited by solutions of sucrose, lactose, and saccharin (Hall & Bryan, 1981; Jacobs, 1964; Vigorito & Sclafani, 1988). Rat pups are also attracted to the taste of polysaccharides at an early age (Vigorito & Sclafani, 1988). Figure 4.2 illustrates that 9-day old rat pups display similar concentration-dependent increases in mouthing behavior when infused with Polycose and sucrose solutions.

The rat pups used in these experiments were not completely naive to carbohydrates in that they had previously suckled dam's milk, which contains lactose. It is unlikely, however, that this influenced their ingestive responses to the sucrose, saccharin, and Polycose solutions; lactose at the concentration found in dam's milk (2.8%) elicits little ingestive behavior in rat pups (Jacobs, Smutz, & DuBose, 1977). Thus, it appears that rats have innate preferences for sweet and polysaccharide tastes. Other species (hamsters, rabbits, pigs, humans) are also

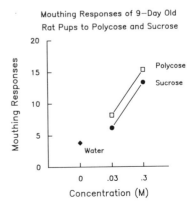

FIG. 4.2. Mean number of mouthing responses evoked by intraoral infusions of water (0 M), Polycose (.03 or .3 M), and sucrose (.03 or .3 M) in 9-day old rat pups. Adapted from Vigorito and Sclafani (1988). With permission of *Developmental Psychobiology.* Copyright John Wiley & Sons, Inc.

attracted to sweet solutions at very early ages (Ganchrow & Matzner, 1979; Ganchrow et al., 1983; Houpt & Houpt, 1977; Jacobs et al., 1977) but their response to polysaccharide solutions remains to be determined.

Adult rats.   The palatability response to carbohydrate tastes has been most extensively studied in adult rats. Taste effects have been isolated by using procedures that minimize postingestive effects (e.g., brief intake, sham-feeding, and bar-pressing tests). By minimizing postingestive influences, these procedures also reduce the possibility of conditioned alterations in the palatability response. However, since carbohydrate absorption can occur within minutes of eating (Steffens, 1969), and since the sham-feeding preparation does not necessarily block absorption (Sclafani & Nissenbaum, 1985), it is difficult to completely eliminate the influence of postingestive factors on the palatability response. Nevertheless, with postingestive and conditioned effects minimized, and the animal maintained in a relatively constant body energy state, "orosensory palatability" (the palatability response to orosensory stimulation) can be assessed.

(1) Taste Intensity.   It is well documented that the hedonic response to sweet taste varies as a function of taste intensity. This effect is illustrated for sucrose in Fig. 4.3, which summarizes results obtained with three different response measures (orofacial reactivity, licking rates, bar-pressing rates) using minimally deprived rats (Collier & Willis, 1961; Davis, 1973; Schwartz & Grill, 1984).

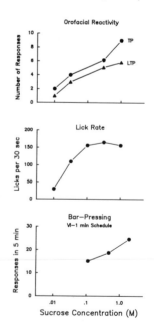

FIG. 4.3. Hedonic response of adult rats to sucrose as measured by orofacial reactivity, lick rate, and bar-pressing tests. **Top:** Mean number of rhythmic tongue protrusions (TP) and lateral tongue protrusions (LTP) elicited by intraoral infusions of sucrose (1 ml) at .01 to 1.0 M concentrations. Adapted from Schwartz & Grill (1984). With permission of *Chemical Senses.* Copyright IRL Press Limited. **Middle:** Mean number of licks/30 sec elicited by sucrose at .01 to 1.0 M concentrations during 2.5-min drinking tests. Adapted from Davis (1973). With permission of *Physiology and Behavior.* Copyright Pergamon Press, Inc. **Bottom:** Mean number of bar presses on VI-1 min schedule during first 5 min of 30-min tests with sucrose at .11 to 1.87 M concentrations. Adapted from Collier & Willis (1961). With permission of *Journal of Experimental Psychology.* Copyright American Psychological Association.

With all three measures, as sucrose concentration increased, the rats' behavioral response increased. The only deviation from this pattern is that lick rates reached an asymptote at the higher sucrose concentrations as the rats reached their maximal rate of licking. The hedonic responses elicited by other sugars (glucose, fructose, maltose, lactose, and galactose) also increase monotonically with concentration as measured by lick rate and sham-feeding tests (Davis, 1973; Davis & Levine, 1977; Davis, Collins, & Levine, 1976; Joyner, Smith, Shindledecker, & Pfaffman, 1985). This is not the case with saccharin, however; as saccharin concentration increases licking rates and sham-intakes increase but then decrease as concentration exceeds .5% (Sclafani & Nissenbaum, 1985; Young & Trafton, 1964). The reduced palatability of the more concentrated saccharin solutions has been attributed to the bitter taste component of saccharin (Pfaffman, 1969), although this interpretation is open to question (see Stewart & Krafczek, 1988).

The relative palatability of different sugars is, in general, consistent with the notion that palatability increases as sweet taste intensity increases. That is, based on the gustatory nerve responses evoked by sugars, sucrose is assumed to be sweeter than fructose and glucose to rats, and it is also the most preferred of the three sugars (Pfaffman, 1982; see also Nejad, 1986). However, the correlation between the gustatory nerve response and the hedonic response breaks down with other sugars, In particular, maltose evokes a relatively weak neural response (Nejad, 1986; Pfaffman, 1982) but is the most preferred sugar at low concentrations (Sclafani & Mann, 1987). This discrepancy may occur because maltose stimulates polysaccharide taste receptors as well as sweet receptors (Nissenbaum & Sclafani, 1987b).

There is also a discrepancy between the gustatory nerve response and the palatability response evoked by saccharin solutions. That is, chorda tympani nerve recordings indicate that saccharin at maximally preferred concentrations (e.g., .4%) produce neural responses equivalent to those produced by 18% to 36% sucrose (Ogawa, Sato, & Yamashita, 1969). Yet, behavioral data indicate that the most preferred saccharin solutions (.2 to .4%) are isohedonic to sucrose solutions of only 2 to 4% (Collier & Novell, 1967; Young & Madsen, 1963). Whether the relatively low palatability of saccharin is due to its having an aversive taste component (see Morrison & Jessup, 1977; Stewart & Krafczek, 1988) or because it is simply not as sweet as sucrose (see Sclafani & Nissenbaum, 1985) remains to be clarified. Although saccharin is a relatively poor sugar substitute, it is the only known artificial sweetener that rats respond to.

While less extensively studied than the sweet taste system, the available data indicate that the hedonic response to polysaccharide taste varies directly as a function of taste intensity as measured by lick rate, brief intake, and sham-feeding measures (Lucas & Sclafani, 1988; Nissenbaum & Sclafani, 1987a; Sclafani & Clyne, 1987). As discussed shortly, however, the taste intensity–hedonic response functions of the polysaccharide taste and sweet taste systems appear to differ.

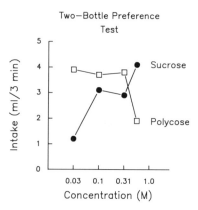

FIG. 4.4. Mean intake of sucrose and Polycose during 3-min, two-bottle preference tests at concentrations of .03 to .5 M. Adapted from Sclafani & Mann (1987). With permission of *Physiology and Behavior.* Copyright Pergamon Press, Inc.

(2) Taste quality. The palatability response elicited by carbohydrates varies as a function not only of taste intensity but also taste quality. In particular, the results of two-bottle preference tests indicate that at low molar concentrations Polycose is more palatable than sucrose whereas at high concentrations sucrose is more palatable than Polycose (Nissenbaum & Sclafani, 1987a; Sclafani & Clyne, 1987; Sclafani & Mann, 1987) (Fig. 4.4). A similar concentration-dependent preference reversal effect is observed with sucrose and maltose. In contrast, sucrose is preferred to glucose and fructose at low to high concentrations (Sclafani & Mann, 1987). The Polycose and maltose results are consistent with the hypothesis that these saccharides stimulate a taste system different from that activated by sucrose and other sugars (Sclafani, 1987). The preference reversal effect further suggests that the taste intensity—hedonic response functions of the two carbohydrate taste systems differ. That is, at low concentrations polysaccharides elicit a stronger hedonic response than does sucrose, but as concentration increases, the hedonic response to sucrose increases at a faster rate than does the hedonic response to polysaccharides (Sclafani & Clyne, 1987).

Cephalic Phase Responses

As indicated in Fig. 4.1, the hedonic response elicited by carbohydrate taste can be modulated by a variety of factors. Cephalic-phase digestive responses represent one potential influence that may have an immediate effect on carbohydrate palatability. It is well known that the taste, smell, texture, and even the sight of food can trigger pancreatic and gastrointestinal secretions that facilitate digestion (Powley, 1977). Some of these reflexes, the cephalic insulin response (CIR) in particular, may have feedback effects on the brain that modulate the palatability response. This is suggested by the findings that adding a nonnutritive sweetener to the rat's diet increased both food intake and the magnitude of the cephalic insulin response, and that blocking the CIR with vagotomy prevented the feeding stimulatory effect of sweet taste (Louis-Sylvestre & LeMagnen, 1980; Louis-

Sylvestre, Giachetti, & LeMagnen, 1983). Other studies report that the sham-feeding response to sucrose is attenuated by atropine, a drug that blocks cholinergically mediated cephalic responses (Nissenbaum & Sclafani, 1988; Weingarten & Watson, 1982b). However, whether these suppressive effects of vagotomy and atropine were due specifically to their attenuation of the cephalic insulin response to sweet taste is not certain.

Much remains to be learned about the relationship between carbohydrate taste, the CIR, and the palatability response. Some data indicate that not all sweet tastants trigger a cephalic insulin release (Grill, Berridge, & Ganster, 1984), and the effect of polysaccharide taste on the CIR has not yet been investigated. Furthermore, recent findings indicate that elevated insulin levels attenuate the gustatory response to sweet taste, which would be expected to reduce rather than enhance palatability (Giza & Scott, 1987). However, the relevance of these findings to the CIR, which involves smaller elevations in plasma insulin, is unclear.

Satiety

Postingestive Satiety.   While taste intensity and quality influence the animal's initial hedonic response to sugar and starch, the amount of carbohydrate consumed in a meal depends largely on other factors. These include feeding inhibitory signals generated by the postingestive actions of carbohydrates. The impact of postingestive satiety on carbohydrate intake is clearly demonstrated with the sham-feeding preparation (Mook & Wagner, 1988; Nissenbaum & Sclafani, 1987a; Weingarten & Watson, 1982a). Figure 4.5 shows that sucrose solution intake in sham-feeding rats, in which ingested solution drains out a gastric fistula, increased monotonically as concentration increased (Nissenbaum & Sclafani, 1987a). The same rats tested with the gastric fistula closed ("real-feeding") increased and then decreased their sucrose intake as the concentration increased, as is seen in intact rats (Cagan & Maller, 1974). As discussed in detail elsewhere (Smith & Gibbs, 1979), there are several components to postingestive

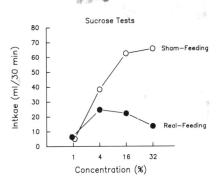

FIG. 4.5. Mean intake of sucrose at concentrations of 1 to 32% during 30 min/day real-feeding and sham-feeding tests. Adapted from Nissenbaum & Sclafani (1987a). With permission of *Physiology and Behavior.* Copyright Pergamon Press, Inc.

satiety, and feeding inhibitory cues can originate at gastric, intestinal, and postabsorptive sites.

While it is well documented that the postingestive actions of carbohydrates can inhibit consumption, their effect on the palatability response is open to question. According to one view, postingestive satiety cues do not inhibit the palatability response *per se,* but suppress consumption by acting on a central "ingestive control mechanism" that integrates palatability, satiety, and other factors (Davis & Levine, 1977; see also Mook & Brandsey, 1982). An alternative view is that postingestive satiety attenuates the hedonic response elicited by carbohydrate taste. This effect of satiety has long been recognized in humans as illustrated by the poetry of Shakespeare: "Enough! no more: 'Tis not so sweet now as it was before" (*Twelfth Night*). Laboratory studies have confirmed that the postingestive effects of carbohydrates can suppress the hedonic response in humans. That is, human subjects reduce their pleasantness ratings of sweet solutions after oral or intragastric preloads of glucose (Cabanac, 1979). The term alliesthesia ("changed sensation") has been used to describe the modulation of sensory pleasure by internal physiological signals such as those produced by glucose loads (Cabanac, 1979).

Whether alliesthesia occurs in rats is difficult to establish with certainty. There is suggestive evidence, though, that postingestive satiety signals reduce the rat's hedonic response to carbohydrates. For example, as a rat consumes a sucrose solution to satiety, the number of ingestive orofacial responses elicited by the sucrose declines while the number of aversive responses (e.g., head shakes, gapes) increases (Grill & Berridge, 1985). Also intraduodenal or intravenous infusions of glucose reduce the rat's initial licking response to sugar solutions (Campbell & Davis, 1974), and intraperitoneal glucose injections reduce sucrose sham-feeding (Bedard & Weingarten, 1989). Similarly, injections of the putative satiety hormone cholecystokinin (CCK) suppress sucrose licking rates during the very first minute of drinking (Waldbillig & O'Callaghan, 1980).

The phenomenon of sensory-specific satiety also suggests that satiety involves a reduction in the palatability response elicited by foods. In an early example of this type of satiety, Young (1940) observed that prefeeding rats sucrose prior to a sucrose vs. wheat powder preference test caused the animals to reverse their preference and select the normally nonpreferred wheat powder. In a more recent study, rats that were satiated for a 36% glucose solution were observed to consume additional glucose when offered the sugar in powdered form (Mook, Brane, Kushner, & Whitt, 1983). The willingness of animals to resume eating when offered a different food, or a new form of the same food, indicates that the animals stopped eating the initial food not because they were completely satiated, but because they *lost* their appetite for that food, i.e., the food no longer elicited a hedonic response.

One means by which postingestive satiety signals may attenuate carbohydrate palatability in rats is by modulating the transmission of gustatory information in the brainstem. This is indicated by the findings that intravenous glucose infusions or gastric distention suppress taste-evoked activity in the NTS (Giza & Scott, 1983; Glenn & Erickson, 1976). This suppressive effect is specific to sweet taste since the NTS responses evoked by sugars are reduced more than the responses evoked by NaCl, HCl, or quinine. Behavioral experiments further indicate that intravenous glucose infusions reduce the rat's perceived sweetness of sugar solutions as measured by conditioned taste aversion tests (Giza & Scott, 1987). In contrast to these effects, CCK injections are reported not to alter sweet taste evoked activity in the NTS (Giza, Scott & Antonucci, 1987) although CCK suppresses the licking response to sucrose (Waldbillig & O'Callaghan, 1980). Taken together, these results suggest that some but not all satiety signals inhibit the rat's hedonic response to sugars by suppressing the perceived sweetness of the sugars. Whether postingestive satiety signals produce similar alterations in the gustatory response to polysaccharide taste remains to be established.

It should be noted that whereas in rats satiety signals may suppress the hedonic response to sugars by reducing perceived sweetness, this appears not to be the case in primates. For example, satiety-induced reductions in pleasantness ratings in humans are not associated with reductions in taste intensity ratings (Cabanac, 1979; Moskowitz, Kumraiah, Sharma, Jacobs, & Sharma, 1976). Also, studies of the macaque monkey indicate that gustatory-evoked activity in the NTS is not altered by satiety signals (Yaxley, Rolls, Sienkiewicz, & Scott, 1985). Thus, there may be fundamental differences in the mechanisms by which postingestive satiety modifies the hedonic evaluation of taste stimuli in rodent and primate species (Scott & Mark, 1986).

Conditioned Satiety.   In addition to having an immediate inhibitory effect on carbohydrate intake, postingestive satiety signals can modulate the animal's subsequent responses to carbohydrates through conditioning processes. This is demonstrated by results obtained with rats fed differently flavored concentrated (50%) and dilute (10%) starch solutions (Booth, 1972). Over the course of several training trials the rats came to consume larger meals of the dilute starch than of the concentrated starch. When subsequently tested with an intermediate starch concentration (30%), the rats consumed more of the starch when it had the *dilute* flavor (i.e., flavor previously paired with the dilute starch) than when it had the *concentrated* flavor (i.e., flavor previously paired with the concentrated starch). The rats did not differ in their feeding rate or preference for the two flavored starches at the start of the test meal, which indicates that their initial hedonic responses to the two flavors were similar. However, as the meal progressed the rats slowed down their rate of feeding and displayed a reduced preference for the starch with the concentrated flavor as compared to the starch with the dilute flavor (Booth, 1972; 1985).

These results demonstrate that rats can learn to associate orosensory cues with the postingestive satiating effect of carbohydrates and use this information to control their meal size. Furthermore, conditioned satiety appears to involve a reduction in the palatability response during the later part of the meal. This effect distinguishes conditioned satiety from toxicosis-induced conditioned aversions since with conditioned aversions a reduced hedonic response is apparent at the beginning of a meal (Booth, 1985).

Oral Satiety. With calorically dilute solutions, the oral cavity rather than postingestive sites appears to be the primary source of satiety. This is indicated by studies in which manipulations of the postingestive effects of noncaloric saccharin solutions or dilute carbohydrate solutions had no effect on the amount of solution consumed. In particular, Mook, Kushner, & Kushner (1981) reported that hungry rats consumed saccharin solutions in discrete "meals" and that intragastric infusions of water prior to or during the meal did not alter the amount of saccharin consumed. In another study, hungry rats were observed to consume the same amount of saccharin whether the saccharin solution remained in the stomach (real-feeding condition) or drained out an open gastric fistula (sham-feeding condition) (Sclafani & Nissenbaum, 1985). Similar results have been obtained with dilute carbohydrate solutions: Rats consumed similar amounts of 1% sucrose or Polycose solutions in real-feeding and sham-feeding tests (Nissenbaum & Sclafani, 1987a) (see Fig. 4.4). In addition, prefeeding rats a .25% saccharin solution was found to reduce their subsequent intake of a 3% glucose solution; this effect disappeared when the presentation of the glucose solution was delayed by 30 min (Hsaio & Tuntland, 1971). Taken together, these findings indicate that postingestive factors (e.g., gastric distention, systemic hydration) are not normally responsible for satiating the animal for saccharin and dilute carbohydrate solutions. Rather, it appears that rats satiate to the *taste* of the saccharin and dilute carbohydrate solutions; that is, the rats no longer find the solutions to be palatable.

Oral factors alone are not sufficient to satiate the rat's ingestive response to concentrated (4%–32%) carbohydrate solutions, as indicated by the observations that rats consume substantially more sucrose or Polycose in sham-feeding tests than in real-feeding tests (Fig. 4.4) (Nissenbaum & Sclafani, 1987a; Weingarten & Watson, 1982a). Note, however, that the rats' rate of ingestion declined during the 30-min sham-feeding tests with concentrated solutions and this may reflect the action of oral satiety. Interestingly, the rate of decline is faster with a 4% sucrose solution than with a 4% Polycose solution, which suggests that rats satiate more rapidly for sweet taste than for polysaccharide taste (Nissenbaum & Sclafani, 1987a). Rats also show much more oral satiety to saccharin solutions then they do to sucrose solutions. This is indicated by the finding that, in contrast to their overconsumption of concentrated sucrose solutions, sham-feeding rats consume normal amounts of saccharin at all concentrations tested (.05–.8%) (Sclafani & Nissenbaum, 1985). One explanation for this effect is that saccharin is only as palatable as dilute sucrose solutions (Collier & Novell, 1967; Young & Madsen, 1963).

The mechanism(s) responsible for oral satiety is not well understood but gustatory adaptation may be one factor. This is suggested by the finding that rats that are orally satiated for a .3% saccharin solution will resume drinking when given a 1% saccharin solution even though the 1% solution is normally less preferred than the .3% solution (Mook et al., 1981). Other results indicate that gustatory adaptation to saccharin occurs at the level of the central nervous system rather than at the taste receptor. That is, Wilcove (1973) reported that prolonged intraoral infusions of saccharin that were effective in reducing the rat's licking response to saccharin did not alter saccharin-evoked activity in the chorda tympani nerve.

Oral–Postingestive Interactions

In addition to having a satiating effect by itself, orosensory stimulation can enhance the satiety produced by postingestive signals. It has long been known that food is more satiating when it is ingested orally than when it is intra- gastrically infused (Berkun, Kessen, & Miller, 1952; see also Smith & Gibbs, 1979). Evidence that sweet taste can potentiate the satiety effect of postingestive signals was recently reported by Bedard and Weingarten (1989). These investi- gators observed that an intraperitoneal glucose injection 5 min prior to a sucrose sham-feeding test did not reduce the amount of sucrose consumed. However, when the glucose injection was paired with a priming sham-feed (i.e., 5-min access to sucrose) the subsequent sham-intake of sucrose was reduced by 40%. These results indicate that postabsorptive glucose can attenuate the hedonic response to sweet taste and that this effect is most pronounced when the rise in plasma glucose is temporally associated with sweet taste.

Using a different paradigm, Sclafani & Kirchgessner (1986) obtained evi- dence that orosensory and postingestive cues can interact over a longer time span to influence the hedonic response to sweet taste (see also Mook, 1981). In this study, rats were given 1 hr/day meals of 16% glucose solution. During 4-day control periods chow and water were available ad libitum, and during 4-day test periods the rats were given, in addition to chow and water, access (22 hr/day) to different test solutions; the test solutions were removed 1 hr prior to the daily glucose meal. Giving the rats daily access to either a noncaloric .2% saccharin solution or a calorically rich 32% Polycose solution had no effect on the size of their daily glucose meals. However, giving the rats daily access to a saccharin- sweetened 32% Polycose solution reduced their daily glucose meals by more than 50%. Further analysis revealed that the availability of the saccharin-Poly- cose solution reduced the rats' initial licking response to the 16% glucose solu- tion. This latter finding indicates that the palatability of the 16% glucose solution was reduced when the rats had the saccharin-Polycose solution to drink 22 hr/day. Note that this suppression in glucose palatability occurred over a relatively long time span since the saccharin-Polycose solution was removed from the cages 1 hr prior to the glucose test and the rats may not have consumed any of the solution for some time prior to its removal.

The rats did not consume more of the saccharin-Polycose solution than of the Polycose solution and therefore nutritional factors alone were not responsible for reduced glucose meal size observed with the saccharin-Polycose solution. The sweet taste of the saccharin-Polycose solution was not by itself responsible for the reduced glucose intake since the saccharin solution alone had no effect on glucose meal size. Rather, the results suggest that it was the interaction between the sweet taste and the postingestive effects of the saccharin-Polycose solution that attenuated the rats' hedonic response to the glucose solution. This interpretation is consistent with the sham-feeding findings described above (Bedard & Weingarten, 1989).

Nimiety and Conditioned Aversions

The term *satiety* is commonly used in the experimental literature to refer in a favorable sense to a state of satisfaction, i.e., lack of hunger, but the term is also used to refer to a state of revulsion or disgust caused by overeating (Webster, 1975). It has recently been suggested that the word *nimiety* (meaning excess or too much) be used to refer to the unpleasant state resulting from overconsumption, and satiety be reserved to refer to the pleasant state associated with satisfaction of hunger or appetite (Kulkosky, 1985). The distinction between satiety and nimiety is particularly appropriate in discussing the postingestive effects of carbohydrates since these effects can have either positive or negative hedonic consequences.

The potential aversive postingestive effects of carbohydrates are demonstrated by the conditioned taste aversions that can be induced by intragastric, intraduodenal or intraperitoneal infusions of hypertonic glucose solutions (Deutsch, Molina, & Puerto, 1976; LeMagnen, 1969). While it could be argued that these treatments represent artificially induced pathological states, there is suggestive evidence that voluntarily consumed concentrated carbohydrate solutions can have discomforting effects in rats. Booth, Lovett, and McSherry (1972) reported that rats given the choice (24 hr/day) between concentrated (25–50%) and dilute (5–10%) glucose solutions initially preferred the concentrated solution but after several days switched their preference to the dilute solution, that is, the rats came to prefer the less sweet of the two solutions. An extensive analysis of this preference reversal indicated that it is due to the rats learning to avoid the concentrated glucose solutions; these solutions, because of their hypertonicity, had aversive postingestive consequences (Booth et al., 1972). Consistent with this interpretation, rats given the choice of 32% glucose and Polycose solutions rapidly develop a preference for the Polycose solution which has a much lower osmolarity (Sclafani, unpublished findings). The aversive effects of concentrated glucose solutions must be relatively mild, however, since rats given only a concentrated glucose solution (plus chow and water) consume substantial amounts of glucose solution over several weeks of testing (e.g., Castonguay, Hirsch, & Collier, 1981).

Another more pronounced case of carbohydrate-induced aversion is that seen in rats fed high-lactose diets. Postweanling rats lack the enzyme (lactase) needed to digest lactose and they will experience lower gut distress (distention, cramps, flatulence) if fed a high-lactose diet. Naive rats will readily consume a lactose diet or solution, but after only a few meals they will avoid the lactose diet or solution in preference for a low-lactose diet or water (Blake & Henning, 1985; Pelchat, Grill, Rozin, & Jacobs, 1983). This learned lactose aversion may be an integral part of the weaning process (Pelchat et al., 1983). Interestingly, although rats learn to avoid lactose, the sugar does not appear to become distasteful to the animals. That is, rats that have learned to avoid lactose do not display aversive orofacial responses to the taste of lactose (Pelchat et al., 1983). This suggests that rats may avoid lactose because they anticipate the lower gut discomfort produced by the lactose malabsorption, *not* because of a shift in the hedonic response elicited by lactose. Alternatively, lactose malabsorption may reduce the palatability response but not sufficiently to make lactose distasteful (see Pelchat et al., 1983).

The most profound carbohydrate aversions are obtained when carbohydrate ingestion is associated with poison-induced visceral malaise (Garcia, Hankins, & Rusiniak, 1974). Rats rapidly learn to avoid sucrose or Polycose solutions when the solutions are paired with a toxic agent such as LiCl (Nissenbaum & Sclafani, 1987b). Of particular interest here is the observation that aversions conditioned by LiCl are associated with a distaste response. That is, pairing sucrose consumption with LiCl injections causes rats to display aversive orofacial responses to sucrose; in fact, the rats respond to the sucrose as if it had a bitter taste (Berridge, Grill, & Norgren, 1981; Pelchat et al., 1983). In contrast, rats trained to avoid sucrose by pairing sugar consumption with electric shock do not display aversive orofacial responses to the sucrose. Following sucrose-shock pairing, rats display a fear rather than a distaste response to the sucrose (Pelchat et al., 1983). Poison-induced and shock-induced taste avoidance responses also differ in that rats will reject poison-paired solutions wherever they encounter them, whereas they reject shock-paired solutions only in the original training environment (Garcia, Kovner, & Green, 1966).

These findings indicate that when a carbohydrate taste is paired with poison-induced visceral malaise there is a shift in the hedonic response to the taste and it becomes unpalatable to the rat. On the other hand, when a taste is paired with painful shock the palatability of the taste does not change but rather the taste serves as a danger signal to the rat. Not all forms of visceral malaise, however, produce a distaste response since, as noted above, lactose avoidance is not associated with aversive orofacial responses. Although additional confirmatory results are needed, these findings suggest that the distaste reaction is produced primarily by upper GI distress (e.g., LiCl-induced nausea), while a qualitatively different aversive response is produced by lower GI distress (e.g., lactose malabsorption) (Pelchat et al., 1983).

The conditioned distaste response produced by LiCl injections may be mediated by changes in the gustatory response to sweet tastants. This is indicated by the finding that conditioning a taste aversion to saccharin in rats results in changes in the taste-evoked neural activity in the NTS (Chang & Scott, 1984). In particular, the clear distinction between the neuronal response patterns elicited by sweet and bitter tastants observed in normal animals is greatly diminished in rats with a conditioned saccharin aversion. These electophysiological data are consistent with the behavioral observations that rats with a conditioned sucrose aversion respond to sweet stimuli as if they had a bitter taste (Berridge et al., 1981; Pelchat et al., 1983). Conditioned changes in the hedonic evaluation of taste stimuli in rats, therefore, may involve changes in perceived taste quality.

In view of the apparent differences in the taste aversions produced by upper and lower gut distress, it would be of interest to compare the NTS taste response profiles in rats with lactose-induced and LiCl-induced taste aversions. An analysis of the changes produced in gustatory evoked activity in rats with conditioned sucrose aversions and Polycose aversions would also be of considerable interest given the evidence that these carbohydrates have qualitatively different tastes.

Trophophilia and Conditioned Preferences

The postingestive actions of carbohydrates can not only be satiating and in some cases (e.g., hypertonic glucose, lactose) aversive, but can also be rewarding to rats. This postingestive reward effect, which has been referred to as trophophilic ("love of nourishment") reward (Booth et al., 1972), can have a major influence on carbohydrate palatability.

Carbohydrate-induced trophophilia is demonstrated by the findings that rats acquire preferences for arbitrary flavors paired with the consumption of sugar solutions, Polycose solutions or high-starch diets (Boakes & Lubart, 1988; Bolles, Hayward, & Crandall, 1981; Capaldi, Campbell, Sheffer, & Bradford, 1987; Fedorchak & Bolles, 1987; Mehiel & Bolles, 1984). For example, hungry rats that consumed a grape-flavored sucrose solution on some days and cherry-flavored water on other days, subsequently preferred grape-flavored water to cherry-flavored water in two-choice tests (Fedorchak & Bolles, 1987). These conditioned flavor preference effects were attributed to the nutritive rather than the taste properties of the carbohydrates. Consistent with this interpretation, preference conditioning for a flavor paired with Polycose is blocked when Polycose digestion is inhibited with the drug acarbose (Elizalde & Sclafani, 1988).

The most direct evidence for the postingestive rewarding effects of carbohydrate is provided by reports of conditioned preferences produced by pairing the consumption of flavored solutions or foods with intragastric (IG) or intravenous (IV) carbohydrate infusions. Conditioned flavor preferences have been obtained using IG and IV glucose infusions (Mather, Nicolaidis, & Booth, 1978; Sherman, Hickis, Rice, Rusiniak, & Garcia, 1983; Tordoff & Friedman, 1986) although this is not a consistent finding (e.g., Koopmans & Maggio, 1978; Puerto, Deutsch, Molina, & Roll, 1976; Revusky, Smith, & Chalmers, 1971). The failure to obtain conditioned preferences in some studies may be related to the use of hypertonic glucose solutions; such solutions can have aversive consequences which would counteract any reward effects (see Booth, 1985). In recent studies reliable conditioned flavor preferences have been produced by pairing flavored solutions with IG infusions of Polycose, which is much lower in osmolality than glucose (Nissenbaum & Sclafani, 1987c; Sclafani & Nissenbaum, 1988). Figure 4.6 illustrates that after only two pairings of a flavored solution with IG Polycose rats preferred that flavor over a different flavor that had been paired with IG water infusion. Hungry rats have also been observed to develop preferences for flavored Polycose solutions that are real-fed over differently flavored Polycose solutions that are sham-fed (and thus provide little or no nourishment) (Nissenbaum, Sclafani, Vigorito, & Cassouto, 1988).

Robust conditioned preference effects have been obtained in a paradigm in which rats were given ad libitum access to chow and flavored water (23 hr/day); consumption of one flavor (e.g., cherry) was paired with IG infusions of 16% Polycose while consumption of a different flavor (e.g., grape) was paired with IG water infusions (Sclafani & Nissenbaum, 1988). After four training days, the rats displayed an overwhelming preference (96%) for the flavor paired with IG

FIG. 4.6. Mean intake (10 min/day) of conditioned stimulus (CS) solutions during one-bottle training and two-bottle test sessions. On training trials 2 and 4 consumption of the CS+ flavored solution was followed by intragastric (IG) infusions of 14% Polycose (7 ml); on trials 1 and 3 consumption of the CS-flavored solution was followed by IG water infusions (7 ml). On trials 5 and 6 the rats were given two-bottle preference tests between the CS+ and CS- flavored solutions. For half the rats the CS+ solution was a grape-flavored 2% Polycose solution, and the CS- was a cherry-flavored 2% Polycose solution; the CS+ and CS- flavors were reversed for the remaining rats. From Nissenbaum & Sclafani (1987c).

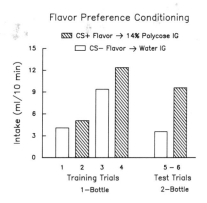

Polycose over the flavor paired with IG water during 23 hr/day two-bottle tests. Comparable results were obtained with rats trained with IG infusions of 32% Polycose although more training trials were required to produce a maximum preference (Elizalde & Sclafani, 1988). Once established, the Polycose-conditioned flavor preferences were very persistent: the rats continued to prefer the Polycose-paired flavor during extinction tests 4 to 43 days in length in which the consumption of both flavors was paired with either IG water infusions or no infusions (Elizalde & Sclafani, 1990; Sclafani & Nissenbaum, 1988).

These findings demonstrate that the postingestive effects of carbohydrates can condition strong flavor preferences. They do not establish, however, that the conditioned preferences involve changes in the hedonic evaluation of the flavor paired with IG Polycose. That is, the rats may have learned to prefer the flavor because they anticipated the nutritional benefits produced by the IG Polycose rather than because they acquired a liking for the flavor (see Rozin & Zellner, 1985). Although further work is needed to distinguish between these two alternatives, the fact that the conditioned preferences can be obtained in nondeprived as well as deprived rats and are resistant to extinction (Nissenbaum & Sclafani, 1987c; Sclafani & Nissenbaum, 1988) suggests that the preferences were mediated by shifts in the hedonic response to the flavors paired with Polycose.

If, as proposed, carbohydrate-induced trophophilia produces an acquired liking for a flavor paired with IG Polycose, how does this acquired liking compare with the animal's innate preference for sugar or polysaccharide tastes? A definitive answer cannot be given because of the limited number of flavors investigated to date and the possibility that the acquired preference may vary as a function of the specific test flavors used (Elizalde & Sclafani, 1988). The available evidence, however, suggests that the acquired preferences are not as strong as the rats' inborn taste preference. For example, when given the choice between their conditioned flavor (e.g., cherry-water paired with IG Polycose infusion) and a Polycose solution (paired with IG water) rats displayed an immediate preference for the Polycose solution over the cherry-water even though they had never tasted the Polycose solution prior to the preference test (Elizalde & Sclafani, 1990).

The trophophilic reward effect of carbohydrates varies as a function of the concentration and type of carbohydrate. This is demonstrated by the finding that IG infusions of dilute (8% or 16%) Polycose solutions have a more rapid reward effect than do concentrated (32%) Polycose solutions (Elizalde & Sclafani, 1990; Nissenbaum & Sclafani, 1987c). Differential reward effects are also suggested by the preference reversals observed when rats are given 24 hr/day two-choice tests between concentrated vs. dilute glucose solutions (Booth et al., 1972), powdered starch vs. powdered Polycose (Sclafani et al., 1987c), 32% glucose vs. 32% Polycose (Sclafani, unpublished), and 32% sucrose vs. 32% Polycose (Sclafani, Hertwig, Vigorito, & Feigin, 1987a). In each of the foregoing examples, the rats initially preferred the first saccharide of the pair but then switched their preference to the second saccharide over the course of several days; Fig. 4.7

FIG. 4.7. Mean intake (24 hr/day) of 32% sucrose and 32% Polycose solutions during two-bottle preference tests. Adapted from Sclafani, Hertwig, Vigorito, & Feigin (1987a). With permission of *Physiology and Behavior.* Copyright Pergamon Press, Inc.

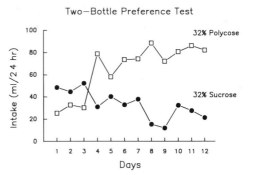

Two—Bottle Preference Test

illustrates this effect with 32% sucrose and 32% Polycose solutions. Osmolarity differences may account for some but not all of these shifts in carbohydrate preference. Much further work is needed to elucidate the postingestive mechanisms responsible for carbohydrate-induced trophophilia. Whatever the mechanisms may be, these preference reversals demonstrate how the rat's initial hedonic response to carbohydrates can be substantially modified by experiential factors.

Body Energy State

Earlier discussion has focused on how orosensory and postingestive factors influence the hedonic response to sugar and starch. Another important determinant of the palatability response is the energy state of the animal. It is well known that food deprivation increases sugar and saccharin intake in rats (Collier & Bolles, 1968; Gilbert & Sherman, 1970; Smith & Duffy, 1957), and recent findings demonstrate that it increases Polycose intake as well (Lucas & Sclafani, 1988). Deprivation-induced reductions in body weight also increase sugar and saccharin intake (Mook & Cseh, 1981). The facilitating effect of deprivation on sugar intake is seen in neonatal rats and thus does not appear to represent a learned response based on prior experience with deprivation and caloric repletion (Hall & Bryan, 1981). Another means of inducing an energy need state is to inject rats with insulin at doses that produce hypoglycemia. Insulin-induced hypoglycemia, like food deprivation, increases sugar and Polycose intake in rats (Jacobs, 1958; Lucas & Sclafani, 1988; Soljacic, Gabric, & Pokrajac, 1978).

The increased carbohydrate intake produced by food deprivation and insulin treatment appears to be due, at least in part, to an increase in the attractiveness of sweet taste and polysaccharide taste. This is indicated by the observations that both treatments increase the rats' initial licking response to sugar and Polycose solutions (Davis, 1973; Davis & Levine, 1977; Lucas & Sclafani, 1988; see also Grill & Berridge, 1985). In addition, food deprivation increases the sham-feeding response to sugar and Polycose solutions (Joyner et al., 1985; Sclafani, unpublished observations). Thus, the hedonic evaluation of sugar and starch is influenced by the animal's energy state. Food deprivation and weight loss may also affect carbohydrate intake by slowing down the satiation process, and decreasing the duration of postprandial satiety (Mook & Cseh, 1981).

Whereas undernutrition increases carbohydrate intake, overnutrition can have the opposite effect. That is, Mook and Cseh (1981) reported that rats force-fed (by intragastric infusions) to mild obesity decreased their voluntary intake of sugar as well as saccharin solutions during 1 hr/day test periods. The impact of this treatment on the hedonic response to the sweet solutions is not certain since initial lick rates or orofacial responses were not measured but it seems likely that the overfeeding reduced the attractiveness of the sweet taste. The suppressive effect of overnutrition on sweet solution intake, however, may be specific to the force-feeding situation. In an experiment by Maller (1964) short-term (2 hr/day) intakes of glucose and saccharin solutions were not altered in rats that voluntarily overate and became obese when fed a high-fat diet. Note also that in the Sclafani and Kirchgessner (1986) study described earlier, the rats did not reduce their 1 hr/day glucose intake when given a 32% Polycose solution 22 hr/day although their daily caloric intake increased by more than 50%. This apparent distinction between the effects of forced and voluntary overeating on short-term reactivity to sugar solutions is most interesting and deserves further study.

SUMMARY

Based on the findings reviewed earlier, the palatability response of rats to sugars and starches can be summarized as follows. The hedonic evaluation of carbohydrates begins in the mouth where multiple taste receptors exist to detect sugars and starch-derived polysaccharides. The brain analyzes the incoming gustatory information in terms of taste quality and intensity. A sugar or polysaccharide taste sensation will evoke an immediate and unconditioned hedonic response that is modulated by the energy state of the animal, i.e., by satiety signals generated by its last meal and by depletion/repletion signals reflecting the state of body fat stores. As the animal begins to ingest, its hedonic evaluation of the carbohydrate may be modified by cephalic reflexes activated by the orosensory stimulation, although this is not certain. If the carbohydrate source is very dilute (or if it is a sugar substitute, i.e., saccharin) the sweet or polysaccharide taste will soon lose its hedonic appeal and the animal will stop eating. If the carbohydrate source is not dilute, its taste will drive the animal to consume sufficient amounts to activate postingestive satiety mechanisms. Gastrointestinal and postabsorptive detectors will respond to the carbohydrate load and send satiety signals to the brain. These signals will reduce the hedonic evaluation of the carbohydrate taste, in part by reducing the perceived taste intensity, to the point that the taste is no longer able to sustain ingestive behavior. However, the animal's satiety is specific and if offered a carbohydrate of a different type or form the new orosensations produced may renew the palatability response.

Postingestive satiety signals, in addition to having an immediate effect on carbohydrate palatability, may produce conditioned alterations in the hedonic evaluation of the carbohydrate that influence the animal's subsequent responses to the food. The animal may, in effect, learn to anticipate the postingestive consequences of a concentrated sugar or starch meal, and as a result its hedonic response to the carbohydrate may dissipate at a faster rate as the meal progresses. The postingestive signals generated by some carbohydrate sources (e.g., concentrated glucose, lactose) may be sufficiently intense to condition relative aversions to the carbohydrates. In the most severe cases, if the intake of a carbohydrate is associated with upper GI distress (e.g., nausea), the animal will develop a conditioned distaste to the sugar or polysaccharide and respond to the carbohydrate as if it were bitter. In most instances, however, a carbohydrate meal is not accompanied by nimiety or nausea. Instead, the postingestive feedback generated by the meal may have a trophophilic reward effect that produces a conditioned enhancement in the hedonic evaluation of the carbohydrate. The trophophilic effect varies as a function of carbohydrate type and form and this will lead to modifications in the animal's preferences for different sugars and starches.

The foregoing description provides only a partial account of the factors that influence carbohydrate palatability. The rat's hedonic response will be determined not only by the orosensory and nutritive properties of the carbohydrate it is presently eating but also by what other carbohydrates it has recently consumed. Furthermore, although not discussed in this chapter, it is possible that the intake of other macronutrients (protein and fats) and micronutrients (minerals, vitamins, etc.) influence the hedonic evaluation of sugars and starches. Still other factors to be considered include the animal's sex, reproductive state, and age, and the day–night cycle. Much remains to be learned about carbohydrate palatability in the rat and how hedonic factors are integrated with other factors (e.g., diet availability) in the control of daily food intake.

Finally, while the rat is a useful laboratory model, significant species differences exist, particularly between rodents and primates, in the gustatory and palatability responses evoked by carbohydrates. These differences limit the generalizations that can be made from rat studies to other species. The findings obtained with rats, however, can serve as a guide in the investigation of carbohydrate palatability in other animals.

ACKNOWLEDGMENTS

The preparation of this chapter was supported by grants from the National Institutes of Diabetes and Digestive Kidney Diseases (DK-31135) and the Faculty

Research Award Program of the City University of New York. The author thanks Dr. Karen Ackroff for her helpful comments on this chapter.

REFERENCES

Bedard, M., & Weingarten, H. P. (1989). Postabsorptive glucose decreases excitatory effects of taste on ingestion. *American Journal of Physiology, 256*, R1142–R1147.

Beidler, L. M., & Tonosaki, K. (1984).   Multiple sweet receptor sites. In D. W. Pfaff (Ed.), *Taste, olfaction, and the central nervous system* (pp. 47–64). New York: Rockefeller University Press.

Berkun, M. M., Kessen, M. L., & Miller, N. E. (1952). Hunger-reducing effects of food by stomach fistula versus food by mouth measured by a consummatory response. *Journal of Comparative and Physiological Psychology, 45*, 550–554.

Berridge, K. C., & Fentress, J. C. (1985). Trigeminal-taste interaction in palatability processing. *Science, 228*, 747–750.

Berridge, K. C., & Grill, H. J. (1984). Isohedonic tastes support a two-dimensional hypothesis of palatability. *Appetite, 5*, 221–231.

Berridge, K. C., Grill, J. H., & Norgren, R. (1981). Relation of consummatory responses and preabsorptive insulin release to palatability and learned taste aversions. *Journal of Comparative and Physiological Psychology, 95*, 363–382.

Blake, H. H., & Henning, S. J. (1985). Basis for lactose aversion in the weanling rat. *Physiology and Behavior, 35*, 313–316.

Boakes, R. A., & Lubart, T. (1988). Enhanced preference for a flavour following reversed flavour glucose pairing. *Quarterly Journal of Experimental Psychology, 40*, 49–62.

Bolles, R. C., Hayward, L., & Crandall, C. (1981). Conditioned taste preferences based on caloric density. *Journal of Experimental Psychology: Animal Behavior Processes, 7*, 59–69.

Booth, D. A. (1972). Conditioned satiety in the rat. *Journal of Comparative and Physiological Psychology, 81*, 457–471.

Booth, D. A. (1985). Food-conditioning eating preferences and aversions with interoceptive elements: conditioned appetites and satieties. *Annals of the New York Academy of Sciences, 443*, 22–41.

Booth, D. A. (1987). How to measure learned control of food or water intake. In F. M. Toates & N. E. Rowland (Eds.), *Feeding and drinking* (pp. 111–149). Amsterdam: Elsevier.

Booth, D. A., Lovett, D., & McSherry, G. M. (1972). Postingestive modulation of the sweetness preference gradient in the rat. *Journal of Comparative and Physiological Psychology, 78*, 485–512.

Cabanac, M. (1979). Sensory pleasure. *Quarterly Review of Biology, 54*, 1–29.

Cagan, R. H., & Maller, O. (1974). Taste of sugars: Brief exposure single-stimulus behavioral method. *Journal of Comparative and Physiological Psychology, 87*, 47–55.

Campbell, C. S., & Davis, J. D. (1974). Peripheral control of food intake: Interaction between test diet and postingestive chemoreception. *Physiology and Behavior, 12*, 377–384.

Capaldi, E. D., Campbell, D. H., Sheffer, J. D., & Bradford, J. P. (1987). Conditioned flavor preferences based on delayed caloric consequences. *Journal of Experimental Psychology: Animal Behavior Processes, 13*, 150–155.

Castonguay, T. W., Hirsch, E., & Collier, G. (1981). Palatability of sugar solutions and dietary selection? *Physiology and Behavior, 27*, 7–12.

Chang, F. T., & Scott, T. R. (1984). Conditioned taste aversions modify neural responses in the rat nucleus tractus solitarius. *Journal of Neuroscience, 4*, 1850–1862.

Collier, G., & Bolles, R. (1968). Some determinants of intake of sucrose solutions. *Journal of Comparative and Physiological Psychology, 65*, 379–383.

Collier, G., Hirsch, E., & Hamlin, P. H. (1972). The ecological determinants of reinforcement in the rat. *Physiology and Behavior, 9,* 705–716.

Collier, G., & Novell, K. (1967). Saccharin as a sugar surrogate. *Journal of Comparative and Physiological Psychology, 64,* 404–408.

Collier, G., & Willis, F. N. (1961). Deprivation and reinforcement. *Journal of Experimental Psychology, 62,* 377–384.

Davis, J. D. (1973). The effectiveness of some sugars in stimulating licking behavior in the rat. *Physiology and Behavior, 11,* 39–45.

Davis, J. D., Collins, B. J., & Levine, M. W. (1976). Peripheral control of meal size: Interaction of gustatory stimulation and postingestional feedback. In D. Novin, W. Wyrwicka, & G. A. Bray (Eds.), *Hunger: Basic mechanisms and clinical implications.* (pp. 395–408). New York: Raven Press.

Davis, J. D., & Levine, M. W. (1977). A model for the control of ingestion. *Psychological Review, 84,* 379–412.

Deutsch, J. A., Molina, F., & Puerto, A. (1976). Conditioned taste aversion caused by palatable nontoxic nutrients. *Behavioral Biology, 16,* 161–174.

Elizalde, G., & Sclafani, A. (1988). Starch-based conditioned flavor preferences in rats: Influence of taste, calories, and CS-US delay. *Appetite, 11,* 179–200.

Elizalde, G., & Sclafani, A. (1990). Flavor preferences conditioned by intragastric Polycose: A detailed analysis using an electronic esophagus preparation. *Physiology and Behavior, 47,* 63–77.

Fedorchak, P. M., & Bolles, R. C. (1987). Hunger enhances the expression of calorie- but not taste-mediated conditioned flavor preferences. *Journal of Experimental Psychology: Animal Behavior Processes, 13,* 73–79.

Feigin, M. B., Sclafani, A., & Sunday, S. R. (1987). Species differences in polysaccharide and sugar taste preferences. *Neuroscience and Biobehavioral Reviews, 11,* 231–240.

Ganchrow, J. R., & Matzner, H. (1979). Development of sucrose preference in rabbit pups. *Chemical Senses and Flavor, 4,* 241–248.

Ganchrow, J. R., Steiner, J. E., & Daher, M. (1983). Neonatal facial expressions in response to different qualities and intensities of gustatory stimuli. *Infant Behavior and Development, 6,* 473–484.

Garcia, J., Hankins, W. G., & Rusiniak, K. W. (1974). Behavioral regulation of the milieu interne in man and rat. *Science, 85,* 824–831.

Garcia, J., Kovner, R., & Green, K. F. (1966). Cue properties vs. palatability of flavors in avoidance learning. *Psychonomic Science, 20,* 313–314.

Gilbert, R. M., & Sherman, I. P. (1970). Palatability-induced polydipsia: Saccharin, sucrose, and water intake in rats, with and without food deprivation. *Psychological Reports, 27,* 319–325.

Giza, B. K., Antonucci, R. F., Sclafani, A., & Scott, T. R. (1988). Gustatory neural responses to polysaccharide and starch in the rat. *Society for Neuroscience Abstracts, 14,*

Giza, B. K., & Scott, T. R. (1983). Blood glucose selectively affects taste-evoked activity in the rat nucleus tractus solitarius. *Physiology and Behavior, 31,* 643–650.

Giza, B. K., & Scott, T. R. (1987). Intravenous insulin infusions in rats decrease gustatory-evoked responses to sugars. *American Journal of Physiology, 252,* R994–R1002.

Giza, B. K., Scott, T. R., & Antonucci, R. F. (1987). Choleystokinin administration does not influence taste-evoked activity in rat NTS. *Society for Neuroscience Abstracts, 13,* 880.

Glenn, J. F., & Erikson, R. P. (1976). Gastric modulation of gustatory afferent activity. *Physiology and Behavior, 16,* 561–568.

Grill, H. J., & Berridge, K. C. (1985). Taste reactivity as a measure of the neural control of palatability. In J. M. Sprague & A. N. Epstein (Eds.), *Progress in psychobiology and physiological psychology* (pp. 1–61). New York: Academic Press.

Grill, H. J., Berridge, K. C., & Ganster, D. J. (1984). Oral glucose is the prime elicitor of preabsorptive insulin secretion. *American Journal of Physiology, 246,* R88–R95.

Hall, W. G., & Bryan, T. E. (1981). The ontogeny of feeding in rats: IV. Taste development as measured by intake and behavioral responses to oral infusions of sucrose and quinine. *Journal of Comparative and Physiological Psychology, 95,* 240–251.

Houpt, K. A., & Houpt, T. R. (1977). The neonatal pig: A biological model for the development of taste preferences and controls of ingestive behavior. In J. M. Weiffenbach (Ed.), *Taste and development* (pp. 86–98). Washington, DC: U.S. Government Printing Office.

Hsiao, S., & Tuntland, P. (1971). Short-term satiety signals generated by saccharin and glucose solutions. *Physiology and Behavior, 7,* 287–289.

Jacobs, H. L. (1958). Studies on sugar preference: I. The preference for glucose solutions and its modification by injections of insulin. *Journal of Comparative and Physiological Psychology, 51,* 304–310.

Jacobs, H. L. (1964). Observations on the ontogeny of saccharine preference in the neonate rat. *Psychonomic Science, 1,* 105–106.

Jacobs, H. L., Smutz, E. R., & DuBose, C. N. (1977). Comparative observations on the ontogeny of taste preference. In J. M. Weiffenbach (Ed.), *Taste and development* (pp. 99–107). Washington, DC: U.S. Government Printing Office.

Jakinovich, W., Jr. (1984). Sugar taste reception in the gerbil. In D. W. Pfaff (Ed.), *Taste, olfaction, and the central nervous system* (pp. 65–91). New York: Rockefeller University Press.

Jakinovich, W., Jr., & Sugarman, D. (1988). Sugar taste reception in mammals. *Chemical Senses, 13,* 13–31.

Joyner, K., Smith, G. P., Shindledecker, R., & Pfaffman, C. (1985). Stimulation of sham feeding in the rat by sucrose, maltose, glucose and fructose. *Society for Neuroscience Abstracts, 11,* 1223.

Kare, M. (1971). Comparative study of taste. In L. M. Beidler (Ed.), *Handbook of sensory physiology, Vol. IV, Chemical Senses, Part 2, Taste* (pp. 278–292). Berlin: Springer-Verlag.

Koopmans, H. S., & Maggio, C. A. (1978). The effects of specified chemical meals on food intake. *American Journal of Clinical Nutrition, 31,* S267–S272.

Kulkosky, P. J. (1985). Conditioned food aversions and satiety signals. *Annals of the New York Academy of Science, 443,* 330–347.

Kunstyr, I., Peters, K., & Gartner, K. (1976). Investigations on the function of the rat forestomach. *Laboratory Animal Science, 26,* 166–170.

LeMagnen, J. (1969). Peripheral and systemic actions of food in the caloric regulation of intake. *Annals of the New York Academy of Sciences, 157,* 1126–1156.

LeMagnen, J. (1987). Palatability: Concept, terminology, and mechanisms. In R. A. Boakes, D. A. Popplewell, & M. J. Burton (Eds.), *Eating habits* (pp. 131–154). Chichester, England: Wiley.

Louis-Sylvestre, J., Giachetti, I., & LeMagnen, J. (1983). Vagotomy abolishes the differential palatability of food. *Appetite, 4,* 295–299.

Louis-Sylvestre, J., & LeMagnen, J. (1980). Palatability and preabsorptive insulin release. *Neuroscience and Biobehavioral Reviews, 4,* Suppl. 1, 43–46.

Lucas, F., & Sclafani, A. (1988). Polycose and sucrose appetite in rats: Influence of food deprivation and insulin treatment. *Appetite, 11,* 201–213.

Maller, O. (1964). The effect of hypothalamic and dietary obesity on taste preference in rats. *Life Sciences, 3,* 1281–1291.

Mather, P., Nicolaidis, S., & Booth, D. A. (1978). Compensatory and conditioned feeding responses to scheduled glucose infusions in the rat. *Nature, 273,* 461–463.

Mehiel, R., & Bolles, R. C. (1984). Learned flavor preferences based on caloric outcome. *Animal Learning and Behavior, 12,* 421–427.

Mook, D. G. (1981). Taste-evoked drinking in the rat: The influence of maintenance diet. *Physiology and Behavior, 26,* 595–599.

Mook, D. G., & Brandsey, S. A. (1982). Preference–aversion drinking in the rat: The nature of postingestive satiety for sugar solutions. *Appetite, 3,* 297–307.

Mook, D. G., Brane, J. A., Kushner, L. R., & Whitt, J. A. (1983). Glucose solution intake in the rat: The specificity of postingestive satiety. *Appetite, 4,* 1–9.

Mook, D. G., & Cseh, C. L. (1981). Release of feeding by the sweet taste in rats: The influence of body weight. *Appetite, 2,* 15–34.

Mook, D. G., Kushner, B. D., & Kushner, L. R. (1981). Release of feeding by the sweet taste in rats: The specificity of oral satiety. *Appetite, 2,* 267–280.

Mook, D. G., & Wagner, S. (1988). Sham drinking of glucose solutions in rats: some effects of hydration. *Appetite, 10,* 71–87.

Morrison, G. R., & Jessup, A. (1977). Does saccharin have a dual taste for the rat? In J. M. Weiffenbach (Ed.), *Taste and development* (pp. 42–48). Washington, DC: U.S. Government Printing Office.

Moskowitz, H. R., Kumraiah, V., Sharma, K. N., Jacobs, H. L., & Sharma, S. D. (1976). Effect of hunger, satiety and glucose load upon taste intensity and taste hedonics. *Physiology and Behavior, 16,* 471–475.

Nejad, M. S. (1986). The neural activities of the greater superficial petrosal nerve of the rat in response to chemical stimulation of the palate. *Chemical Senses, 11,* 283–293.

Nissenbaum, J. W., & Sclafani, A. (1987a). Sham-feeding response of rats to Polycose and sucrose. *Neuroscience and Biobehavioral Reviews, 11,* 215–222.

Nissenbaum, J. W., & Sclafani, A. (1987b). Qualitative differences in polysaccharide and sugar tastes in the rat: A two-carbohydrate taste model. *Neuroscience and Biobehavioral Reviews, 11,* 187–196.

Nissenbaum, J. W., & Sclafani, A. (1987c). Conditioned flavor preference produced by intragastric Polycose infusions in rats. *Proceedings of the Eastern Psychological Association Meeting, 58,* 62.

Nissenbaum, J. W., & Sclafani, A. (1988). A comparison of the effects of atropine on real-feeding and sham-feeding of sucrose in rats. *Pharmacology Biochemistry and Behavior, 29,* 231–238.

Nissenbaum, J. W., Sclafani, A., Vigorito, M., & Cassouto, K. (1988). Conditioned flavor preferences in sham-feeding rats. *Proceedings of the Eastern Psychological Association Meeting, 59,* 18.

Nowlis, G. H., Frank, M. E., & Pfaffmann, C. (1980). Specificity of acquired aversions to taste qualities in hamsters and rats. *Journal of Comparative and Physiological Psychology, 94,* 932–942.

Ogawa, H., Sato, M., & Yamashita, S. (1969). Gustatory impulse discharges in response to saccharin in rats and hamsters. *Journal of Physiology (London), 204,* 311–329.

Pelchat, M. L., Grill, H. J., Rozin, P., & Jacobs, J. (1983). Quality of acquired responses to tastes by *Rattus norvegicus* depends on type of associated discomfort. *Journal of Comparative Psychology, 97,* 140–153.

Pfaffmann, C. (1969). Taste preference and reinforcement: In J. Tapp (Ed.), *Reinforcement and Behavior.* (pp. 215–240). New York: Academic Press.

Pfaffmann, C. (1982). Taste: A model of incentive motivation. In D. W. Pfaff (Ed.), *The physiological mechanisms of motivation* (pp. 61–97). New York: Springer-Verlag.

Powley, T. L. (1977). The ventromedial hypothalamic syndrome, satiety, and a cephalic phase hypothesis. *Psychological Review, 84,* 89–126.

Puerto, A., Deutsch, J. A., Molina, F., & Roll, P. (1976). Rapid rewarding effects of intragastric injections. *Behavioral Biology, 18,* 123–134.

Revusky, S. H., Smith, M. H., Jr., & Chalmers, D. V. (1971). Flavor preference: Effects of ingestion-contingent intravenous saline or glucose. *Physiology and Behavior, 6,* 341–343.

Ross Laboratories. (1977). *Polycose.* Columbus, OH: Ross Laboratories.

Rozin, P., & Zellner, D. (1985). The role of Pavlovian conditioning in the acquisition of food likes and dislikes. *Annals of the New York Academy of Sciences, 443,* 189–202.

Schwartz, G. J., & Grill, H. J. (1984). Relationship between taste reactivity and intake in the neurologically intact rat. *Chemical Senses, 9,* 249–272.

Sclafani, A. (1987). Carbohydrate taste, appetite, and obesity: An overview. *Neuroscience and Biobehavioral Reviews, 11*, 131–153.

Sclafani, A., & Clyne, A. E. (1987). Hedonic response of rats to polysaccharide and sugar solutions. *Neuroscience and Biobehavioral Reviews, 11*, 173–180.

Sclafani, A., Hertwig, H., Vigorito, M., & Feigin, M. B. (1987a). Sex differences in polysaccharide and sugar preferences in rats. *Neuroscience and Biobehavioral Reviews, 11*, 241–251.

Sclafani, A., Hertwig, H., Vigorito, M., Sloan, H., & Kerzner, B. (1987b). Influence of saccharide length on polysaccharide appetite in the rat. *Neuroscience and Biobehavioral Reviews, 11*, 197–200.

Sclafani, A., & Kirchgessner, A. L. (1986). Influence of taste and nutrition on the sugar appetite of rats. *Nutrition and Behavior, 3*, 57–74.

Sclafani, A., & Nissenbaum, J. W. (1985). On the role of the mouth and gut in the control of saccharin and sugar intake: A reexamination of the sham-feeding preparation. *Brain Research Bulletin, 14*, 569–576.

Sclafani, A., & Nissenbaum, J. W. (1987a). Taste preference thresholds for Polycose, maltose and sucrose in rats. *Neuroscience and Biobehavioral Reviews, 11*, 181–185.

Sclafani, A., & Nissenbaum, J. W. (1987b). Oral versus postingestive origin of polysaccharide appetite in the rat. *Neuroscience and Biobehavioral Reviews, 11*, 169–172.

Sclafani, A., & Nissenbaum, J. W. (1988). Robust conditioned flavor preference produced by intragastric starch infusions in rats. *American Journal of Physiology, 255*, R672–R675.

Sclafani, A., Nissenbaum, J. W., & Vigorito, M. (1987c). Starch preference in rats. *Neuroscience and Biobehavioral Reviews, 11*, 253–262.

Sclafani, A., & Mann, S. (1987). Carbohydrate taste preferences in rats: Glucose, sucrose, maltose, fructose and Polycose compared. *Physiology and Behavior, 40*, 563–568.

Scott, T. R., & Mark, G. P. (1986). Feeding and taste. *Progress in Neurobiology, 27*, 293–317.

Sherman, J. E., Hickis, C. F., Rice, A. G., Rusiniak, K. W., & Garcia, J. (1983). Preferences and aversions for stimuli paired with ethanol in hungry rats. *Animal Learning and Behavior, 11*, 101–106.

Smith, G. P., & Gibbs, J. (1979). Postprandial satiety. In J. M. Sprague & A. N. Epstein (Eds.), *Progress in psychobiology and physiological psychology, Vol. 8* (pp. 179–242). New York: Academic Press.

Smith, M., & Duffy, M. (1957). Consumption of sucrose and saccharine by hungry and satiated rats. *Journal of Comparative and Physiological Psychology, 50*, 65–69.

Soljacic, M., Gabric, D., & Pokrajac, N. (1978). Effect of insulin on sex differences in the intake of glucose solutions in rats. *Physiology and Behavior, 21*, 307–311.

Spector, A. C., & Grill, H. J. (1988). Differences in the taste quality of maltose and sucrose in rats: Issues involving the generalization of conditioned taste aversions. *Chemical Senses, 13*, 95–114.

Steffens, A. B. (1969). Rapid absorption of glucose in the intestinal tract of the rat after ingestion of a meal. *Physiology and Behavior, 4*, 829–832.

Stewart, C. N., & Krafczek, S. A. (1988). The taste characteristics of sodium-saccharin in the rat: a re-examination of the dual taste hypothesis. *Chemical Senses, 13*, 205–212.

Sunderland, G., & Sclafani, A. (1988). Taste preferences of squirrel monkeys and bonnet macaques for Polycose, maltose and sucrose. *Physiology and Behavior, 43*, 685–690.

Tordoff, M. G., & Friedman, M. I. (1986). Hepatic-portal glucose infusions decrease food intake and increase food preference. *American Journal of Physiology, 251*, R192–R196.

Travers, S. P., Pfaffmann, C., & Norgren, R. (1986). Convergence of lingual and palatal gustatory neural activity in the nucleus of the solitary tract. *Brain Research, 365*, 305–320.

Vigorito, M., & Sclafani, A. (1988). Ontogeny of Polycose and sucrose appetite in neonatal rats. *Developmental Psychobiology, 21*, 457–465.

Waldbillig, R. J., & O'Callaghan, M. (1980). Hormones and hedonics, cholecystokinin and taste: a possible behavioral mechanism of action. *Physiology and Behavior, 25*, 25–30.

Webster's New Collegiate Dictionary (1975). Springfield, MA: Merriam Co.

Weingarten, H. P., & Watson, S. D. (1982a). Sham feeding as a procedure for assessing the influence of diet palatability on food intake. *Physiology and Behavior, 28,* 401–407.

Weingarten, H. P., & Watson, S. D. (1982b). Effects of atropine methyl nitrate on sham feeding in the rat. *Pharmacology Biochemistry and Behavior, 17,* 863–867.

Wilcove, W. G. (1973). Ingestion affected by the oral environment: The role of gustatory adaptation on taste reactivity in the rat. *Physiology and Behavior, 11,* 297–312.

Yaxley, S., Rolls, E. T., Sienkiewicz, Z. J., & Scott, T. R. (1985). Satiety does not affect gustatory activity in the nucleus of the solitary tract of the alert monkey. *Brain Research, 347,* 85–93.

Young, P. T. (1940). Reversal of food preference of the white rat through controlled pre-feeding. *Journal of General Psychology, 22,* 33–66.

Young, P. T. (1961). *Motivation and Emotion.* New York: Wiley & Sons.

Young, P. T. (1967). Palatability: The hedonic response to foodstuffs. In C. F. Code (Ed.), *Handbook of physiology; section 6: Alimentary canal* (pp. 353–366). Washington, DC: American Physiological Society.

Young, P. T. (1977). Role of hedonic processes in the development of sweet taste preferences. In J. M. Weiffenbach (Ed.), *Taste and development* (pp. 399–417). Washington, DC: U.S. Government Printing Office.

Young, P. T., & Madsen, C. H., Jr. (1963). Individual isohedons in sucrose-sodium chloride and sucrose-saccharin gustatory areas. *Journal of Comparative and Physiological Psychology, 56,* 903–909.

Young, P. T., & Trafton, C. L. (1964). Activity contour maps as related to preference in four gustatory stimulus areas of the rat. *Journal of Comparative and Physiological Psychology, 58,* 68–75.

5 Hedonic Consequences of Salt Hunger

Jay Schulkin
University of Pennsylvania

One essential property of many kinds of animals is that they make judgments about the world. For example, they make spatial and temporal judgments (Gallistel, 1989), and predict the probability of events (Rescorla & Wagner, 1972) that may be causally related (Dickinson, 1980). Much of the learning that animals show is dependent upon these judgments, or computations. Animals also recognize ingesta that are of biological significance (Krieckhaus, 1970). Recognition is an evaluation, a judgment.

The appreciation of a sweet taste is also a judgment. A sweet taste can be appreciated or not. This depends in part upon the physiological state, and past experience of the animal (Grill & Berridge, 1986; Le Magnen, 1985; Stellar, 1987). These hedonic evaluations are not the same as the sensory properties of the stimulation, that is, whether something tastes salty or not (Sabini & Schulkin, 1990). In other words, a palatability judgment is made about the value of the salty or sweet taste (Berridge & Grill, 1983). The mechanisms that make this possible are unconscious to the animal.

SALT HUNGER: A MODEL MOTIVATION SYSTEM

Curt Richter reported in 1936 that adrenalectomized rats (who are chronically losing sodium and therefore in a state that will be fatal) ingested sodium salts. And therefore they survived. The phenomenon has been replicated many times (e.g., Epstein & Stellar, 1955), and there are a number of less drastic ways to induce a salt hunger (Denton, 1982; Wolf, 1982).

By the 1940s and 1950s a number of physiological psychologists interested in motivation realized that salt hunger, and other basic regulatory drives, were ideal behaviors to study (Miller, 1957; Morgan & Stellar, 1950; Young, 1949). Salt hunger in particular seemed simple, and easily elicited and controlled. And therefore one could ask questions about motivation, learning and perception (see also Denton, 1982). George Wolf, a student of Neal Miller, envisioned salt hunger as a "Model Motivational System." Such motivational systems are inherently related to hedonic events (Epstein, 1982), and are tied to the regulation of biological drives (Cabanac, 1971; Stellar, 1987).

Salt hunger, therefore, has several unique properties that make it especially interesting. There is an innate hunger for salt following sodium depletion. The detection mechanisms for finding sodium in the environment are tied to a specific psychophysical property: Saltiness. Sodium and its value can be recognized when the animal is not sodium depleted. And when the animal needs the sodium it shows anticipatory behavior that is driven by a change in the incentive value of the salty ingesta. The behavior is driven by a hedonic change in the perception of

FIG. 5.1. Drinkometer records of individual rats. Every fifty lick is represented by a vertical mark. Records within the upper brackets are from 9 sodium-depleted rats drinking solutions of sodium salts. Records within the middle brackets are from 6 sodium-depleted rats drinking solutions of nonsodium salts. Records within the lower brackets are from 3 nondepleted rats drinking a sodium salt solution. From Handal (1965); Wolf (1969).

salt that reflects the needs and motivation the animal has for sodium and possibly other minerals. Consider some of these facts.

INNATENESS

One of the most interesting observations made of the salt-hungry rat (or sheep, the other species extensively studied) is that the first time it is in that state it avidly ingests salt (Bare, 1949; Bolles, Sulzbacher, & Arent, 1964; Denton, 1982; Epstein & Stellar, 1955; Nachman, 1962). This is expressed best, I think, by the observation that salt-hungry rats ingest sodium salts within seconds after their first exposure to them (Handal, 1965; Fig. 5.1).

Richter (1943, 1956), rooted in the German tradition of innate ideas, thought there were many innate specific hungers. Those rooted in British associationism (e.g., Harris, Clay, Hargreaves, & Ward, 1933), envisioned the specific hungers as learned associations between ingestion and amelioration of tissue need. But the hunger for salt is unique. There appear to be few other examples of innate recognition of what is needed to repair a physiological deficit (Rozin, 1976).

LATENT LEARNING AND SENSORY
PRECONDITIONING STUDIES

Rats are prepared to recognize the significance of salt. It is part of their innate endowment. This was demonstrated in an elegant experiment by Krieckhaus and Wolf (1968), who trained thirsty rats to bar press for dilute sodium salts, or water. When rendered salt hungry and no longer thirsty, those rats previously exposed to the saline demonstrated greater bar pressing (in extinction conditions) than those that had been exposed to the water, despite the fact that neither was available in the test (Fig. 5.2). The phenomenon has been replicated a number of

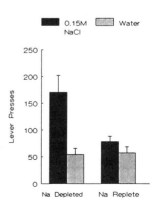

FIG. 5.2. Mean (SEM) number of lever presses of rats during a 1-hr extinction test. Rats either tasted NaCl or water during the training, and are now sodium depleted or sodium replete. From Krieckhaus and Wolf (1968).

times (e.g., Dickinson, 1986; Weisinger, Woods, & Skorupski, 1970). In addition, just a brief exposure of up to 2–5 licks of the NaCl is enough to get this effect (Bregar, Strombakis, Allan, & Schulkin, 1983; Wirsig & Grill, 1982). Moreover, one can find similar effects in a runway (Krieckhaus, 1970). That is, thirsty rats having tasted NaCl return to where it was located when they are salt hungry and no longer thirsty. An analogous phenomena was found in rats with central gustatory damage, which will ingest salt when sodium depleted, but only if the salt is in the same position both pre and postoperatively (Paulus, Eng, & Schulkin, 1984).

In addition, rats are capable of preferring what the NaCl was associated with (Rescorla, 1981). Thirsty and nonthirsty rats were given a compound ingesta of Na and almond or banana (Fudim, 1978), or Na and quinine or citric acid alone (Berridge & Schulkin, 1989; Rescorla & Freiberg, 1978). Those rats exposed to the compound stimulus ingested the arbitrary taste that had been associated with the sodium when salt hungry (Fig. 5.3). Rats are therefore prepared to associate other taste properties with the saltiness of NaCl. In nature, the sodium-deficient animal ingesting at mineral licks or dirt rich in minerals would find a number of taste properties associated together (Goodall, 1986; Schaller, 1963).

SEARCHING FOR SOMETHING SALTY: APPETITIVE

Wallace Craig (1918), a noted American naturalist, distinguished an appetitive from a consummatory phase in ingestive behavior. The appetitive phase is the search for what is wanted or needed, which is followed by the consummatory phase- the actual ingestion. Consider the appetitive phase first.

It has been known for some time that rats and other animals have endogenous biological clocks that help organize their behavior (Richter, 1965). Rats are known to anticipate the availability of a food or water source (e.g., Bolles, 1965, 1968). A circadian clock plays a role in this anticipatory behavior (see review by Rosenwasser & Adler, 1986). There is evidence of anticipatory behavior to the availability of NaCl in sodium-hungry rats (Fig. 5.4; Ronsenwasser, Schulkin &

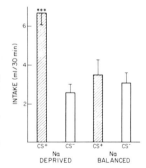

FIG. 5.3. Mean (SEM) amounts consumed of the CS (quinine or citric acid) and CS solutions in a 30 minute intake test while either sodium balanced or when sodium depleted. From Berridge and Schulkin (1989).

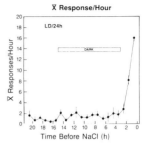

FIG. 5.4. Mean number of non-reinforced leverpresses per hour under salt-access schedules in adrenalectomized rats. From Rosenwasser, Schulkin, and Adler (1988).

Adler, 1988). That is, adrenalectomized rats whose access to NaCl is restricted to a 3-hr period begin to bar press for the salt before it is available (but only within the circadian schedule).

There is also evidence that the amount of bar pressing that salt-hungry rats or sheep demonstrate is related to the strength of the natriorexigenic treatment, or drive for salt (Denton, 1982; Quartermain, Miller, & Wolf, 1967; Fig. 5.5). Salt-hungry rats are also willing to run down an alley for very small quantities of salt (about 0.1 ml for each run, Schulkin, Arnell, & Stellar, 1985; Fig. 5.6). The intensity of running is related to the strength of natriorexigenic treatment and the concentration of the salt solution at the end of the runway (Fig. 5.7). They run for salty tasting sodium salts as well as for lithium salts (Fig. 5.8).

This last finding is consistent with those of others (Nachman, 1963; Schulkin, 1982) where sodium deficient rats will ingest LiCl and even prefer it over sodium salts: But only if it tastes saltier than the sodium salt (Schulkin, 1982). After all, it is the taste quality of saltiness that the sodium deficient rat is searching for. It is this search for saltiness that may organize the appetitive behavior of other mineral deficiencies. A number of mineral deficiencies elicit NaCl ingestion (Adam & Dawborn, 1972; Lewis, 1968; Schulkin, 1981). NaCl is a prototypical salty taste (Bartoshuk, 1980; Schulkin, 1982). And in nature sodium is found largely in mineral composites (Jones & Hanson, 1985). Saltiness may be a marker for other minerals. Therefore, perhaps, the one innate hunger for sodium, where animals are searching for something salty is also the same strategy used when deficient in other minerals.

FIG. 5.5. Mean cumulative bar presses for 4 groups of rats injected with 0 ml, 0.5 ml, or 1.0 ml of 1.5% formalin (sodium depletion) and given 0.33 M NaCl solution as reinforcement, and 1 group injected with 1.0 ml of 1.5% formalin and given water as reinforcement. From Quartermain, Miller, and Wolf (1967).

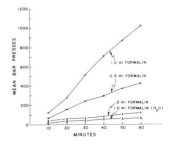

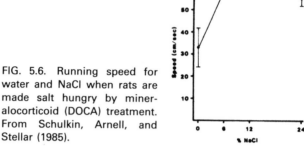

FIG. 5.6. Running speed for water and NaCl when rats are made salt hungry by mineralocorticoid (DOCA) treatment. From Schulkin, Arnell, and Stellar (1985).

ORAL-FACIAL RESPONSES: CONSUMATORY

Once the sodium deficient animal finds salt, it ingests the salt rapidly (Denton, 1982). The response is clearly under hedonic control; consider the evidence. Infusions of ingesta into the oral cavity reveal a pattern of facial responses for ingestion and rejection (Grill & Norgren, 1978a) that are in fact governed by the caudal brainstem (Grill & Norgren, 1978b; Steiner, 1977; see also Flynn & Grill, 1988; Fig. 5.9). A sweet taste elicits an ingestive sequence, a bitter taste a rejection sequence. Hypertonic NaCl elicits a mixed ingestive-rejection sequence

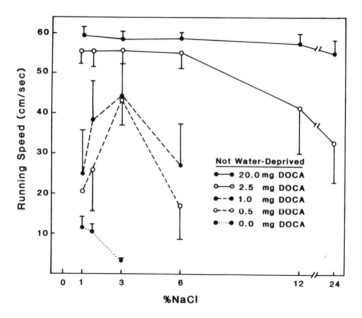

FIG. 5.7. Running speed for NaCl under different degrees of salt hunger, produced by different doses of DOCA. From Schulkin, Arnell, and Stellar (1985).

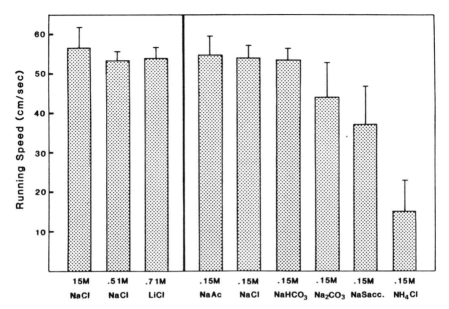

FIG. 5.8.   Running speed for different salt solutions when salt hungry by DOCA. The salt solutions tested were NaCl (sodium chloride), LiCl (lithium chloride), NaAc (sodium acetate), $NaHCO_3$ (sodium bicarbonate), Na_2CO_3 (sodium carbonate), NaSacc (sodium saccharine), and NH_4Cl (ammonium chloride). From Schulkin, Arnell, and Stellar (1985).

FIG. 5.9.   Taste-elicited consummatory responses. (Ingestive responses (top) are elicited by continuous oral infusions of glucose, sucrose, and other palatable solutions and include rhythmic mouth movements, tongue protrusions, lateral tongue protrusions, and paw licking. Aversive responses (bottom) are elicited by infusions of quinine solutions and include gapes, chin rubs, head shakes, face washing, forelimb flailing, and locomotion (not shown). From Grill and Norgren (1978).

in the rat that is in sodium balance. But when rats are salt hungry the oral-facial response to NaCl is changed. The response is now largely ingestive; the rejection responses decreases (Berridge, Flynn, Schulkin, & Grill, 1984; Berridge & Schulkin, 1989; Grill & Bernstein, 1988; Fig. 5.10). Sodium-depleted humans also report that salty foods are more pleasing (Beauchamp, 1989). This effect, at least in rats, is specific. Other tastants (e.g., HCl) which elicit equally mixed ingestive-aversive responses are not changed when the rat is salt hungry (Berridge et al., 1984). Moreover, the oral-facial change to intraoral infusions of hypertonic NaCl is not dependent upon experience. The first time rats are sodium depleted they demonstrate the phenomenon (Berridge et al., 1984). Therefore, this hedonic change, like the hunger for salt itself, is innate.

There is also evidence that the sensory-preconditioning effect (Rescorla, 1981) manifests itself in a change in the hedonic response of the rat. Rats were intraorally infused with NaCl along with citric acid or quinine. Then they were rendered salt hungry for the first time. They showed a positive facial profile to the infusion of either quinine or citric acid when they were given alone (Berridge & Schulkin, 1989; Fig. 5.11). That is, the arbitrary taste quality associated with the saltiness of NaCl is now more palatable to the rat when it needs sodium. Interestingly, the negative profile elicited by the quinine or citric acid did not change. This is unlike the response to NaCl itself where negative responses decrease. This dissociation could be construed as support for the independence of the ingestive and rejection sequence, and how they both can be expressed under some conditions (Berridge & Grill, 1983; Berridge & Schulkin, 1989).

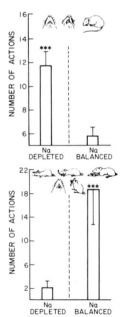

FIG. 5.10. Taste reactivity profile to 0.5 M NaCl while in either sodium balanced or when sodium depleted. Top: Combined mean (SEM) number of ingestive actions (rhythmic tongue protrusions, non-rhythmic lateral tongue protrusions and paw licks). Bottom: Combined mean (SEM) number of aversive actions (chin, rubs, head shakes, paw treads, gapes, face washes and forelimb flails. From Berridge and Schulkin (1989).

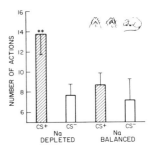

FIG. 5.11.   Ingestive taste reactivity to conditioned tastes. Mean (SEM) number of combined ingestive actions emitted to the CS (quinine or citric acid) and CS while either sodium depleted or when sodium replete. From Berridge and Schulkin (1989).

SALT PREFERENCE

Following P. T. Young (1949), one should distinguish preference from appetite. Animals prefer sucrose, even when they are not hungry. That is, Young wanted his colleagues to know that not all ingestive behavior is driven by tissue need. There are ingesta that are not needed, and yet preferred. Sodium may be one of them. It has long been observed that dilute NaCl solutions are actually preferred over water (e.g., Weiner & Stellar, 1951). The dilute NaCl is roughly the concentration of extracellular sodium (Denton, 1982), so it is interesting that it is preferred over water.

Rats, however, will not run to NaCl if they do not need it, nor will they run for concentrations of dilute NaCl that they are known to prefer over water in home cage consumption tests (Schulkin et al., 1985; Stellar, 1987; Fig. 5.12). By contrast, rats that are hungry will run for a sweet taste (Stellar, 1987). In fact, rats do not prefer the saline unless there are postingestive consequences that result from its ingestion (Mook, 1963). Therefore, the preference for dilute NaCl

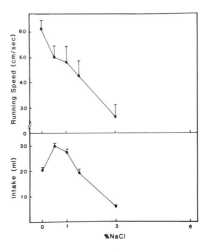

FIG. 5.12.   Top. Running speed for water and NaCl when rats are thirsty (dashed line). Bottom. Amount of water and saline consumed during the 1-hr test when thirsty, as a function of salt concentration. From Schulkin, Arnell, and Stellar (1985).

is based on something other than its hedonic properties (Deutsch & Jones, 1960; Stellar, Hyman, & Samet, 1954), since it does not provide a powerful incentive except when rats are salt hungry, or when it is readily accessible.

HEDONIC NEURAL SUBSTRATES

The 7th, 9th and 10th cranial nerves transmit gustatory information to the central nervous system, and terminate in the rostral portion of the solitary nucleus. Gustatory signals are then transmitted to the medial region of the parabrachial nucleus (Norgen, 1984). From this region there are two main gustatory projection systems: A dorsal projection to the ventral basal thalamus and insular cortex, and a ventral projection which courses through the lateral hypothalamus into the central nucleus of the amygdala, in addition to the bed nucleus of the stria terminalis. The anatomical connections of the gustatory system in the rat are depicted in Fig. 5.13 (Norgren, 1984). It was suggested (Pfaffman, Norgren, & Grill, 1977) that the sensory evaluation of a food or fluid—whether it is sweet or salty—is made by the dorsal projection, and that the organization of the drive, and the hedonic value of the stimulation, is made by the ventral projection.

Interestingly, "sweet neurons," or rather, "hedonic neurons," in the gustatory region of the solitary nucleus increase their firing pattern when the oral cavity is infused with NaCl while the rat is salt hungry (Jacobs, Mark, & Scott, 1988). "Salt neurons" decrease their firing rate when the rat is salt hungry (as

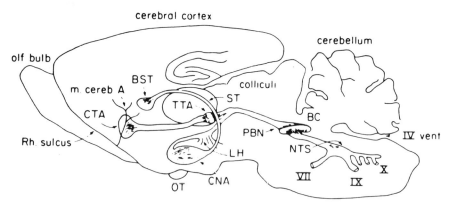

FIG. 5.13. Schematic outline of thalamo-cortical and limbic connections for taste in rat brain. NTS, nucleus of solitary tract; PTA, pontine taste area; BC, brachium conjunctivum; TTA, thalamic taste area; CTA, cortical taste area; CNA, central nucleus of the amygdala; ST, Stria terminalis; BST, bed nucleus of stria terminalis; OT, optic tract; IV vent, fourth ventricle; V11, 1X, X, taste afferents of 7th, 9th, and 10th crainial nerves; Rh, sulcus, rhinal sulcus; m. cereb, A, middle cerebral artery. From Norgren (1984).

they do in the chorda tympani nerve, e.g., Contreras, 1977), while "sour" and "bitter" neurons tend to stay the same. This shift towards sweetness, or the reward neurons, is further reflected by the salt hungry rats' oral facial profile-a face that appears as if they are ingesting something rewarding.

These gustatory hedonic responses may not be on a contiuum, as P. T. Young (1959) had suggested. He thought that there could not be an expression of both positive and negative responses at the same time. But in fact there appear to be two separate systems for hedonic evaluation, one for approach and acceptance and one for avoidance and rejection. More generally, animals of many kinds approach pleasant stimulation, and avoid noxious stimulation (Schnierla, 1959).

Good evidence for separate systems for the hedonic evaluation of pleasant and unpleasant gustatory stimulation is provided by the work of Berridge and colleagues (e.g., Berridge & Grill, 1983; Berridge & Schulkin, 1989). They discovered (by using the taste reactivity test and recording the oral-facial profile of the rat) that both acceptance and rejection responses can be manifested at the same time. Both responses also competed for expression at the same time. The ingesta is then evaluated, or computed, for both its positive and ingestive characteristics. The weighted hedonic value of the ingesta determines the extent to which positive or negative facial responses are expressed. The decision about whether the event is pleasurable or painful, revealed in part by the competition between the two responses, was also suggested by a much earlier thinker (Hobbes, 1651). A hedonic decision is made that values one response more than another.

An approach and avoidance system is also expressed in terms of taste responses at the level of the oral cavity, which I believe is under centrifugal control. There is a system to accept ingesta by the chorda tympani nerve which innervates the anterior end of the oral cavity, and a rejection system innervated by the glossopharyngeal nerve at the posterior end of the oral cavity (Nowlis, 1977; Fig. 5.14). Stimulation of anterior portions of the tongue of the decerebrate cat elicited acceptance tongue movements. Stimulation of the posterior portion of the tongue elicited rejection responses. This corresponds to the 7th and 9th cranial nerves respectively (Nowlis, 1977).

Infusions of ingesta into the oral cavity activate classical hypothalamic regions involved in motivated behavior (Norgren, 1984). These hypothalamic areas are involved in approach and avoidance. Stimulation of the lateral area promotes approach, and stimulation of the medial hypothalamic area promotes avoidance of ingesta; lesions of either area have the opposite effects (Stellar, Brooks, & Mills, 1979).

In addition, approach and avoidance responses may also be represented at the level of the prefrontal cortex. Damage to these regions are known to result in changes in hedonic evaluation (Davidson, 1984). There is rich anatomical connectivity between the prefrontal cortex, hypothalamus, amygdala and the solitary nucleus (e.g., Schwaber, Kapp, Higgens, & Rapp, 1982).

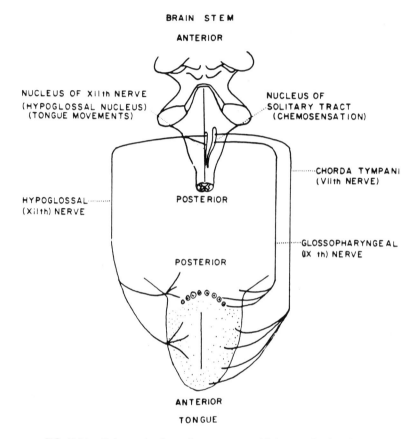

FIG. 5.14. Schematization of structures which may be involved in taste-elicited tongue reflexes. From Nowlis (1977).

Moreover, approach may be related to the activation of the left prefrontal cortex, and avoidance to the right prefrontal cortex (Davidson, 1984). This assymetry in hedonic evaluations has been suggested for positive and negative ingesta. If it tastes sweet there is greater activity in the left prefrontal cortex (measured by EEG), while with bitter tastes there is greater activity in the right prefrontal cortex (Fox & Davidson, 1986).

Probably the one anatomical site that is most importantly involved in the hedonic evaluation of ingesta is the amygdala, and perhaps the central nucleus. It receives the majority of taste-visceral projections to the ventral forebrain (Herrick, 1948; Norgren, 1984). And there has long been thought to be two separate anatomical systems with in the amygdala in the approach or avoidance of ingesta (Fonberg, 1974). The central nucleus is directly connected to the gustatory regions of the solitary nucleus and the parabrachium (e.g., Norgren, 1976;

Ricardo & Koh, 1978; Schwaber et al., 1982), in addition to the classical hypothalamic regions (e.g., Deolmos, Alheid, & Beltramino, 1985). The anatomical circuit for the acceptance and rejection of ingesta therefore includes the 7th and 9th cranial nerves, the gustatory region of the solitary nucleus, classical hypothalamic regions, in addition to the amygdala and the prefrontal cortex. The endogenous opiates, known to influence ingestive behavior and the palatability of fluids (including saline intake, e.g., Bertino et al., 1988; Cooper & Gilbert, 1984), are highly localized in many of these regions. It is therefore conceivable that the endorphins act as neurotransmitters in the evaluation of ingesta.

CONCLUSION

Rats and also sheep (Denton, 1982; Krieckhaus, 1970) innately recognize the significance of salt. This recognition is expressed in their immediate ingestion of it when salt hungry, and learning where the salt is and what it is associated with. Salt hunger also results in a change in the hedonic evaluation of concentrated salt solutions that reflects both appetitive as well as consummatory responses. Moreover, this hedonic evaluation insures the behavioral regulation of the needed sodium. Therefore, the pleasure of salt taste, and the motivation to search for it, are intimately tied to the biology of the animal and the restoration of body sodium. The approach or avoidance of ingesta are organized by palatability judgments. If the palatability judgment is pleasant, central states potentiate movement for ingestion- that is, approach and consummatory behavior. If the judgment is unpleasant then the central state potentiates rejection and avoidance behavior (Gallistel, 1980).

REFERENCES

Adam, W. R., & Dawborn, J. K. (1972). Effect of potassium depletion on mineral appetite in the rat. *Journal of Comparative and Physiological Psychology, 418,* 51–58.

Bare, J. K. (1949). The specific hunger for sodium chloride in normal and adrenalectomized rats. *Journal of Comparative and Physiological Psychology, 42,* 242–253.

Bartoshuk, L. M. (1980). Sensory analysis of the taste of NaCl. In M. Kare, M. Fregly, & R. Bernard (Eds.), *Biological and behavioral aspects of salt intake.* New York: Academic Press.

Beauchamp, G. E. (1989). *Human salt preference.* Unpublished Manuscript.

Berridge, K. C., & Grill, H. J. (1983). Alternating ingestive and aversive consummatory responses suggest a two-dimensional analysis of palatability in rats. *Behavioral Neuroscience, 97,* 563–573.

Berridge, K. C., Flynn, F. W., Schulkin, J., & Grill, H. J. (1984). Sodium depletion enhances salt palatability in rats. *Behavioral Neuroscience, 98*(4), 652–660.

Berridge, K. C., & Schulkin, J. (1989). Palatability shift of a salt-associated incentives during sodium depletion. *Quarterly Journal of Experimental Psychology.* 41B (2) 121–138.

Bertino, M., Abelson, M. L., Marglin S. H., Neuman, R., Burkhardt, C. A., & Reid, L. D. (1988). A small dose of morphine increases intake of and preferences for isotonic saline among rats. *Pharmacology, Biochemistry and Behavior, 29,* 617–623.

Bolles, R. C., Sulzbacher, S. I., & Arent, H. (1964). Innateness of the adrenalectomized rat's acceptance of salt. *Psychonomic Science, 1,* 21–22.

Bolles, R. C. (1965). Rat's anticipation of diurnal and a-diurnal feeding. *Journal of Comparative and Physiological Psychology, 60,* 290–294.

Bolles, R. C. (1968). Anticipatory general activity in thirsty rats. *Journal of Comparative and Physiological Psychology, 65,* 511–513.

Bregar, R. E., Strombakis, N., Allan, R. W., & Schulkin, J. (1983). Brief exposure to a saline stimulus promotes latent learning in the salt hunger system. *Neuroscience Abstracts.* (8) 1220.

Cabanac, M. (1971). Physiological role of pleasure. *Science, 173,* 1103–1107.

Contreras, R. J. (1977). Changes in gustatory nerve discharges with sodium deficiency: A single unit analysis. *Brain Research, 121,* 373–378.

Cooper, S. J., & Gilbert, D. B. (1984). Naloxone suppresses fluid consumption in tests of choice between sodium chloride solutions and water in male and female water deprived rats. *Psychopharmacology, 84,* 362–367.

Craig, W. (1918). Appetites and aversions as constituents of instincts. *Biological Bulletin, 34,* 91–107.

Davidson, R. (1984). Affect, cognition and hemispheric specialization. In C. E. Izard, J. Kagan, & R. Zajonc (Eds.), *Emotion, cognition and behavior.* Cambridge, MA: Cambridge University Press.

Denton, D. A. (1982). *The hunger for salt.* New York: Springer.

Deolmos, J. D., Alheid, G. F., & Beltramino, C. A. (1985). Amygdala. In G. Pavinos (Ed.). The rat neuron system. New York: Academic Press.

Deutsch, J. A., & Jones, A. D. (1960). Diluted water: An explanation of the rat's preference for saline. *Journal of Comparative Physiological Psychology, 53,* 122–127.

Dickinson, A. (1980). Contemporary animal learning theory. New York: Cambridge University Press.

Dickinson, A. (1986). Re-examination of the role of instrumental contingency in the sodium appetite irrelevant incentive effect. *The Quarterly Journal of Experimental Psychology, 36,* 161–172.

Epstein, A. N., & Stellar, E. (1955). The control of salt preference in the adrenalectomized rat. *Journal of Comparative and Physiological Psychology, 48,* 167–172.

Epstein, A. N. (1982). Instinct and motivation as explanations for complex behavior. In D. Pfaff (Ed.), The physiological mechanisms of motivation. New York: Springer-Verlag.

Flynn, F. W., & Grill, H. J. (1988). Intraoral intake and taste reactivity responses elicited by sucrose and sodium chloride in chronic decerebrate rats. *Behavioral Neuroscience, 102*(6).

Fonberg, E. (1974). Amygdala functions within the alimentary systems. *Acta Neurobiol Exp, 34,* 435–466.

Fox, N. A., & Davidson, R. J. (1986). Taste-elicited changes in facial signs of emotion and the asymmetry of brain electrical activity in human newborns. *Neuropsychologia, 24,* 417–422.

Fudim, O. K. (1978). Sensory preconditioning of flavors with a formalih-produced sodium need. *Journal of Experimental Psychology: Animal Behavior Processes, 4,* 276–285.

Gallistel, C. R. (1980). From muscle to motivation. *American Psychologist, 68,* 398–409.

Gallistel, C. R. (1989). Animal cognition: The representation of space, time and number. *Annual Review of Psychology, 40,* 155–189.

Goodall, J., (1986). The chimpanzees of Gombe. Cambridge, MA: Belknap Press of Harvard University Press.

Grill, H. J., & Norgren, R. (1978a). The taste reactivity test: 1. Mimetic responses to gustatory stimuli in neurologically normal rats. *Brain Research, 143,* 263–279.

Grill, H. J., & Norgren, R. (1978b). The taste reactivity test:11. Mimetic responses to gustatory stimuli in chronic thalamic and chronic decerebrate rats. *Brain Research, 143,* 281–297.

Grill, H. J., & Berridge, K. C. (1986). Taste reactivity as a measure of the neural control of palatability. In J. M. Sprague & A. N. Epstein (Eds.), *Progress in psychobiology and physiological psychology,* Vol. 11, Orlando, FL: Academic Press.

Grill, H. J., & Bernstein, I. (1988). Strain differences in taste reactivity to NaCl. *American Journal of Physiology, 14* R424–430.

Handal, P. J. (1965). Immediate acceptance of sodium salts by sodium deficient rats. *Psychonomic Science, 3,* 315–316.

Harris, L. J., Clay, J., Hargreaves, F., & Ward, A. (1933). Appetite and choice of diet. The ability of the vitamin B deficent to discriminate between diets containing and lacking the vitamin. *Proceeding of the Royal Society Series 113,* 161–190.

Herrick, C. J. (1948). *The brain of the tiger salamander.* Chicago: University of Chicago Press.

Hobbes, T. (1651 1958). *Leviathan,* New York: Library of Liberal Arts Bobbs-Merrill.

Jacobs, K. M., Mark, G. P., & Scott, T. R. (1988). Taste responses in the nucleus tractus solitarius of sodium-deprived rats. *Journal of Physiology, 406,* 393–410.

Jones, R. L., & Hanson, H. C. (1985). *Mineral locks, geophagy, and biogeochemistry or North American ungulates.* Ames: Iowa State University Press.

Krieckhaus, E. E. (1970). Innate recognition aids rats in sodium regulation. *Journal of Comparative and Physiological Psychology 73,* 117–122.

Krieckhaus, E. E., & Wolf, G. (1968). Acquisition of sodium by rats: Interaction of innate mechanisms and latent learning. *Journal of Comparative and Physiological Psychology, 65,* 197–201.

Le Magnen, J. (1985). Hunger. Cambridge, MA: Cambridge University Press.

Lewis, M. (1968). Discrimination between drives for sodium chloride and calcium. *Journal of Comparative and Physiological Psychology, 65,* 208–212.

Miller, N. E. (1957). Experiments on motivation; Studies combining psychological physiological and pharmacological techniques. *Science, 126,* 1271–1278.

Mook, D. (1963). Oral and posingestional determinants of the intake of various solutions in rats with esophageal fistulas. *Journal of Comparative and Physiological Psychology, 56,* 645–659.

Morgan, C. T., & Stellar, E. (1950). *Physiological psychology.* New York: McGraw-Hill.

Nachman, M. (1962). Taste preference for sodium salts by adrenalectomized rats. *Journal of Comparative and Physiological Psychology, 55,* 1124–1129.

Nachman, M. (1963). Taste preference for lithium chloride by adrenalectomized rats. *American Journal of Physiology, 205,* 219–221.

Norgren, R. (1976). Taste pathways to hypothalamus and amygdala. *Journal of Comparative Neurology, 166,* 17–30.

Norgren, R. (1984). Section 1. The nervous system, Vol. 3, Sensory processes, pt. 2. Darian-Smith, vol. In J. M. Brookhart & V. B. Mountcastle (Eds.), Bethesda, MD: American Physiological Society, 1087–1128.

Nowlis, G. H. (1977). From reflex to representation: taste-elicited tongue movements in the human newborn. In J. M. Weiffenbach (Ed.), Taste and development. Bethesda, MD: U.S. Department of Health, Education and Welfare.

Paulus, R. A., Eng, R., & Schulkin, J. (1984). Preoperative latent place learning preserves salt appetite following damage to the central gustatory system. *Behavioral Neuroscience, 98*(1), 146–151.

Pfaffmann, C., Norgren, R., & Grill, H. J. (1977). Sensory affect and motivation. In B. M. Wenzel & H. P. Zeigler (Eds.), Tonic functions of sensory systems Vol. 290. New York: Academy of Sciences.

Quartermain, D., Miller, N. E., & Wolf, G. (1967). Role of experience in relationship between sodium deficiency and rate of bar pressing for salt. *Journal of Comparative Physiological Psychology, 63,* 417–420.

Rescorla, R. A., & Wagner, A. R. (1972). A theory of Pavlovian conditioning: Variations in the effectiveness of reinforcement and nonreinforcement. In A. H. Black & W. F. Prokasy (Eds.), Classical conditioning 11: Current research and theory. New York: Appleton-Century-Crofts.

Rescorla, R. A., & Freiberg, L. (1978). The extinction of within-compound flavor associations. *Learning and Motivation, 9,* 411–427.

Rescorla, R. A. (1981). Simultaneous associations. In P. Harzen & M. D. Zeiler (Eds.), *Predictability, correlation and contiguity.* New York: Wiley.

Ricardo, J. A., & Koh, E. T. (1978). Anatomical evidence of direct projections from the nucleus of the solitary tract to the hypothalamus, amygdala, and other forebrain structures in the rat. *Brain Research, 153,* 1–26.

Richter, C. P. (1936). Increased salt appetite in adrenalectomized rats. *American Journal of Physiology, 115,* 151–161.

Richter, C. P. (1943). Total self regulatory functions in animals and human beings. *Harvey Lecture Series, 38,* 63–103.

Richter, C. P. (1956). Salt appetite of mammals: Its dependence on instinct and metabolism. In M. Autuori (Ed.), *L'instinct dans le comportement des animaux et de l'homme.* Paris: Masson et Cie.

Richter, C. P. (1965). *Biological clocks in medicine and psychiatry.* Springfield, IL: Charles C. Thomas.

Rosenwasser, A. M., & Adler, N. T. (1986). Structure and function in circadian timing systems: Evidence for multiple coupled circadian oscillators. *Neuroscience and Biobehavioral Reviews, 10,* 431–448.

Rosenwasser, A. M., Schulkin, J., & Adler, N. T. (1988). Anticipatory appetitive behavior of adrenalectomized rats under circadian salt-access schedules. *Animal Learning and Behavior, 16*(3), 324–329.

Rozin, P. (1976). The selection of foods by rats, humans and other animals. J. S. Rosenblatt, R. A. Hinde, E. Shaw, & C. Beer (Eds.), Advances in the study of behavior. New York: Academic Press.

Sabini, J., & Schulkin, J. (1990). Mind-body issues in contemporary psychology. *Scientia,* in press.

Schaller, G. B. (1963). *The mountain gorilla.* Chicago: University of Chicago Press.

Schulkin, J. (1981). The appetite for salts in mineral and vitamin deficient rats. FASEB.

Schulkin, J. (1982). Behavior of sodium deficient rats: The search for a salty taste. *Journal of Comparative and Physiological Psychology, 96,* 628–634.

Schulkin, J., Arnell, P., & Stellar, E. (1985). Running to the taste of salt in mineralocorticoid-treated rats. *Hormones and Behavior, 19,* 413–425.

Schwaber, J., Kapp, B. S., Higgens, G. A., & Rapp, P. R. (1982). Amygdaloid and basal forebrain direct connections with the nucleus of the solitary tract and the dorsal motor nucleus. *Journal of Neuroscience, 10,* 1424–1438.

Shipley, M. T., & Sanders, M. S. (1982). Special senses are really special: Evidence for a reciprocal, bilateral pathway between insular cortex and nucleus parabrachialis. *Brain Research Bulletin, 8,* 493–501.

Steiner, J. (1977). Facial expressions of the neonate infant indicating the hedonics of food-related chemical stimuli. In J. M. Wiffenbach (Eds.), Taste and development: The genesis of sweet preference. Bethesda, MD: U.S. Department of Health, Education, and Welfare.

Stellar, E., Hyman, R., & Samet, S. (1954). Gastric factors controlling water and salt solution drinking. *Journal of Comparative and Physiological Psychology, 57,* 220–226.

Stellar, E. (1987). The internal environment and appetitive measures of taste function in the rat. In R. F. Chapman, E. A. Bernays, & J. G. Stoffolano Jr. (Eds.), Perspectives in chemoreception and behavior. New York: Springer-Verlag.

Stellar, J. R., Brooks, F. H., & Mills, L. E. (1979). Approach-withdrawal analysis of the effects of hypothalamic stimulation and lesions in rats. *Journal of Comparative and Physiological Psychology, 93,* 446–466.

Weiner, I. H., & Stellar, E. (1951). Salt preference of the rat determined by a single stimulus method. *Journal of Comparative Physiological Psychology, 44*(4), 394–401.

Weisinger, R. S., Woods, S. C., & Skorupski, J. D. (1970). Sodium deficiency and latent learning. *Psychonomic Science, 19,* 307–308.

Wirsig, C. R., & Grill, H. (1982). Contribution of the rat's neocortex to ingestive control: 1. Latent learning for the taste of sodium chloride. *Journal of Comparative and Physiological Psychology, 96,* 615–627.

Wolf, G. (1969). Innate mechanism for regulation of sodium intake. In C. Pfaffman (Eds.), Olfaction and taste. New York: Rockefeller University Press.

Wolf, G. (1982). Refined salt appetite methodology for rats demonstrated by assessing sex differences. *Journal of Comparative and Physiological Psychology, 96,* 1016–1021.

Young, P. T. (1949). Studies of food preference, appetite and dietary habit. *Comparative Psychology Monographs, 19,* 1–74.

Young, P. T. (1959). The role of affective processes in learning and motivation. *Psychological Review, 66,* 104–125.

6 Hedonic-Shift Conditioning with Calories

Ron Mehiel
Shippensburg University

The acquisition and consumption of food occupies a large portion of the behavior of many species including humans and rats. Both humans and rats are omnivores and are capable of extracting energy and nutritional benefit from a wide variety of foods. Yet each particular food has unique properties of taste, smell, and texture, and these and other properties contribute to its palatability. But taste is perhaps the primary identifying characteristic of food. Sweet tastes are innately preferred by humans (Steiner, 1977) and other species. However, we believe that most of the richness and variety of acceptance and preferences of flavors is learned.

A number of different mechanisms for learning to prefer flavors have been identified in rats. One is the "medicine effect" (Zahorick, Maler, & Pies, 1974) whereby flavors that are paired with relief from illness are later preferred. Another is the "flavor-flavor effect" (Holman, 1975; Fanselow & Birk, 1982; Zellner, Rozin, Aron, & Kulish, 1983), which occurs when neutral flavors are paired with flavors that have unconditioned hedonic value and some of the hedonic valence from the unconditioned flavor "rubs off" on the new flavor. The concept of "mere exposure" (Zajonc, 1968) has been applied to changes in hedonic ratings for flavors by humans, for both positive (Thorndike, 1935; Pliner, 1982), and negative changes (Stang, 1975).

BEHAVIORAL EVIDENCE OF CALORIE CONDITIONING

Our research has focused on the acquisition of preferences for flavors that are paired with calories. This focus was born from the observation that sweet tastes are innately preferred, and that sweet foods tend to be calorically dense. It was reasonable to assume that evolutionary pressure had developed a preference for sweetness in animals because sweetness represented and thus served as a label for calories (Bolles,1983).

Calorie Conditioning: Our General Method

Our method in most of the experiments described here follow what we refer to as our general method. Naive male Long Evans rats are brought into the lab and placed on a regimen of ad libitum water and 14 g of rat chow per day. During conditioning, housekeeping chores are done; the rats are fed, and solutions are presented, in that order, at the same time every day. Typically, the rats alternate between a flavored caloric solution and a flavored noncaloric solution with a few 24-hour exposures to each. Paired flavors, order of presentation, and position on the cage front are always counterbalanced. Most often, the rats have a few days off with ad libitum chow and water between the conditioning and test phases. Two-bottle tests for conditioned preference are usually between the two paired flavors and do not include the conditioning solutions. In other words, we typically leave out the calories during the tests. Our interest is in the specific hedonic changes to the flavors, not the caloric solution.

Bolles, Hayward, and Crandall (1981) reported that when a flavor was paired with rat chow that had been made more calorically dense by the addition of vegetable fat, rats learned to prefer that flavor over another that was paired with calorically dilute chow. However it was possible that the dilutants (powdered chalk and petroleum jelly) had caused a learned aversion to the flavor paired with the dilute chow.

In order to circumvent the possibility of conditioning an aversion, we replicated Bolles et al. but used sucrose solution as the calorie source, and saccharin solution as the "dilute" source (Mehiel & Bolles, 1984). We let rats drink as much as they wanted for 8 days (four 1-day long exposures to each) with novel flavors paired with each in a counterbalanced design. Following this conditioning phase, we tested for flavor preference with a two-bottle test between the paired flavors without any sugar or saccharin. Every rat preferred the sugar-paired flavor to the saccharin-paired flavor. (See Fig. 6.1.)

Our design in the foregoing experiment allowed for several explanations of its results in addition to caloric repletion. During conditioning the rats drank about twice as much sugar solution as saccharin solution. This difference in consumption introduced the possibility of mere exposure effects. In addition, sugar is preferred to saccharin by rats, thus the flavor–flavor effect could have been operating. Holman (1975) reported evidence that argues against the mere exposure hypothesis. He had rats drink saccharin with a paired flavor for 5 min and with another flavor for 60 min over a number of trials. No preference for the highly exposed flavor over the low exposed flavor developed. Pliner (1982) did get an

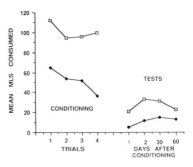

FIG. 6.1 Intake of flavored solutions during conditioning and flavors only during the tests. Rats were tested four times. Open squares represent sucrose and the flavor paired with it, filled diamonds represent saccharin its paired flavor.

increase in hedonic ratings for sweetness-paired flavors that was related to amount of exposure with humans, but in that experiment the subjects were ingesting sucrose solutions, not saccharin. While we were concerned with the mere exposure effects, the flavor–flavor explanation seemed particularly fatal to our calorie hypothesis.

Ethanol as a Source of Calories

If rats have evolved a learning mechanism to insure that flavors serving as labels for calories are preferred, then it should be possible to see such conditioning even when the flavor of the calorie source is not unconditionally preferred. With that in mind, we looked for a calorie source that is unpalatable to rats. Pairing ethanol with neutral flavors typically produces a learned aversion for the flavor (Cappell, LeBlanc, & Endrenyl, 1972; Cunningham, 1978; Lester, Nachman, & Le Magnen, 1970). This occurs even though ethanol is a dense source of calories. In addition, liking for the flavor of ethanol is something that needs to be acquired. That is, most of us remember our first sip of liquor, and its disagreeable taste. But alcohol is unique stuff. Generally, if you drink enough of it, you come to like it. If we could condition a preference for an alcohol-paired flavor utilizing the same design as in the earlier experiment, we could be sure that flavor–flavor effects were not responsible.

We substituted 5% ethanol solution for sugar and once again the rats preferred the flavor associated with the calorie source over the saccharin-paired flavor. However, it was possible that the rats were getting a pharmacological dose of ethanol during the day's drinking, and that the resulting "high" was serving to reinforce intake of the ethanol solution and the resultant preference for the paired flavor. We ran four additional groups of rats to look at this question. Each group received the same conditioning sequence of alternating between flavored ethanol and flavored saccharin, but differed in the concentration of ethanol used (5, 7.5, 10, and 12.5%). During the conditioning phase, we drew blood samples at random times around the clock and assayed for blood alcohol level. No rat ever had a measurable amount of ethanol in its blood. The two-bottle flavor test after conditioning revealed that the two low concentration groups preferred the ethanol-paired flavor, and the two high concentration groups did not. We gave the rats an additional test between unflavored ethanol and saccharin and interestingly, all the rats preferred the saccharin. A flavor–flavor analysis of the learned preference would have predicted that the saccharin-paired flavor should be preferred. It seemed that the caloric property of the ethanol was reinforcing the preference, but that in higher concentrations, the hedonically negative taste of the ethanol was overshadowing any learned preference. (See Fig. 6.2.)

Further work with ethanol and sucrose solutions (Mehiel & Bolles, 1984) revealed that when the two calorie sources were juxtaposed in a conditioning process I described earlier, no preference for either paired flavor resulted. In other words, even though each solution was capable of conditioning a preference when it offered a caloric advantage over an alternate saccharin or water solution, when there was no advantage because the solutions were isocaloric, no preference was conditioned. This was in spite of the fact that sucrose was always preferred to ethanol.

Exposure Effects

We replicated the initial sucrose-saccharin experiment and the ethanol-saccharin experiments but controlled for exposure by yoking the amounts of solutions available during conditioning. In other words, the amount of sucrose solution available on a particular conditioning trial was equal to the rat's intake of saccharin solution the day before. In the ethanol study, we reversed the contingency. Each rat's saccharin was yoked to its ethanol intake. There was no impact on conditioned preference.

Another way to examine the issue of exposure during conditioning is to systematically vary the available amounts of solutions. In the next experiment we

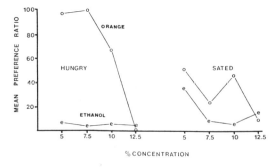

FIG. 6.2.   Preference ratios for the four groups tested when hungry and sated. Half the rats were given a two-bottle test between the ethanol and saccharin paired flavors (O), while the other half chose between unflavored saccharin and ethanol (e).

FIG. 6.3. Intake of the conditioning solutions and Polycose and saccharin paired flavors during the preference test. During conditioning the 40 POLY group drank all of the solutions daily. Group 80 POLY did not and the intakes are shown above (p = Polycose, s = saccharin).

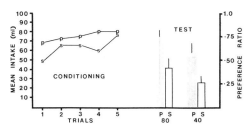

offered one group of rats twice as much flavored saccharin as flavored starch, and reversed the relationship in the other group. Once again the method was as already described, with flavors and order of presentation balanced within groups. One group got 40 ml saccharin (.25% w/v) and 80 ml Polycose (hydrolized corn starch, Ross Labs, 8% w/v), while the other got 40 ml Polycose and 80 ml saccharin. After 5 days exposure to each in an alternating sequence, we tested for preference between the paired flavors in a two-bottle test.

Figure 6.3 shows that both groups learned to prefer the Polycose-paired flavor over the saccharin-paired flavor. However, the 80 POLY group that had twice as much Polycose available during conditioning as the 40 POLY group, drank more than twice as much of the Polycose paired flavor in the test (means of 13 ml vs. 5 ml). Although this looked like evidence for an exposure effect, intake of the saccharin-paired flavors was almost equal between the groups. Why was there no exposure effect operating on the saccharin-paired flavor?

We replicated the experiment with naive rats and got essentially the same results. Again there was evidence of an exposure effect on the Polycose-paired flavor and no evidence of such an effect on the saccharin-paired flavor. In fact, in both replications, the rats receiving twice as much saccharin drank less of its paired flavor than the other rats. How could we explain a mere exposure effect that selectively operated on caloric solutions? Perhaps the effect was due to exposure to calories, not to solutions.

One possibility is that if there was an exposure effect sensitive to calories, then perhaps rats might learn to prefer a flavor paired with a calorically large meal over a flavor paired with a calorically small meal. For 6 days we restricted rats to a liquid diet consisting of an 8% Polycose solution. Each rat was fed at 10::30 AM and 10:30 PM. For half the rats the morning meal contained 20 calories with one flavor, and the evening meal 40 calories with another flavor. For the other half the schedule was reversed. Lime and orange flavors were counterbalanced across rats. Following the six conditioning days we tested for preference in a two-bottle test between the two flavored Polycose solutions, offering the rats 10 mls of each for 20 min. Intake of the two flavored solutions was equal. No preference had developed.

Although these data seem to contradict the effects of exposure, there were important differences between the experiments. In the two-meal experiment, both flavors were paired with calories, there was no noncaloric solution. Both flavored solutions were offered within a single day. In the mere exposure experiment, solutions were always offered on different days. We know that hunger and eating behavior in rats is under the influence of diurnal cycles (Bolles & Stokes, 1965; Richter, 1927). It seems likely that incentive quality or hedonic value of foods may interact with hunger and thus also be constrained by these circadian rhythms.

Motivational Effects

The notion that circadian rhythms may be tied to learned preferences led us to look at the effects of deprivation on flavor preferences. We had noticed in some of the early experiments that when rats were tested hungry, their preference for the calorie-paired flavor was robust. However, when rats were fed just prior to the flavor test, or were living under ad libitum chow conditions, the preference was not displayed. Analysis of the data revealed that ingestion of the calorie-paired flavor was depressed; the saccharin or water-paired flavor showed no change across motivational states (Fig. 6.4.). Fedorchak and Bolles (1987) reported similar data.

It would be interesting to establish a predictive relationship between level of hunger and degree of preference for a calorie-paired flavor. In order to examine this relation we used our general method to condition a preference for a sugar-paired flavor. But 24 hours before the test we fed different amount of Purina Rat Chow to independent groups of rats. The groups were fed either 0, 5, 10, 15, 20, 25, 30, or 40 grams of chow and the next day were given a two-bottle preference test between a sugar-paired flavor and a saccharin-paired flavor. Intake of the sugar-paired flavor decreased monotonically across groups with the 0-gram group consuming the most. Intake of the saccharin-paired flavor did not differ across groups (Fig. 6.5.)

In summary, then, rats learn to preferentially consume a flavor paired with a calorie source (sucrose, starch, ethanol) over a flavor paired with either saccharin or water. There seems to be an exposure effect that operates only on the calorie-

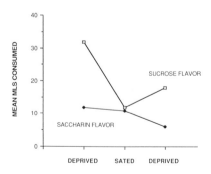

FIG. 6.4.   Test intake of an ethanol and a saccharin paired flavor across motivational states. Each rat was tested three times with motivational state counterbalanced across tests.

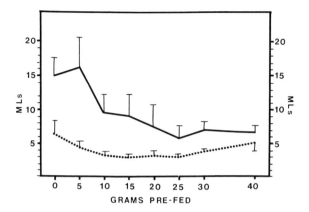

FIG. 6.5.   Test intake of a calorie-paired flavor and a saccharin-paired flavor as a function of amount of chow prefed 24 hours before the test.

paired flavor. Additionally, display of that learned preference is dependent on motivational constraints. So the rat learns to like a flavor that predicts calories (not necessarily sweetness) and the preference is strongest when the rat is hungriest. We may ask if the rat needs to be hungry in order to learn about flavors associated with calories.

Westerfeld and Lawrow (1953) examined the intake of ethanol by rats when they were free feeding or restricted to a proportion of baseline chow intake. Their animals had ethanol, water, and chow available at all times, and reacted to decreased chow availability by drinking more ethanol than the 100% baseline group. When the animals were switched from half rations to full and from full to half rations, ethanol intake by the rats switched, too. Westerfeld and Lawrow's (1953) experimental design seemed appropriate to examine the learning of an ethanol-paired flavor preference under different conditions of deprivation. We replicated their experiment, adding a flavor to the ethanol, then tested for learned flavor preferences at the end of each period.

Both groups started under ad libitum chow and water conditions for a 3-day baseline period. On the fourth day, one group remained on ad libitum rations of chow, and a flavor was added to their water. In addition, flavored 5% (w/v) ethanol was made available. The other group also got ethanol and water with flavors added, but were offered half their baseline intake of chow. On the succeeding conditioning days, the restricted group was always offered half the amount of chow eaten by the ad libitum group the day before. Conditioning lasted 10 days. The next 2 days were test days.

On the first test day the rats were given either ad libitum or the yoked half rations and two water bottles. One bottle was flavored with the ethanol-paired flavor, the other with the water-paired flavor. The ad libitum group displayed an aversion to the ethanol-paired flavor and the half ration group drank equal amounts of both flavors. The rats were then deprived of food for 24 hours prior to test 2. Test 2 was the same as test 1 except that no plain water or chow was available during the test. The second test, in which the rats were hungry, revealed a robust and equal preference for the ethanol-paired flavor in both groups.

Following the first test session, we reversed the availability of chow between the groups. The group that had been on ad libitum intake was now restricted to 50% of the other group's consumption, which was now ad libitum. Conditioning and testing proceeded as during the first phase. Once again, no preference was displayed in the nondeprived test and a robust preference was evident during the hungry test. (See Fig. 6.6.)

The results of this experiment, in which we varied hunger level during conditioning, revealed that deprivation does have an effect on the manifestation of the preference, but not on the preference learning. The rats learned to prefer the calorie-paired flavor whether they were on restricted rations or not. These results indicate that it was not caloric repletion per se that was responsible for the preference. Perhaps it was some effect of calories, some phase of the digestive process itself, that served to increase the hedonic value of the calorie-paired flavor.

Stimulus Order Effects

Our general method in these experiments was to alternate the rats daily between a caloric solution and a noncaloric solution. One might wonder what part this alternation played in the hedonic learning. Did the rats need to alternate in order to make the discrimination? We ran 16 rats in a modified design to address that question. Instead of alternating daily, we gave half the rats the caloric solution for a week and the other half the noncaloric solution. The following week the

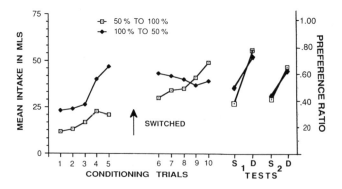

FIG. 6.6.   Intake of a flavored ethanol solution during both ad libitum and restricted chow access phases, and preference ratios from deprived and sated tests after each phase.

conditions were reversed. In this manner there was only one alternation. When we tested for preference in the usual two-bottle test, the preference was as robust as ever. Apparently there was nothing special about the daily switching from the caloric to the noncaloric solution.

Higher Order Effects

Everything we had done pointed to calories being responsible for the hedonic shift. Exposure seemed to contribute little. Unconditioned taste preference for the solutions seemed to contribute very little. Timing of the alternations seemed to contribute little. We began to wonder how amenable the preferences were to influences once they were learned. In other words, was it possible to impact the learning once it was in place?

One way to think about these learned preferences is that the flavor paired with calories comes to represent the calories. That is, due to conditioning trials, the flavor serves as a label, or stimulates an expectancy of the caloric solution. A different way to think of it is that the paired flavor itself undergoes a hedonic shift. If the association between the caloric solution and the paired flavor is such that the flavor comes to represent the solution, then after conditioning, if we devalue the solution, the flavor, if it is linked, should likewise be devalued. However, if the learned hedonic value of the flavor is not linked to the solution, then changes in the value of the solution should not effect the value of the flavor.

We conditioned rats to prefer one flavor or another based on its association with starch. We then sought either to inflate or devalue the preference by pairing the starch solution with either a good taste (saccharin) or a bad taste (quinine). This was similar in concept to Fanselow and Birk (1982), who paired a novel flavor with either saccharin or quinine and showed that changes of intake of the neutral flavor moved in the direction of the hedonic value of the saccharin or quinine. The difference was that we were starting with a flavor that was already hedonically positive due to learning based on association with calories. Following the standard conditioning phase the rats were tested for calorie-based preference as usual. Then we deprived the rats of water for 23.5 hours per day. After 4 days of drinking water 30 min per day, we gave half the rats experience with the starch laced with quinine, and half starch plus saccharin. The solutions did not contain the flavors that had been paired with them in conditioning. This inflation/devaluation phase consisted of four 30-min trials, and provided the only liquid available to the rats. Following the inflation/devaluation phase we again tested for preference between the starch- and water-paired flavors.

The test revealed that the postconditioning manipulation had no impact on the learned preference. The group that had received the saccharin-starch pairings had a preference that was 98% of their baseline preference. The quinine group's preference was 93% of baseline. These percentages were not reliably different.

These data looked like evidence that the change in hedonic value for the calorie-paired flavor was not linked to the caloric solution per se but rather was a function of the calories. In fact, our manipulation of changing the taste of the starch solution really had not changed its caloric value at all. A calorie is a calorie whether it is sweet or bitter. If the original flavor preference learning is due to association with calories, and not the taste of the caloric solution, then our manipulation should not have affected the preference. This experiment failed as a critical test between the idea of caloric expectancy and hedonic shift because we did not impact the value of the calories in the inflation/devaluation phase. However, the results suggest that the preference for calorie-paired flavors is not due to association with the unconditioned hedonic value of the taste of the caloric solution.

Unconditioned Flavor Effects

It seemed plausible that if caloric value was of prime importance in conditioning the hedonic value of the paired flavors, then isocaloric solutions should condition equal preferences. The unconditioned hedonic value of a caloric solution should contribute very little to the learned preference. On the other hand, if the unconditioned hedonic value of a solution was a good predictor of the learned preference for a flavor paired with it, then a flavor–flavor explanation of the learning would be parsimonious. To test these explanations, we offered free feeding rats five solutions simultaneously to get a ranking of hedonic value. Four of the solutions were isocaloric and one was saccharin. Intake of the solutions revealed reliable differences between them. Sucrose was preferred to starch, to saccharin, to ethanol, to oil, in that order. We then ran four groups of naive rats through our standard flavor conditioning procedure. Each group had one of the caloric solutions paired with a flavor and saccharin paired with a second flavor. The two-bottle test at the end of the conditioning revealed that there was no difference between groups. All the rats had learned a preference for the calorie-paired flavor and preferences did not differ between groups, even though the caloric solutions did differ in unconditioned hedonic value (Mehiel & Bolles, 1988a).

Extinction

If the rat learns to like a flavor because it is paired with calories, what happens to that preference if we stop pairing it with the caloric solution? We conditioned a preference for a flavor paired with an 8% sucrose solution, then tested every other day for over a month. Figure 6.7 shows the test intake over 20 tests. The tests were short, lasting only 20 minutes, and came at the same time every day. Following test 14, we gave the rats overnight experience with the sugar solution again but reversed the paired flavor. The next test revealed no preference, but the original preference came back on succeeding tests.

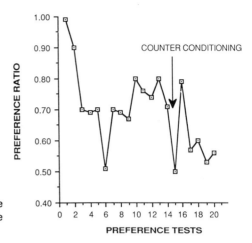

FIG. 6.7. The extinction curve for a calorie-based preference ratio over 20 tests.

Stimulus Modality and Context Effects

Everything to this point implied a general kind of learning mechanism based on calories that is relatively resistant to extinction. The hedonic shift may be a general one, that is, not tied to any specific sensory dimension of the caloric solution. Would a preference for a calorie-paired flavor transfer from solutions to chow? We conditioned a preference for a flavor based on sucrose solution, and tested for preference between two flavored chows (Mehiel & Bolles, 1988b). The rats preferred to eat the chow that had the calorie-paired flavor. This was in spite of the gross changes in sensory modality of the food, mash versus liquid. These data argued strongly against the notion of caloric expectency (Fedorchak & Bolles, 1988). The rats had eaten chow all their lives. Any learned expectancies about chow and calories must have already been in place at the time of the test. Perhaps a better way to think about these data is that the rats learn to like the calorie-paired flavor. We need not invoke any specific expectencies about calories.

We conditioned another group of rats to prefer a calorie-paired flavor in the usual manner and then tested them in their home cage and in a new context. The new context was wooden boxes in a separate room. The rats had not been out of their home cages since their arrival at the lab. There was no difference in intake between the two tests. The hedonic value of the paired flavor seemed to be independent of both food modality and context. But this is what we would expect. If you like chocolate, you like it in candy, cake, a milkshake, or at grandma's house.

The behavioral data that we had gathered in our investigations of the learned flavor preference for calorie-paired flavors compelled us to rule out as relatively unimportant all the variables except calories. Exposure, context, food modality, meal size, flavor–flavor mechanisms, unconditioned hedonic value, extinction trials, level of hunger during the learning; none of these variables seem to impact the learning of the preference. The caloric value of the solution seemed to be of prime importance. So we may wonder what it is about calories that could serve in an associative mechanism to condition these preferences?

A MODEL OF THE PHYSIOLOGICAL SUBSTRATE FOR HEDONIC SHIFTS

When the stomach is loaded with a glucose or other caloric solution, its rate of emptying is under the control of a reflex involving endocrine cells of the duodenum and their effect on the pyloric sphincter at the base of the stomach. Cholecystokinin (CCK), the peptide involved in this reflex, was discovered and named by Ivy and Oldberg (1928) as a blood factor involved in satiety. CCK causes the muscle cells of the pyloric sphincter to contract and thereby controls the emptying rate of the stomach. The more calorically dense the load is in the stomach, the more vigorous is the CCK response. In this way caloric emptying is regulated precisely at a constant rate. For example, glucose is emptied at a constant rate of .4 calories per minute, while saline is emptied exponentially (McHugh & Moran, 1981, 1986).

CCK receptors on the vagal axons enervating the hepatic area bind CCK and transport it rostrally to the area postrema (AP) at the base of the nucleus of the solitary tract (NTS) (Sankaran, Deveney, Goldfine, & Williams, 1979; Zarbin, Wamsley, Innis, & Kuhar, 1981). The AP is a circumventricular organ and thus receives input from both blood and synaptic transmission. Moran, Robinson, Goldrich, and McHugh (1986) have identified two types of receptors for CCK in the AP, one for CCK in cerebrospinal fluid, and one for axonally transported CCK. This CCK pathway runs from the AP through the midbrain to at least three nuclei of the hypothalamus: the paraventricular nucleus (PVN), the ventromedial nucleus (VMH), and the dorsomedial nucleus (DMN). Nuclei in the amygdala are also involved. Some of these connections are reciprocal. That is, the higher centers send axons to the NTS and AP (Kott, 1987; Ricardo & Koh, 1978; Norgren, 1978; Borone, Wayner, Scharoun, Guerra-Aguilar, & Aguilar-Baturoni, 1981; Hosoya & Mashushita, 1981; van der Kooy & Koda, 1983; van der Kooy, 1984; Shapiro & Miselis, 1985). Lesions in the AP, DMN, and PVN disrupt the satiety effects of exogenously administered CCK (Crawley, Kiss, & Mezey, 1984).

When CCK is administered exogenously to the interperotineal cavity deprived rats eat less than saline administered controls and go through a behavioral satiety sequence of drinking, grooming, drinking again, and finally sleeping (Gibbs, Young, & Smith, 1973). This suppression of intake effect has been reported in a variety of animals including humans, cats, dogs, chicks, hamsters, sheep, and baboons (Zadina, Banks, & Kastin, 1986). Additionally, exogenous CCK elicits the satiety sequence from sham feeding rats fitted with gastric fistulae. In the rat, an intact vagus is necessary for the effect to occur (Smith, Jerome, Kushin, Eterno, & Simansky, 1981).

When CCK is put into the fourth ventricle of hungry or thirsty rats, motivation to run for food is decreased while motivation to run for water is unaffected. (Zhang, Bula, & Stellar, 1986). In sheep, the amount of CCK required to get the suppression of intake effect is related to the amount of deprivation the sheep are under (Baile, McLaughlin, & Della-Fera 1986). CCK antiserum delivered into the lateral ventricles of sheep increases feeding (Della-Fera & Baile, 1984). Schick, Reilly, Roddy, Yaksh, and Go (1987) found CCK-like immunoreactivity (CCL-LI) in the hypothalamus of owl monkeys, which was released following an intragastric carbohydrate/amino acid meal. They found a ten-fold increase in hypothalamic CCK-LI during the first 30 minutes after the meal. During the next 60 minutes, CCK-LI release was still above baseline, but declined to below baseline levels afterwards.

In addition to vagal input to the NTS and related structures about peripheral CCK activity, it is noteworthy that vagally carried taste information from esophagus and throat also impinge on the NTS. Furthermore, taste information from the mouth and tongue is carried via the glossopharyngeal nerve to the taste nucleus that lies adjacent and superior to the NTS (Cajal, 1933).

If the neuronal circuitry described above serves to increase the hedonic value of flavors, how might it work? We propose that when a flavor is paired with a caloric solution as in our general experimental paradigm, the hedonic value of the flavor is shifted upward because it predicts the peripheral CCK reflex at the duodenum and thereby activates various excitatory and inhibitory processes involving the nuclei described above. While we do not understand the exact central mechanisms involved, CCK could be serving ás a modulator of endorphins and norepinepherine (NE) within the hypothalamus, and thereby acting on the reward value of flavors. Ample evidence for a complex functional relationship between CCK and endogenous opioids exists. For example, progulumide, a CCK receptor antagonist blocks morphine induced analgesia (Ambrose, Autry, Liebman, & Barbaz, 1986). CCK and opioid systems enjoy considerable and extensive overlap in their central distribution and receptor colocalization (Gall, Lauterborn, Burks, & Seroogy, 1987). CCK independently causes analgesia and sedation, responses that are probably opioid mediated (Crawley, Hays, Paul, & Goodwin, 1981; Zetler, 1980). However, the nature of the relationship between CCK and endogenous opiates is far from simple, as CCK has also been shown to act as an opiate antagonist (Faris, 1985; Faris, McLauglin, Baile, Olney, & Komisaruk, 1987; Rovati, Sacerdte, & Paneral, 1985; Watkins, Kinscheck, & Mayer, 1985).

Perhaps through Pavlovian conditioning processes, a flavor paired with the reflexive activation of the CCK circuit comes to elicit that activation. If the release and activation of CCK is conditionable, a number of experimental predictions can be made. First, following a conditioning sequence in which a flavor is paired with a caloric solution, the flavor by itself should elicit the CCK response.

Within limits, ingestion of the calorie-paired flavor should be able to suppress feeding. Second, if the calorie-paired flavor elicits CCK, exogenously administering CCK should reveal an additive effect on satiety. The effect should not be seen when a flavor paired with a noncaloric solution is tested. Third, if the CCK reflex is really the unconditioned stimulus that we argue, then if we pair interperitoneal injections of CCK with a flavored noncaloric solution, rats should learn to prefer that flavor. The following experiments sought to test this model. (See Fig. 6.8.)

Experimental Test of the Conditioned CCK Model

We conditioned two groups of rats to prefer either cherry or grape flavor based on its association with either dextrose or starch. The rats alternated daily between the caloric solution and water with the alternate flavor. As usual, order of presentation and paired flavor were balanced within groups. Following the conditioning period, all rats received the standard two-bottle test between the two paired flavors and every rat displayed a preference for the calorie-paired flavor. After a few days of free access to chow and water, the rats were restricted to water and 12 grams of chow for 24 hours. Then they were offered either the preferred flavor or the water flavor for 30 minutes. Ten minutes later all rats were offered access to chow and allowed to eat for 20 minutes. Chow intake was suppressed in those rats that had received the calorie-paired flavor. The next day each rat went through the same testing process, but the flavors were reversed. Once again, the rats that got the calorie-paired flavor ate less. (See Fig. 6.9.)

A second experiment looked at differences in the efficacy of CCK to suppress intake of a calorie-paired flavor, a saccharin-paired flavor, and a water-paired flavor. We conditioned two groups of rats. One group had a flavor paired with sucrose on half the days and a different flavor paired with water on the other half of the days. The other group had a flavor paired with saccharin on half the days

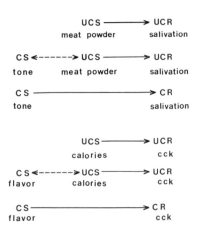

FIG. 6.8. A Pavlovian explanation of conditioning of CCK release by a calorie-paired flavor.

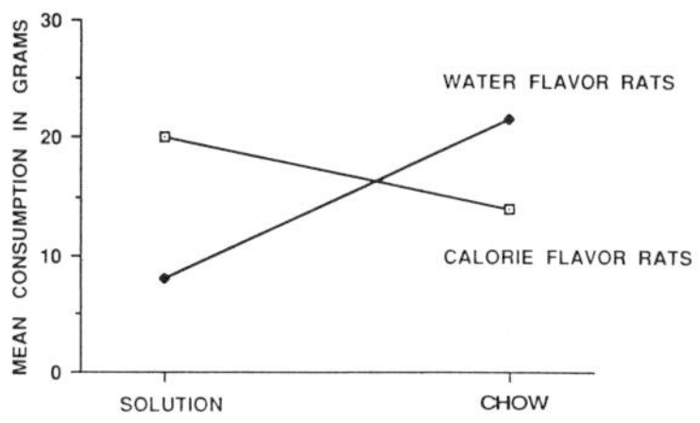

FIG. 6.9. Rats that drink a calorie-paired flavor eat less chow
than rats that drink a water-
paired flavor.

and flavored water on the alternate days. Following conditioning, we tested for flavor preference in the usual way. Only the sugar group displayed a robust preference for the calorie-paired flavor. The results for the saccharin group were surprising in view of the reports in the literature regarding the flavor–flavor effect (Fanselow & Birk, 1982). Perhaps the flavor–flavor effect is only active on short exposures to saccharin. A second two-bottle test between the flavors was of main interest. During that test, half the rats were injected with CCK and half with saline. Only the flavor that had been paired with sucrose was suppressed. Neither the water paired flavor nor the saccharin-paired flavor was affected by the drug.

If calorie-paired flavors come to ellicit a conditioned CCK release, as we have argued, then the present results make sense. The combination of a conditioned release and the exogenous administration would be additive and the drug effects would be enhanced. In the rats drinking their water or saccharin paired flavor, no conditioned release would occur, so there would be no additive effect. (See Fig. 6.10.)

Perhaps the most crucial test for our model of CCK and hedonic value are the two following experiments. We had amply demonstrated that flavors paired with calories were preferred to saccharin-paired flavors. We had conditioned hundreds of rats in numerous experiments using sugar and saccharin with paired flavors. Almost every rat had learned to prefer a sugar-paired flavor to a saccharin-paired flavor. In addition, it looked like preferences for saccharin-paired flavors in a flavor–flavor paradigm were weak, at best. If we could show that the

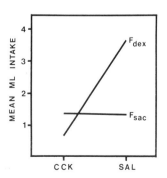

FIG. 6.10. A flavor paired with dextrose is subject to the suppressive effects of a CCK injection: a saccharin-paired flavor is not.

addition of CCK to saccharin "fooled" the rat and disrupted the preference, then that might provide strong evidence for our model.

Eight rats were deprived of water 23.25 hours per day. They were allowed to drink in wooden drinking boxes in a room separate from the vivarium for 45 minutes per day. After a week of training with water the rats' weights had stabilized. We replaced the water with flavored sucrose for half the rats and flavored saccharin for the other half. The next day the solutions and flavors were reversed. Conditioning proceeded for 14 days. We extended the usual amount of conditioning because the rats could only drink a portion of their normal intake when conditioning trials lasted all day. Following the conditioning phase, we tested the rats in the usual manner. All rats preferred the calorie-paired flavor.

After 2 days of ad libitum chow and water in the home cages, the rats began a second conditioning phase that was a replication of the first phase. In phase two, we used two new flavors, and injected the rats with the CCK-blocker proglumide (a gift of Joseph Barrows, Barrows Research Group) on sugar trials, and CCK on saccharin trials. Figure 6.11 shows the change in preference between conditioning phases. Proglumide did not impact the intake of the sugar-paired flavor. However, the addition of CCK to the saccharin trials had a significant effect on intake of its paired flavor. These data are interesting in view of the controversy surrounding the way in which CCK suppresses meal size. Deutch and Hardy (1977) have argued that CCK's suppression of intake effects are due to a conditioned aversion to flavors paired with the drug. This idea now seems unlikely in view of the conditioned preference we obtained in the present experiment.

Perhaps the addition of CCK to saccharin *fools* the rat's digestive system and acts like sugar. It should be possible to condition a preference for a saccharin-CCK flavor over a saccharin-saline flavor. We attempted to do that. We restricted 8 rats to 12 grams of chow and 45 minutes access to water per day. After a week of acclimation to the brief drinking period we gave half the rats grape saccharin and half cherry saccharin. All the rats were injected interperitoneally with CCK. The next day they got saccharin again, but the flavors were reversed across rats and the injection was saline. Conditioning proceeded for 10 days.

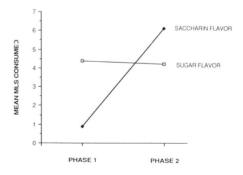

FIG. 6.11.   Intake of a sugar and a saccharin paired flavor during tests. In phase I, rats drank the conditioning solutions under normal circumstances. In phase II, flavored saccharin was paired with CCK and flavored sucrose was paired with Proglumide.

FIG. 6.12.   Test intake of two flavors that had been paired with saccharin during conditioning. One solution was always paired with an injection of CCK, the other with saline. Each test followed 5 exposures to the conditioning solutions and paired drugs.

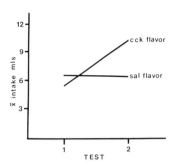

Following conditioning we tested for flavor preference between the two flavored saccharin solutions. We then ran an additional 10 days of conditioning and a second test.

Figure 6.12 shows the development of the preference for the CCK-paired flavor across the conditioning trials and tests. While the magnitude of the preference is not as large as we have seen in more natural circumstances, as when the rat drinks sucrose, the effect is still there. Taken together with the other evidence we have offered here, it seems reasonable to conclude that the reflexive release of CCK, and the activation of the central components of that system, serve to increase the hedonic value of flavors that predict that release and activation.

CONCLUSION

I argue that the satiation effects of CCK should not be considered as resulting only from stimuli such as stomach distention. Rather, CCK should be thought of in more psychological terms, as a peptide involved in the modulation of hedonics within a meal. Cabanac (1971) coined the term "alliesthesia" to describe the reduction in pleasantness ratings given by subjects as they tasted then swallowed sucrose solutions. Perhaps this aversive change in palatability within the meal is due to the activation of CCK. We believe that CCK has both short term (alliesthesia) and long term (conditioned increase in hedonic value) effects.

Rats learn to like flavors that predict calories. This is true when the calorie source is innately preferred (sucrose and starch) or disliked (ethanol). We have examined this learning under a variety of experimental constraints including daily versus weekly alternation between the caloric and non-caloric solutions, the amount of exposure, the amount of available calories, the context of conditioning and testing, the explicit format of the flavor in the test (eating versus drinking), and the unconditioned hedonic value of the solutions. Finally, we have identified and tested a possible physiological substrate for the learning of hedonic value that involves cholecystokinin, a brain-gut peptide.

REFERENCES

Ambrose, F. G., Autry, W. L., Liebman, J. M., & Barbaz, B. S. (1986). Selective antagonism by proglumide and CR-1409 of the antiwrithing actions of CCK-8-S and related peptides in the mouse. *Soc. Neurosci. Abstr., 12,* 1490.

Baile, C. A., McLaughlin, C. L., & Della-Fera, M. A. (1986). Role of cholecysotkinin and opioid peptides in control of food intake. *Physiological Reviews, 66,* 172–234.

Barone, F. C., Wayner, M. J., Scharoun, S. L., Guerra-Aguilar, R., and Aguilar-Baturoni, H. U. (1981). Afferent connections to the lateral hypothalamus: A horseradish peroxidase study in the rat. *Brain Research Bulletin, 7,* 75–88.

Bolles, R. C. (1983). A mixed model of taste preferences. In R. L. Mellgren (Ed.), *Animal cognition and behavior.* Amsterdam: North-Holland.

Bolles, R. C., Hayward, L., & Crandall, C. (1981). Conditioned taste preferences based on caloric density. *Journal of Experimental Psychology: Animal Behavior Processes, 7,* 59–69.

Bolles, R. C., & Stokes, L. W. (1965). Rat's anticipation of diurnal and a-diurnal feeding. *J. Comp. Physiol. Psychol., 60,* 290–294.

Cabanac, M. (1971). Physiological role of pleasure. *Science, 173,* 1103–1107.

Cajal, S. R. (1933). *Histology* (10th ed.). Baltimore: William Wood.

Cappell, N., LeBlanc, A. E., & Endrenyi, L. (1972). Effects of chlordiazepoxide and ethanol on the extinction of a conditioned taste aversion. *Physiology and Behavior, 9,* 167–169.

Crawley, J. N., Hays, S. E., Paul, S. M., & Goodwin, F. K. (1981). Cholecystokinin reduces exploratory behavior in mice. *Physiology and Behavior, 27,* 407–411.

Crawley, J. N., Kiss, J. Z., & Mezey, E. (1984). Bilateral midbrain transection block the behavioral effects of cholesystokinin on feeding and exploration in rats. *Brain Research, 322,* 316–321.

Cunningham, C. L. (1978). Alcohol interacts with flavor during extinction of conditioned taste aversion. *Physiological Psychology, 6,* 510–516.

Della-Fera, M. A., & Baile, C. A. (1984). Control of feed intake in sheep. *Journal of Animal Science, 59,* 1362–1368.

Deutch, J. A., & Hardy, W. T. (1977). Cholecystokinin produces bait shyness in rats. *Nature, 266,* 196.

Fanselow, M., & Birk, J. (1982). Flavor–flavor associations induce hedonic shifts in taste preference. *Animal Learning and Behavior, 10,* 223–228.

Faris, P. L. (1985). Opiate antagonistic function of cholecystokinin in analgesia and energy balance systems. *Annals of New York Academy of Sci., 448,* 437–447.

Faris, P. L., McLauglin, C. L., Baile, C. A., Olney, J. W., & Komisaruk, B. R. (1987). Active immunization against cholecystokinin potentiates and prolongs morphine analgesia, but does not affect development of tolerance. *Science, 226,* 1215–1217.

Fedorchak, P. M., & Bolles, R. C. (1987). Hunger enhances the expression of calorie—but not taste—mediated conditioned flavor preferences. *Journal of Experimental Psychology: Animal Behavior Processes, 13,* 73–79.

Fedorchak, P. M., & Bolles, R. C. (1988). Nutritive expectancies mediate cholecystokinen's suppression-of-intake effect. *Behavioral Neuroscience, 102,* 451–455.

Gall, C., Lauterborn, J., Burks, D., & Seroogy, K. (1987). Colocalization of enkephalin and cholecystokinin in discrete areas of rat brain. *Brain Research, 403,* 403–407.

Gibbs, J., Young, R. C., & Smith, G. P. (1973). Cholecystokinin elicits satiety in rats with open gastric fistulas. *Nature, 245,* 323–325.

Holman, E. (1975). Immediate and delayed reinforcers for flavor preferences in rats. *Learning and Motivation, 6,* 91–100.

Hosoya, Y., & Mashushita, M. (1981). Brainstem projections from the hypothalamus to the area postrema in the rat, as by the HRP and autoradiographic methods. *Brain Research, 214,* 144–149.

Ivy, A. C., & Oldberg, E. (1928). A hormone mechanism for gallbladder contraction and evacuation. *American Journal of Physiology, 86,* 599–613.

Kott, J. N. (1987). *Dorsal medullary factors in pancreatic regulation.* Doctoral dissertation submitted to the Department of Psychology, University of Washington.

Lester, D., Nachman, M., & Le Magnen, J. (1970). Aversive conditioning by ethanol in the rat. *Quarterly Journal of Studies on Alcohol, 31,* 578–586.

McHugh, P. R., & Moran, T. H. (1981). Distinctions among three sugars in their effects on gastric emptying and satiety. *American Journal of Physiology, 241.*

McHugh, P. R., & Moran, T. H. (1986). The stomach, cholecystokinin, and satiety. *Federation Proceedings, 45,* 1384–1390.

Mehiel, R., & Bolles, R. C. (1984). Learned flavor preferences based on caloric outcome. *Animal Learning and Behavior, 12,* 421–427.

Mehiel, R., & Bolles, R. C. (1988a). Learned flavor preferences based on calories are independent of initial hedonic value. *Animal Learning and Behavior, 16,* 383–387.

Mehiel, R., & Bolles, R. C. (1988b). Hedonic shift learning based on calories. *Bulletin of the Psychonomic Society, 26,* 459–462.

Moran, T., Robinson, P. H., Goldrich, M. S., & McHugh, P. R. (1985). Two brain cholecystokinin receptors: Implications for behavioral actions. *Brain Research, 362,* 175–179.

Norgren, R. (1978). Projections from the nucleus of the solitary tract in the rat. *Neuroscience, 3,* 207–218.

Pliner, P. (1982). The effects of mere exposure on liking for edible substances. *Appetite, 3,* 283–290.

Ricardo, J. A., & Koh, E. T. (1978). Anatomical evidence of direct projections from the nucleus of the solitary tract to the hypothalamus, amygdala, and other forebrain structures of the rat. *Brain Research, 153,* 1–26.

Richter, C. P. (1927). Animal behavior and internal drives. *Quart. Rev. Biol., 2,* 307–343.

Rovanti, L. C., Sacerdte, P., & Panerai, A. E. (1985). Effects of proglumide on morphine analgesia and tolerance. *Annals of New York Academy of Science, 448,* 630–632.

Sankaran, H., Deveney, C. W., Goldfine, I. D., & Williams, J. A. (1979). Preparation of biologically active radioiodinated cholecystokinin for radioreceptor assay and radioimmuinoassay. *Journal of Biological Chemistry, 254,* 9349–9351.

Schick, R. R., Reilly, A., Roddy, S., Yaksh, T. L., & Go, V. L. W. (1987). Neuronal CCK-like immunoreactivity is postprandially released from primate hypothalamus. *Brain Research, 418,* 20–26.

Shapiro, R. E., & Miseils, R. R. (1985). The central connections of the area postrema of the rat. *The Journal of Comparative Neurology, 234,* 344–346.

Smith, G. P., Jerome, C., Cushin, B. J., Eterno, R., & Simansky, K. J. (1981). Abdominal vagotomy blocks the satiety effect of cholecystokinin in the rat. *Science, 213,* 1036–1037.

Stang, D. (1975). When familiarity breeds contempt, absence makes the heart grow fonder: Effects of exposure and delay on taste pleasantness ratings. *Bulletin of the Psychonomic Society, 6,* 273–275.

Steiner, J. E. (1977). Facial expressions of the neonate infant indicating the hedonics of food-related chemical stimuli. In J. M. Weiffenbach (Ed.), *Taste and development: The genesis of sweet preference.* (DHEW Publication No. NIH 77-1068). U.S. Government Printing Office: Washington, D.C.

Thorndike, E. (1935). *The psychology of wants, interests, and attitudes.* New York: Appleton-Century.

van der Kooy, D. (1984). Area postrema: Site where cholecystokinin acts to decrease food intake. *Brain Research, 295,* 345–347.

van der Kooy, D., & Koda, L. Y. (1983). Organization of the projections of a circumventricular organ: The area postrema in the rat. *Journal of Comparative Neurology, 219,* 328–338.

Watkins, L. R., Kinscheck, I. B., & Mayer, D. J. (1985). Potentiation of morphine analgesia by the cholecystokinin antagonist proglumide. *Brain Research, 327,* 169–180.

Westerfeld, W. W., & Lawrow, M. S. (1953). The effect of caloric restriction and thiamine deficiency on the voluntary consumption of alcohol by rats. *Quarterly Journal of Studies on Alcohol, 14,* 378–384.

Zadina, J. E., Banks, W. A., & Kastin, A. J. (1986). Central nervous system effects of peptides, 1980–1985: A cross-listing of peptides and their central actions from the first six years of the journal Peptides. *Peptides, 7,* 497–537.

Zajonc, R. (1968). Attitudinal effects of mere exposure. *Journal of Personality and Social Psychology, 9,* 1–27.

Zahorik, D. M., Maier, S. F., & Pies, R. W. (1974). Preferences for tastes paired with recovery from thiamine deficiency in rats: Appetitive conditioning or learned safety. *Journal of Comparative and Physiological Psychology, 87,* 1083–1091.

Zarbin, M. A., Wamsley, J. K., Innis, R. B., & Kuhar, M. J. (1981). Cholecystokinin receptors: Presence and axonal flow in the rat vagus nerve. *Life Sciences, 29,* 697–705.

Zellner, D. A., Rozin, P., Aron, M., & Kulish, C. (1983). Conditioned enhancement of human's liking for flavor by pairing with sweetness. *Learning and Motivation, 14,* 338–350.

Zetler, G. (1980). Analgesia and ptosis caused by caerulein and cholecystokinin octapeptide (CCK-8). *Neuropharmacology 19,* 415–422.

Zhang, D., Bula, W., & Stellar, E. (1986). Brain cholecystokinin as a satiety peptide. *Physiology and Behavior, 36,* 1183–1186.

7 Hunger and the Learning of Flavor Preferences

Elizabeth D. Capaldi
University of Florida

Animals eat for taste and eat for calories. The early work on food intake focused primarily on the importance of calories. As quoted from E. Scott by Jacobs and Sharma (1969), "There is only one known true hunger. This is the appetite for food as such, and in the rat at least, it is satisfied by sufficient calories. There are, to the author's knowledge, no data to contradict the assumption that normally rats eat for calories." This conclusion comes from the early work showing that rats compensate for dilution of their diet by consuming more, thereby maintaining a constant caloric intake (Adolph, 1947). Rats adjust to dilution even when feeding is done intragastrically, bypassing the taste system (Epstein & Teitelbaum, 1962). On the other hand, rats readily consume saccharin solutions, which have no calories, and also sham feed for sugar and other substances (e.g., Joyner, Smith, Shindlehecker, & Pfaffman, 1985), showing that palatability and sensory factors are also major determinants of food intake.

Animals also form flavor preferences based on both categories of reinforcer, sensory, and metabolic. Fanselow and Birk (1983) and Holman (1975) showed rats develop preferences for flavors associated with saccharin, taste–taste learning. Sherman et al., (1983) found preferences for flavors paired with low doses of ethanol directly intubated into the stomach, and flavors associated with intragastric infusion of polycose also came to be preferred (Sclafani & Nissenbaum, 1989), taste-calorie learning.

Fedorchak and Bolles (1987) were concerned with how hunger affects learning of flavor preferences and later expression of these flavor preferences. They found that hunger enhanced the expression of flavor preferences based on calories (sucrose or ethanol) but did not affect the expression of flavor preferences based on taste alone (saccharin). In all their experiments except one animals were trained hungry and tested ad lib or hungry. Because hunger was not varied in training, we do not know if hunger affects learning of flavor preferences as well as the expression of flavor preferences. We were interested in how hunger affects the learning of flavor preferences.

There is reason to believe hunger should affect learning of flavor preferences. Hunger increases consumption of sweet substances. As long ago as 1944, Soulairac showed that hunger induced by insulin increases consumption of 10% solutions of maltose, sucrose, and glucose in direct proportions to their sweetness (Soulairac, 1944). Since then many studies have shown that hunger increases sugar consumption in rats (e.g., Collier & Bolles, 1968; Davis, 1973; Smith & Duffy, 1957). The increased sugar intake produced by hunger could be due to an increase in the attractiveness of the sweet taste or to a reduction in the satiating effects of sugar, or to an increased value of calories, or all of these (e.g., Davis & Levine, 1977). If hunger increases the reinforcing effect of a sweet taste, or of calories or of both, increasing hunger during learning should produce stronger conditioned flavor preferences for flavors associated with sweet caloric substances.

Fedorchak and Bolles (1987), in one study varying hunger during formation of conditioned flavor preferences, found no effects of hunger during training on strength of preference for a flavor associated with ethanol. Ethanol is preferred because of its calories, not because of its taste (Sherman et al., 1983). Thus this result suggests that learning of taste-calorie associations is not enhanced by hunger. Hunger may, however, enhance learning of taste–taste associations, if, as many suggest, hunger increases the palatability of pleasant tastes. In the experiments reported here, we varied hunger during training and test of conditioned flavor preferences based on a number of different substances: saccharin, sucrose and polycose.

EXPERIMENT 1

Method

In Experiments 1A and 1B we measured conditioned preferences for saccharin as a function of hunger in training and in test. If hunger increases the reinforcement produced by sweet tastes stronger conditioned preferences should be formed with high hunger in training. We used the same procedures as Fedorchak and Bolles (1987). In all the experiments reported here subjects were naive male Sprague-Dawley rats purchased from the Harlan Co., Indianapolis, Indiana. Experiments began within 3 weeks after arrival. Liquid foods were presented in 50 ml Nalgene centrifuge tubes with rubber stoppers and metal spouts. Positions of the substances were reversed daily in test on an ABBA sequence. Feeding occurred 90 min after each daily session.

In Experiment 1A, there were 40 subjects that were 60 days old upon arrival at the laboratory; the 20 subjects in Experiment 1B were 73 days old upon arrival. The solutions were flavored .15% saccharin or flavored deionized water. Flavorings consisted of 1% wintergreen (2% wintergreen oil in 100% ethanol) or 1% cinnamon (2% cinnamon oil in 100% ethanol).

Half the rats were maintained on ad lib food and the other half were placed on 14 gm daily. Ad lib animals were also given an additional 14 gm daily during the deprived animals feeding time. Rats in Experiment 1A had access to water during the first 10 days of their feeding schedule and bottles were removed on day 11. For Experiment 1B all water bottles were removed on day 1 and the feeding schedule was begun.

The first round of training began on day 12 in Experiment 1A and day 2 for Experiment 1B. During training each rat received wintergreen flavored solution on half the days and cinnamon flavored on the other half. Wintergreen and cinnamon flavors followed a double alternation pattern in Experiment 1A and a single alternation pattern over days in 1B. Two tubes containing 50 ml remained on the cages side by side for 23 hr. Half the rats in each group had wintergreen saccharin and cinnamon water over days and the other half had the opposite flavor pairing. This first round of training lasted 8 days.

The first postconditioning phase lasted 2 days. Water bottles were replaced on the first day. Half the rats in each subgroup were switched to the opposite feeding schedule on the second day to prepare for testing.

The test run on the following day consisted of a two-bottle choice between 50 ml of wintergreen water and cinnamon water side by side for 10 min. Food was removed from all cages during the test. Following the test, all animals were returned to their original training feeding condition overnight. The next day those rats *not* previously switched to the opposite feeding condition before test one were now switched before test two. Test two was run the following day in the same manner as test one. Following the test all rats returned to training feeding conditions and were given access to water.

Water was again removed the next day (day 25 for 1A and day 15 for 1B) and a second complete round of training, postconditioning, and testing was run. All details remained the same except that those switched to new feeding conditions for test one in round one were switched for test four and those switched before test were again switched for test three.

Results

Figures 7.1 and 7.2 show the results of these two experiments. As can be seen, we replicated Fedorchak and Bolles' (1987) finding that hunger in test did not enhance the preferences for the flavor associated with saccharin. In both experiments only one group showed a preference for the flavor associated with saccharin, the group trained hungry and tested ad lib. We repeated this experiment

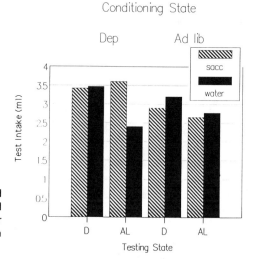

FIG. 7.1. Mean ml consumed in test of the flavor associated with saccharin and the flavor associated with water for each group in Experiment 1A.

because this seemed a surprising finding, but as Fig. 7.2 shows, we obtained the same result. In both experiments, the Reinforced Flavor X Training Deprivation X Test Deprivation interaction was significant, Experiment 1A, $F(1,128) = 4.37, p < .05$; Experiment 1B, $F(1, 128) = 8.97, p < .01$. Newman-Keuls tests showed that in both experiments only Group Deprivation-ad lib drank significantly more of the flavor associated with saccharin, producing the significant interaction mentioned.

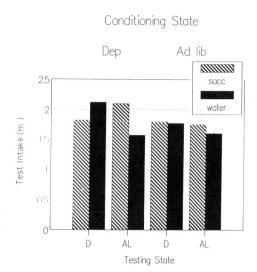

FIG. 7.2. Mean ml consumed in test of the flavor associated with saccharin and the flavor associated with water for each group in Experiment 1B.

Discussion

The data suggest that preference for the sweet taste of saccharin is initially enhanced by hunger, but that with experience rats learn that a particular sweet taste is not reinforcing, perhaps because no caloric consequence follows. Thus, the sweet taste of saccharin and the flavors associated with this taste are preferred in test only if the rat was hungry in training, but was not hungry in test. No single-factor view satisfactorily explains this result. If, for example, we assume that the sweet taste of saccharin is preferred only when the rats are not hungry, it is not clear why the group trained and tested ad lib did not prefer the saccharin flavor. On the other hand, if we assume that training under hunger produced the preference for the flavor associated with saccharin, it is mysterious why this preference appeared only when the test was given under the ad lib condition.

The results of Experiments 1A and 1B show that hunger affects learning of the taste–taste association with saccharin. The higher the hunger in training the stronger the association. We believe that this is because the hedonic reaction to sweet is enhanced by hunger. Taste-calorie learning also occurs with saccharin; specifically, rats learn that caloric restoration is not produced by saccharin. Accordingly, their preference in the test for a flavor associated with saccharin is not enhanced by hunger. Only the group trained hungry and tested ad lib showed a preference for the flavor associated with saccharin, because training hungry is necessary to get the strong positive affective reaction to sweet, and testing ad lib is necessary to reduce the aversiveness of expecting no caloric restoration.

If this is correct, then increasing hunger in training should produce stronger conditioned flavor preferences for sweet substances containing calories, such as sucrose. Experiment 2 measured conditioned preferences for sucrose as a function of hunger in training and test.

EXPERIMENT 2

When trained hungry rats should have a strong positive affective reaction to the sweet taste of sucrose (as they do to saccharin), which should produce a stronger conditioned flavor preference for rats trained hungry than for those trained ad lib. And the sweet taste of sucrose is associated with caloric restoration, so the preference should also be enhanced by hunger in the test as reported by Fedorchak and Bolles (1987). The 40 subjects in this experiment were 77 days old on arrival. Solutions were wintergreen or cinnamon in 2% sucrose or de-ionized water. All other procedures were the same as in Experiments 1A and 1B.

Results

Figure 7.3 shows test consumption of the flavor that was associated with sucrose and the flavor that was associated with water as a function of hunger during

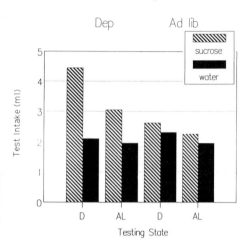

FIG. 7.3. Mean ml consumed in test of the flavor associated with sucrose and the flavor associated with water for each group in Experiment 2.

training and test. As can be seen, hunger in training enhanced later preference for a flavor associated with sucrose, $F(1,32) = 12.98$ $p < .01$. Also, hunger in the test enhanced the preference for a flavor associated with sucrose, $F(1,32) = 4.03$ $p < .05$, as reported by Fedorchak and Bolles (1987).

In training, all rats consumed more sucrose than water, and this difference was larger for the hungry rats. The mean sucrose consumption was 85.67 ml for ad lib rats and 97.39 for hungry rats. This difference in consumption shows that sucrose was more preferred in training for the hungry rats, and thus more reinforcing. Although more sucrose was consumed by the hungry rats, this alone should not produce a subsequent difference in flavor preference. Holman (1975) found no differences in preference produced by different amounts of saccharin and we have obtained the same result varying amount of sucrose solution. We found no difference in preference between a flavor associated with 20 ml of sucrose and one associated with 5 ml of sucrose (unpublished). Thus we believe the enhanced preference in Experiment 2 is not attributable to the greater consumption of sucrose by hungry rats.

Discussion

Experiments 1 and 2 both showed that hunger enhanced conditioning of flavor preferences based on sweet substances. This conditioned preference was also enhanced by hunger in the test if the sweet substance contained calories (sucrose), but not if the sweet substance was non caloric (saccharin). We suggested that hunger enhances initial preference for sweet substances, but that this preference is maintained only if calories follow. Experiment 3 tested these ideas by evaluating the preference for flavors associated with sweet vs nonsweet caloric substances when calories were equated.

EXPERIMENT 3

Experiment 3 evaluated the preference for flavors associated with sucrose or polycose as a function of hunger. Polycose is a glucose polymer calorically equivalent to sucrose but minimally sweet. Preference for sucrose over polycose gives a measure of what the preference for a sweet taste is when caloric reduction occurs equally with and without the sweet taste.

Method

Procedures of the preceding experiments were followed. The 20 subjects in this experiment were 71 days old upon arrival at the laboratory. Solutions were wintergreen or cinnamon flavored 2% sucrose or 2% polycose.

Results

Figure 7.4 show the preference for sucrose over polycose as a function of hunger during training and test. As can be seen, rats trained hungry preferred the flavor associated with sucrose over the flavor associated with polycose, rats trained ad lib showed the reverse preference. The interaction of reinforced flavor X training deprivation was significant $F(1,12) = 13.47$ $p < .01$ as was the interaction of reinforced flavor and testing deprivation $F(1,12) = 7.84$ $p < .02$. Subsequent

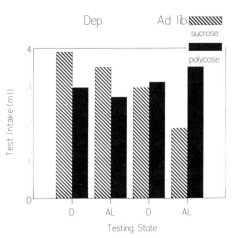

FIG. 7.4. Mean ml consumed in test of the flavor associated with sucrose and the flavor associated with polycose for each group in Experiment 3.

Newman-Keuls tests showed that the group trained and tested deprived preferred the flavor associated with sucrose, while rats trained and tested ad lib preferred the flavor associated with *polycose*. Groups that were trained ad lib and tested deprived or trained deprived and tested ad lib had no significant preference.

Discussion

Experiment 3 shows that hunger enhances the conditioned preferences for a flavor associated with a sweet taste when a difference in caloric restoration is not associated with the sweet taste. This is consistent with our hypothesis that hunger produces a preference for sweet tastes, a preference that is then maintained only if caloric restoration follows the sweet. In addition, Experiment 3 shows that under ad lib conditions sweetness is disliked compared to starch alone. Rats trained and tested ad lib later preferred a flavor associated with polycose over a flavor associated with sucrose. Because the caloric value of polycose and sucrose is the same, apparently the sweet taste of sucrose is disliked under ad lib conditions. Sclafani and Mann (1987) found that ad lib rats preferred polycose to sucrose when equated concentrations were low, as they were here. They also found that if concentrations were high ad lib rats preferred sucrose to polycose. They did not vary deprivation so we do not know if the preference for sucrose would have been enhanced by deprivation.

We have shown that hunger enhances the preference for sweet, even when the sweet is not currently a differential cue for calories. Why is this? Sweetness may be an innate marker for calories that animals use as a "rule of thumb" (e.g., Bolles, 1983). Thus hunger may enhance the preference for sweet because the animal is built to ingest sweet substances. Normally this rule of thumb will produce ingestion of calories, with the unnatural substance of saccharin being an exception.

If hungry rats naturally prefer sweet substances because they are tracking sweet as a marker for calories what would happen if they had experience with two substances, one sweet but low calorie, the other bitter but high calorie? Which would they prefer? We asked that question in Experiment 4.

EXPERIMENT 4

Experiment 4 pitted 20% polycose plus quinine against 2% polycose plus Nutrasweet in a flavor preference experiment. For half the rats, one flavor was associated with the high calorie, bad tasting 20% polycose plus .2% quinine. The other flavor was associated with the good tasting, low calorie 2% polycose plus 2% nutrasweet. The other half of the rats had one flavor associated with 20% polycose and the other with 2% polycose.

Method

Procedures of the preceding experiments were followed. There were 40 rats, half of each group was on a 14 gm/day deprivation schedule for eleven days before training began and during training, the other half of the rats remained on ad lib food. There were eight days of training and 4 tests, two under each deprivation condition. In the test rats had a choice between cinnamon or wintergreen flavored water with 11% polycose.

Results

Figure 7.5a shows the preference for the flavor associated with 20% polycose and that associated with 2% polycose as a function of training and test deprivation. As can be seen, all rats preferred the flavor associated with 20% polycose over the flavor associated with 2% polycose and this effect was slightly larger the higher the hunger in training and in test. Figure 7.5B shows the effects of adding quinine to the 20% polycose and Nutrasweet to the 2% polycose. This treatment reduced the preference for the flavor associated with 20% polycose for the rats trained ad lib, but actually *reversed* the preference for rats trained deprived. When trained deprived, rats preferred a flavor associated with a sweet tasting low calorie substance over a flavor associated with a bitter tasting high calorie substance. They track sweetness, even when it is experienced with fewer calories than an alternative.

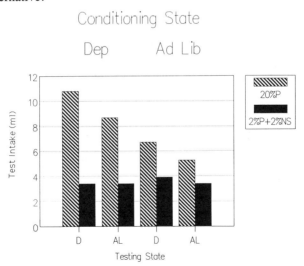

FIG. 7.5a. Mean ml consumed in test of the flavors associated with 20% polycose or 2% polycose as a function of hunger in training and in test in Experiments 4.

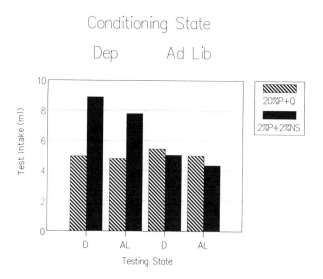

FIG. 7.5b. Mean ml consumed in test of the flavors associated with 20% polycose plus .2% quinine or 2% polycose plus 2% nutrasweet as a function of hunger in training and test in Experiment 4.

Analyses of variance showed that the preference for a flavor associated with 20% polycose over one associated with 2% polycose was larger when they did not contain quinine and Nutrasweet $F(1,36) = 15.28$ $p <. 001$. Also, the reduction in preference for the flavor associated with 20% polycose produced by adding quinine to it and Nutrasweet to the 2% polycose was significantly larger for rats trained deprived than for rats trained ad lib $F(1,36) = 7.28$ $p < .01$.

Because we added quinine to the 20% polycose as well as adding Nutrasweet to the 2% polycose, it is of course possible that the hungry rats were avoiding quinine more than the nonhungry rats, rather than approaching Nutrasweet more. To determine if this was so, in Experiment 5 we did not use quinine. We paired flavors with 20% polycose and 2% polycose for half the rats and with 20% polycose and 2% polycose plus 4% Nutrasweet for the other half of the rats.

EXPERIMENT 5

The procedures of the preceding experiment were followed precisely.

Results

Figures 7.6a and 7.6b show the results of this experiment. As can be seen in Fig. 7.6a, rats preferred a flavor associated with 20% polycose over a flavor associ-

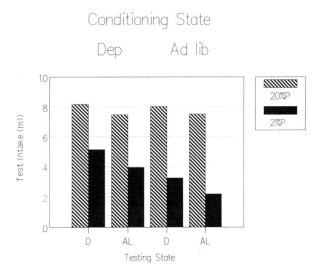

FIG. 7.6a.   Mean ml consumed in test of the flavors associated with 20% polycose or 2% polycose as a function of hunger in training and test in Experiment 5.

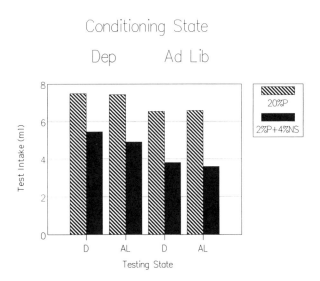

FIG. 7.6b.   Mean ml consumed in test of flavors associated with 20% polycose or 2% polycose plus 4% nutrasweet as a function of hunger in training and test in Experiment 5.

ated with 2% polycose, as we found in Experiment 4. Figure 7.6b shows that adding 4% Nutrasweet to the 2% polycose reduced this preference, but not significantly so. The only significant effect was a greater preference for the flavor associated with 20% polycose over the flavor associated with 2% polycose $F(1,36) = 27.69 \ p < .001$. This preference did not vary with deprivation or with whether or not Nutrasweet was in the 2% polycose.

Discussion

It is interesting that the preference for a flavor associated with more calories (20% vs 2% polycose) did not vary significantly with deprivation in either Experiment 4 or 5. This is consistent with the idea that hunger increases the role of rules of thumb, such as tracking sweet, and does not necessarily increase successful tracking of calories per se. Yet in Experiment 5 adding 4% Nutrasweet to the 2% polycose did not significantly reduce the preference for 20% polycose for any group. We expected increasing hunger would lead to increased tracking of sweet and accordingly a reduced preference for 20% polycose over 2% polycose when Nutrasweet was added to the polycose. Perhaps, however, Experiment 5 did not use a high enough concentration of Nutrasweet to affect preference, or perhaps not enough training was given for the rats to learn the relationships between flavors and consequences. In Experiment 6 we increased the amount of training to see if we could recruit greater tracking of sweet in hungry animals if they had more experience with the flavor solution combinations.

EXPERIMENT 6

In Experiment 6 all rats had one flavor associated with 20% polycose and the other flavor associated with 2% polycose + 4% Nutrasweet. Either 8 days of training or 32 days of training were given. Procedures were the same as Experiments 4 and 5 with the short training groups being run simultaneously with the last days of the training of the extended training group. Deprivation started at the same time for all deprived rats.

Results

Figures 7.7a and 7.7b show the results of this experiment. Examining first Fig. 7.7a which shows the short training groups we can see that all groups showed a small preference for the flavor associated with 20% polycose except for the group trained and tested deprived which showed a small preference for the flavor associated with 2% polycose plus Nutrasweet. For the extended training groups (Fig. 7.7b) those groups trained ad lib continued to show a preference for the

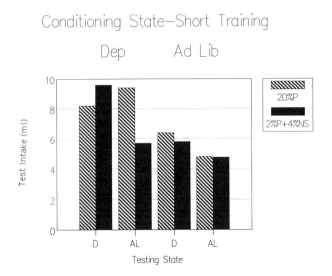

FIG. 7.7a. Mean ml consumed in test of the flavors associated with 20% polycose or 2% polycose plus 4% nutrasweet for the short training groups in Experiment 6.

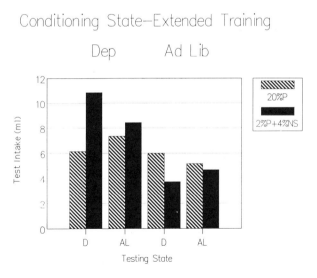

FIG. 7.7b. Mean ml consumed in test of the flavors associated with 20% polycose or 2% polycose plus 4% nutrasweet for the extended training groups in Experiment 6.

flavor associated with 20% polycose, while those trained deprived showed a preference for the flavor associated with 2% polycose plus Nutrasweet, and this was a particularly large effect when they were tested deprived. Analysis of variance including all groups produced a marginally significant interaction of training deprivation, test deprivation and preference for the flavor associated with 20% polycose, $F(1,35) = 3.42$ $p < .07$.

GENERAL DISCUSSION

We showed here that hunger affects learning of conditioned flavor preferences. In our experiments a stronger conditioned flavor preference was produced under hunger than under ad lib conditions using sucrose or saccharin as the US. This appears to be a result of hunger increasing the positive affective reaction to a sweet taste, because hunger did not affect conditioned flavor preferences produced by polycose, which is believed to be reinforcing primarily on the basis of calories (Elizalde & Sclafani, 1989). Also, there was an effect of hunger on the strength of the conditioned flavor preference for a flavor associated with sucrose over a flavor associated with polycose. These two substances differ in taste, not in calories.

When we pitted taste against calories, hunger accentuated the preference for sweet taste even if the sweet taste was not correlated with calories. We suggest that rats may be built to track sweet when hungry as a rule of thumb that will normally produce ingestion of calories.

One would think that with experience rats could learn that a particular sweet substance or taste was not correlated with calories. We speculated that was the case in Experiments 1A and 1B, where only the group trained hungry and tested ad lib preferred a flavor associated with saccharin. We suggested that the rats had learned saccharin had no calories by the time of the test, and thus did not prefer a flavor associated with saccharin when they were tested hungry. Le Magnen (1957) found, measuring single bottle consumption of saccharin or sucrose over a 5-day period without food, that sucrose consumption increased over days, while after day 3, consumption of saccharin decreased.

The greater preference under high hunger for a flavor associated with a sweet taste is maintained only if calories accompany the sweet taste. However, it is not clear that the number of calories matter. In Experiments 4 and 6, hungry rats preferred a flavor associated with 2% polycose plus nutrasweet over one paired with 20% polycose. They tracked sweetness not calories, and this preference for the sweeter substance was maintained as long as calories accompanied the sweetness. It is interesting to speculate whether rats could ultimately learn to prefer a flavor associated with more calories and less sweetness. In Experiment 6, increasing training increased the preference rats had for the flavor associated with a sweeter taste but fewer calories than an alternative. The effects of hunger in tracking sweet are clearly very powerful, more powerful than 32 days of training where higher calories were correlated with the nonsweet substance. We plan on increasing training even more dramatically to see if ultimately rats can overcome their tendency to track sweet when hungry.

There has been previous discussion of how hunger may affect the animal's reaction to sensory and metabolic effects of food. Jacobs and Sharma (1969) suggested that hunger enhances the effects of sensory signals on intake—pleasant foods increase in pleasantness and unpleasant foods increase in unpleasantness. Nisbett (1968) likewise suggested that hunger directly increased sensitivity to taste factors. These theorists suggest that sensitivity to palatability factors in general increases with increased hunger. Our research shows a more specific increased reaction to sweet with increased hunger. We have shown here that hungry rats learn to prefer flavors associated with sweet tastes and that this preference is very persistent when calories accompany the sweet taste. And when sweetness is pitted against calories, they track sweetness. This is not just a general increase in conditioned preferences for all palatable substances because hunger did not affect the strength of conditioned flavor preferences based on polycose, a palatable but nonsweet substance (Sclafani & Clyne, 1987).

Why should conditioned flavor preferences based on sweet substances be enhanced by hunger in training, while those based in starch are not? One hypothesis suggested by Lucas and Sclafani (1989) is that hungry animals prefer sweet foods because sugars are typically more rapidly digested than starches. These investigators failed to find a greater preference for sucrose over polycose with increased hunger, but they used single bottle tests in most of their experiments, a relatively insensitive measure of preference. Here we showed that hungry rats form a stronger conditioned flavor preference for a flavor associated with sweetness than do nonhungry rats, that there must be calories in the sweet substance for this preference to be maintained, and that rats track sweetness, not calories, when the two are pitted against each other.

ACKNOWLEDGMENT

I want to thank Rebecca J. Pulley and Jean D. Sheffer who collected data and contributed a lot to these studies. The research was supported in part by grant MH39453 from the National Institute of Mental Health.

REFERENCES

Adolph, E. F. (1947). Urges to eat and drink in rats. *American Journal of Physiology, 151,* 110–125.

Bolles, R. C. (1983). A "mixed" model of taste preference. In R. L. Mellgren (Ed.) *Animal cognition and behavior.* North-Holland Publishing Co. pp. 65–83.

Collier, G., & Bolles, R. (1968). Hunger, thirst, and their interaction as determinants of sucrose consumption. *Journal of Comparative and Physiological Psychology, 66,* 633–641.

Davis, J. D. (1973). The effectiveness of some sugars in stimulating licking behavior in the rat. *Physiology and Behavior, 11,* 39–45.

Davis, J. D., & Levine, M. W. (1977). A model for the control of ingestion. *Psychological Review, 84,* 379–412.

Elizalde, G., & Sclafani, A. (1989). Starch-based conditioned flavor preferences in rats: Influence of taste, calories, and CS-US delay. *Appetite, 11,* 179–200.

Epstein, A. N., & Teitelbaum, P. (1962). Regulation of food intake in the absence of taste, smell and other oropharyngeal sensations. *Journal of Comparative and Physiological Psychology, 55,* 753–759.

Fanselow, M. S., & Birk, J. (1982). Flavor-flavor associations induce hedonic shifts in taste preference. *Animal Learning and Behavior, 10*(2), 223–228.

Fedorchak, P. M., & Bolles, R. C. (1987). Hunger enhances the expression of calorie, but not taste mediated conditioned flavor preferences. *Journal of Experimental Psychology: Animal Behavior Processes, 13,* 73–79.

Holman, E. W. (1975). Immediate and delayed reinforcers for flavor preferences in rats. *Learning and Motivation, 6,* 91–100.

Jacobs, H. L., & Sharma, K. N. (1969). Taste versus calories: Sensory and metabolic signals in the control of food intake. *Annals of the New York Academy of Science, 157,* 1084–1125.

Joyner, K., Smith, G. P., Shindledecker, R., & Pfaffman, C. (1985). Stimulation of sham feeding in rat by sucrose, maltose, glucose and fructose. *Society of Neuroscience Abstracts, 11,* 1223.

LeMagnen, J. (1954). Le processus de discrimination par le Rat blanc des stimuli sucres alimentaires et non alimentaires. *Journal Physiologie, 46,* 414–418.

Lucas, F., & Sclafani, A. (1989). Polycose and sucrose appetite in rats: Influence of food deprivation and insulin treatment. *Appetite.*

Nisbett, R. E. (1968). Taste, deprivation and weight as determinants of eating behavior. *Journal of Personality and Social Psychology, 10,* 107–116.

Sclafani, A., & Clyne, A. E. (1987). Hedonic response of rats to polysaccharide and sugar solutions. *Neuroscience and Biobehavioral Reviews, 11,* 173–180.

Sclafani, A., & Mann, S. (1987). Carbohydrate taste preferences in rats: Glucose, sucrose, maltose, fructose and polycose compared. *Physiology & Behavior, 40,* 563–568.

Sclafani, A., & Nissenbaum, J. W. (1988). Robust conditioned flavor preference produced by intragastric starch infusions in rats. *American Journal of Physiology, 255,* R672–R675.

Sherman, J. E., Hickis, C. F., Rice, A. G., Rusiniak, K. W., & Garcia, J. (1983). Preferences and aversions for stimuli paired with ethanol. *Animal Learning and Behavior, 11,* 101–106.

Smith, M., & Duffy, M. (1957). Consumption of sucrose and saccharin by hungry and satiated rats. *Journal of comparative and Physiological Psychology, 50,* 65–69.

Soulairac, A. (1944). Action de L'insuline sur la consummation de differents glucides chez la souris. *Comptes Rendus de la Societé de Biologie, 138,* 119–120.

8 Development of Taste Preferences

Ilene L. Bernstein
University of Washington

Developmental studies of taste preference have proven an irresistible approach for addressing some of the most basic issues in the area of taste hedonics. To many, the developmental approach is viewed as the best available for examining nature/nurture questions and demonstrating, unequivocally, that certain preferences, such as the preference for sweet tastes, are innate. There is a very large literature examining taste preferences of human neonates, and neonates of other mammalian species. Some date back to the turn of the century, while many are quite recent. In this chapter I plan a highly selective overview of this work. In particular, the questions I focus on are the following: Does taste preference change through development and can such changes be attributed largely to maturation? Do early taste experiences have particular impact on adult taste preference? If so, what accounts for the importance of early experiences and what types of experiences are important? In the course of examining these questions, I also consider those studies that have exploited the ''taste naive'' neonate to study the innateness of certain taste preferences and aversions.

Development of Gustatory Function

An insightful evaluation and interpretation of the data on taste preferences of mammalian neonates would be aided by a brief examination of what is known about the development of the gustatory system itself. A considerable literature is accumulating which considers changes in gustatory structure and function with age in a number of mammalian species, particularly rat and sheep. Mistretta and Bradley and their colleagues have made major contributions in this research area studying fetal and neonatal lambs, which have a time course of maturation of taste buds that is comparable to that of humans. Detailed coverage of these findings is beyond the scope of this chapter and the interested reader is referred to Mistretta (1981) for a thorough review. Taste buds first appear in human and lamb fetuses during the second to third month of gestation and acquire adult morphology in utero (Bradley, 1972; Bradley & Mistretta, 1975). Functional and anatomical maturation proceeds postnatally and, in lambs, electrophysiological responding to tastants increases with age.

Available anatomical and electrophysiological evidence point to a later time course of taste development in the rat. Taste buds of rats are absent or immature at birth, and considerable maturation occurs during the suckling period (Farbman, 1965; Mistretta, 1972). Electrophysiological assessments of taste function (Hill, Mistretta, & Bradley, 1982) provide evidence of immaturity in response to salty (NaCl) and sweet (sucrose) solutions in neonatal rats, with maturational changes proceeding through the suckling period and on into the postweaning period (to 35–40 days-of-age). Even after the age of weaning, young rats are less responsive than adults to sweet and salty tastes as judged by neural activity in the chorda tympani and nucleus of the solitary tract. On the other hand, electrophysiological responses to sour stimuli such as citric acid and to ammonium chloride do not increase with age (Hill, Mistretta, & Bradley, 1982).

One implication of these findings is that generalization across species with regard to taste development requires consideration of species differences in maturity of the system at the time of birth. Another implication is that the dramatic differences in functional maturity of the gustatory system evident in immature animals relative to adults are likely to be expressed behaviorally in their taste preferences. However, although sensory maturation may account for some change in taste preference with age, there are other potential causes and one task in this area is to distinguish between the various factors that may be involved in developmental changes in taste preference.

NORMATIVE DEVELOPMENT OF TASTE PREFERENCE

Human Fetus and Neonate

Human fetal taste buds have an adult morphology and the amniotic fluid undergoes frequent changes in chemical composition during gestation. Also, the human fetus apparently engages in periodic swallowing of amniotic fluid beginning around the 12th week of gestation (Davis & Potter, 1946; as reviewed by Cowart, 1981). It would, therefore, appear that human neonates have an opportunity for prenatal taste experience. In an often cited early study, DeSnoo (1937) obtained evidence suggesting that fetal swallowing could be influenced by the composition of the amniotic fluid. He treated a number of pregnant women suffering from an excess of amniotic fluid by injecting saccharin into the amniotic cavity and reported that this treatment improved their condition, presumably by increasing fetal swallowing of the sweetened amniotic fluid. Despite the unorthodox nature of these findings, we might tentatively conclude that humans display a sweetness preference prenatally.

Human newborns have long been considered ideal subjects for studies of innate responses to taste stimuli because their responses were viewed as being relatively uncontaminated by learning experiences and social influences. A number of dependent measures of taste responsiveness have been used with infants. For example, consumption measures, sucking patterns, facial expressions, as well as cardiovascular and respiratory responses have been used with infants and differential responding to different tastants provides clear indication that the infant can discriminate between them. For many of these measures, however, the hedonic or affective meaning of the response remains open to question.

Facial Expressions. Studies of infant facial reactions to taste stimuli have a long history. An early study by Peterson and Rainey (1910) observed infants' facial responses to prototypes of the four basic tastants. They reported that full term and premature infants responded to these tastants with expressions similar to those of adults. More recently, Steiner (1977) has characterized the gustofacial responses of human neonates within the first hours of extrauterine life. Three distinct gustofacial patterns have been characterized which are elicited by small amounts of sweet (25% sucrose), sour (2.5% citric acid) and bitter (.25% quinine sulphate) solutions placed on the tongue. The sweet stimulus elicits an expression of satisfaction, accompanied by licking and sucking movements and often a slight smile. Steiner reports that observers of filmed examples of this expression characterize it as one of appreciation or enjoyment. The sour stimulus produced an expression with pursed lips, wrinkled nose, and blinking of the eyes. The response to a bitter stimulus involved an arching of the mouth with upper lip elevated and was generally viewed as expressive of distaste or disgust. There is a general consensus that these gustofacial patterns are quite similar to those of adults presented with similar tastants, which clearly implicates a strong unlearned component to the hedonic responses to these particular tastants. In addition to normal neonates, Steiner tested some infants with severe developmental malformations such as anencephaly. The responses of these infants were similar to those of normal infants indicating that the neural circuitry underlying these gustofacial patterns or reflexes does not require cortical structures. This conclusion is consistent with studies by Grill and Norgren (1978) who found that gustofacial responses to tastants like sucrose and quinine were similar in decerebrate and intact rats. It is somewhat paradoxical that facial expressions which appear to convey the very essence of hedonic responses to pleasure and disgust can be evoked in a reflexive way in organisms without higher brain structures. It is challenging to examine the implication of these findings as we consider potential dependent measures for assessing taste preferences in nonverbal infants and animals.

Ingestion and Sucking Patterns.   Measuring solution intake of human neo-nates provides data clearly analogous to preference studies at later ages. Where sweet solutions are concerned, measures of ingestion seem to agree with those of facial expression in suggesting a sweetness preference in human neonates at the earliest ages tested. For example, Desor, Maller, and Turner (1973) found that newborns consumed significantly more sweetened water than plain water during a 3-minute presentation. When sour, salty, and bitter taste stimuli were examined the newborns' hedonic responses were more ambiguous. Amounts ingested were not significantly different from plain water and it remains unclear whether such findings should be interpreted as indicating that newborns find such tastes hedonically neutral or whether the solution concentrations offered were simply too low to be aversive. To further complicate matters, very young infants may be limited in their ability to inhibit sucking even when they dislike a taste since their sucking for sour, salty, and bitter stimuli was reported to be accompanied by frequent grimaces (Peterson & Rainey, 1910). An accidental poisoning of infants in a neonatal nursery when salt was added to formula in place of sugar, indicates that high levels of salt may not completely inhibit ingestion (Finberg, Kiley, & Luttrell, 1963). Using a somewhat different approach, Crook (1978) examined effects of discrete, intraoral fluid presentations on sucking bursts and pauses in neonates. When .04 ml of sucrose solution was presented during a pause, the length of the subsequent sucking burst was lengthened, relative to bursts which followed water. In contrast, NaCl presentation shortened sucking bursts, a find-ing that indicates that salt is hedonically negative to newborns. In attempting to reconcile the 3-minute intake data indicating indifference with data from indi-vidual sucking bursts, it is unclear why shortened bursts, as detected in discrete trials, would not lead to a cumulatively lower intake in a 3-minute ingestion test.

Autonomic Changes.   Finally, changes in heart rate and respiration have been reported in response to gustatory stimulation in newborns (Cowart, 1981; Lipsitt, 1977), but the meaning of such changes in hedonic terms is still subject to dispute.

Viewed as a whole, the study of human newborns has provided an opportunity which has been exploited by a large number of investigators. Interpretation of these studies is challenging, not only because differences in procedure have led to conflicting findings but also because standard measures of hedonics and pref-erence which have been developed for adults, often cannot be used in infants or may be subject to different interpretations in infants. When a variety of depen-dent measures are in general agreement, it is easier to draw conclusions about taste hedonics. For example, where sweet tastes are concerned, there is virtual unanimity regarding a clear preference for these tastes no matter how early in development testing is done. Questions remain regarding bitter, sour, and salty tastes. Although it is generally agreed that bitter and sour tastes are aversive, the time of appearance of these aversions is uncertain. In the case of salty stimuli, it is not known whether the hedonic response to such stimuli in infants is positive, negative, or neutral.

Human Infancy and Childhood

The basic observation of a preference for sweet and a distaste for bitter and sour persists when taste preferences are studied during later infancy and into childhood. A more interesting issue in studying children concerns whether the general impression of striking differences in food preference between children and adults can be attributed to maturational changes in sensation or in preference for basic tastes. Relatively little is known regarding this question although there is some evidence from developmental studies which supports the idea that, where children are concerned, nothing is "too sweet." Desor, Greene, and Maller (1975) had children (aged 9 and 15 years) rank sucrose solutions (.075 to .6M) from least to most preferred. The majority of the children chose the most concentrated solution as the one they preferred, whereas adults given the same task preferred the lower concentrations. In agreement with this observation, other studies have reported a negative correlation between age and preferred concentration of sucrose (Cowart, 1981).

Beauchamp and Cowart (1985; Beauchamp, Cowart, & Moran, 1986) have studied infants and young children, focusing on the question of whether preference for salty tastes is largely innate or acquired. They note that the indifference often displayed by young infants toward salt stimuli could indicate that they find these stimuli hedonically neutral or that they cannot taste them. Although the latter suggestion is not consistent with the occasional reports of aversive responses to salty tastes in newborns, it is consistent with evidence of relative insensitivity of the gustatory system to NaCl stimulation around the time of birth in sheep and rats (Hill & Almli, 1980; Hill, Mistretta, & Bradley, 1982; Mistretta & Bradley, 1983). Because sensitivity to NaCl increases with age, Beauchamp, Cowart, and Moran (1986) assessed the responses to salt solutions of infants and children of various ages through the use of ingestion measures. They found that infants 2½- to 4-months-of-age were similar to newborns in displaying indifference to NaCl solutions; that is, they ingested these solutions in amounts comparable to water. In contrast, older infants (4- to 24-months-of-age) displayed a preference for salt solutions, ingesting significantly more saline than water. An interesting parallel can be seen between these findings and the evidence for salt preference in neonatal rats discussed in the next sections. As children get older (3–6 years-of-age) they begin to reject saline solutions but not necessarily salty tastes. Like adults they will prefer salted to unsalted versions of soup, indicating that, with age (or perhaps with experience), the context in which a taste is experienced becomes important in determining preference (Cowart & Beauchamp, 1986).

Neonatal Rats

In view of the evidence presented earlier that the gustatory development of the rat at birth is considerably retarded relative to that of the human, differences might be expected in the relative maturity of behavioral responses to gustatory stimuli in neonatal rats. Indeed, an initial report by Jacobs and colleagues (Jacobs, Smutz, & DuBose, 1977) suggested that rat pups' ability to discriminate gustatory stimuli did not appear until the second postnatal week. However, subsequent work has provided evidence of gustatory discrimination as early as the first 1 to 4 days postnatal (e.g., Ganchrow, Steiner, & Canetto, 1986; Hall & Bryan, 1981). Differences between quality and concentration of tastants, mode of stimulus delivery, as well as the nature of the dependent measure in these studies have yielded a range of impressions about the functional maturity of the neonatal rat's gustatory system and the hedonic valence of various tastants. A brief review of these approaches and an analysis of critical differences in procedure and interpretation follow.

Ganchrow et al (1986) examined behavioral responses to gustatory stimuli in infant rats during the first 4 days postnatal in a study analogous to that of Steiner (1977) in human newborns. Solutions of sucrose, sodium saccharin, citric acid, and quinine hydrochloride were inserted into the mouth as single droplets. Facial and head movements were scored by observers blind to the experimental condition. Licking and rhythmic mouth movements (ingestive responses) were consistently associated with sweet solutions while sustained mouth openings and head movements (aversive responses) were associated with quinine stimulation. These patterns are similar to the behaviors seen to such tastes in adult rats (Grill & Norgren, 1978). Neonatal responses to citric acid were less clear cut, with elements of both ingestive and aversive responding. Thus, orofacial reactions indicate that rat pups can discriminate between certain tastants in the first days of life and that their hedonic responses to sweet and bitter stimuli are similar to those of adults. The authors conclude that evidence of function in the form of gustatory discrimination appears early in the course of taste bud development, well before actual maturation of the gustatory system.

Studying rats 3- to 15-days-of-age, Hall and Bryan (1981) delivered taste solutions through an implanted intraoral cannula. Dependent measures included solution intake (as determined by body weight gain) and behavioral responses such as mouthing and general activity. Discrimination between water and sucrose appeared at 3-days-of-age in terms of behavioral measures, but not until 6 days of age in terms of differential intake. Discrimination between water and quinine was not evident by either type of measure until 9-days-of-age, clearly a later appearance than was reported by Ganchrow et al. (1986). Responses to concentrated NaCl solutions were only examined at 3-days-of-age and pups ingested significantly less saline than water at that age. The early appearance of NaCl avoidance is an interesting and somewhat paradoxical observation which we return to later in this section.

Intraoral solution delivery was also employed by Kehoe and Blass (1985) in rat pups 5- to 20-days-of-age. However, in this study pups were tested while suckling an anesthetized dam and fluid delivery was contingent upon sucking or nipple attachment. Ingestion (as measured by body weight gain), time spent "attached," and aversive behavioral responses were measured. Quinine, NaCl, and ammonium chloride were the taste solutions delivered and comparisons were made relative to rats receiving water. Because rats receiving water spent some 80–90% of their time attached and showed no aversive reactions at all, this procedure was clearly designed to detect aversions but not preferences. At 5-days-of-age, pups were relatively unresponsive to quinine but were highly disrupted in their sucking responses by NaCl and ammonium chloride delivery. Together with the aversive reactions triggered by these salts, these findings suggest that rat pups are capable of responding to aversive tastes received during suckling by discontinued sucking. Aversive responses to quinine emerged at later ages and the general impression that NaCl and ammonium chloride are aversive to rat pups and inhibit their ingestion persisted in pups 10-days-of-age and older.

Salt Preference.   There appears to be little controversy regarding the nature of the young or adult rat's hedonic responses to sucrose and quinine. On the other hand, the response to salts, particularly NaCl, seems quite a bit more interesting. This is partly due to the display of both preference and aversion to NaCl solutions in adult rats, with the direction and intensity of the response dependent on solution concentration. Furthermore, the hedonic response of young rats (and humans) to NaCl solutions is not at all clear. The following studies specifically focus on the development of salt preference in young rats.

Two methods have been developed by Hall and his colleagues (Hall, 1979; Hall & Bryan, 1980) to study the ingestive capabilities of neonatal rats independent of suckling. One of them is the technique used in the studies discussed previously, involving the surgical implantation of an intraoral cannula through which solutions are slowly infused into the mouth. Rat pups are weighed before and after infusion to determine the amount of infused solution ingested. This method allows rat pups to eject rather than swallow infused solutions and differential ingestion as a function of quality and concentration of infusate has been demonstrated (Hall & Bryan, 1981). However, ingestion via this method appears to be quite dissimilar in form from the ingestive behavior usually measured in weanling and adult rats. Another method, referred to here as "towel testing," has been used less frequently (Hall & Bryan, 1980). It entails testing rat pups in a warm, humid incubator on a piece of toweling or gauze that has been saturated with water, milk, or some taste solution. Active mouthing is seen when solutions are palatable; ingestion can be quantified by weighing the pups before and after the "towel test." This method appears similar to later forms of ingestion in that it requires active responding to accomplish ingestion rather than rejection (as is the case with intraoral cannulas). Both methods have been used to examine NaCl preference of neonatal rat pups and they have yielded similar results.

In my own laboratory, salt (NaCl) preference of 5–20 day old rats was examined using the "towel testing" method (Bernstein & Courtney, 1987). At most ages pups ingested significantly more hypertonic saline than water and at 10 days of age rat pups appeared particularly insensitive to the usual aversiveness of concentrated (4–8%) NaCl solutions. In view of the evidence presented earlier, the demonstration of a strong salt preference in neonatal rats is rather surprising and might suggest that characteristics peculiar to the "towel testing" method were responsible for these findings. However, these findings are quite similar to those of Moe (1986) who used intraoral cannulas to infuse NaCl solution into neonatal rats. She found that neonatal rats 6- to 18-days-of-age showed prefer-ence–aversion functions for NaCl which were shifted to the right along the concentration axis with the 6 day old animals peaking at the highest concentra-tion. Thus, Bernstein and Courtney (1987) and Moe (1986) both found that young rats appear to be insensitive to the aversiveness of hypertonic NaCl solu-tions. It is interesting to consider whether this unusual response is a reflection of the immaturity of the neonatal gustatory system. As previously discussed, dra-matic changes in function occur during the suckling period which are particularly evident when responses to NaCl solutions are examined (Hill, Mistretta, & Bradley, 1982). The gustatory system of the immature rat has been found to be relatively insensitive to NaCl stimulation when assessed electrophysiologically. This insensitivity has been proposed as an explanation of the failure of young rats to avoid hypertonic NaCl solutions as well as their preference. In the case of preference, it has been suggested that reduced sensitivity to hypertonic NaCl would cause these solutions to be perceived as more dilute. As dilute NaCl is generally preferred to water by rats, with a peak preference at isotonic concentra-tions or below, a shift in perceived concentration in young rats could explain their preference for concentrations of NaCl that adult rats shun (Beauchamp et al., 1986; Midkiff & Bernstein, 1983).

Unfortunately, there are several experimental findings that are inconsistent with this straightforward explanation of NaCl preference in neonatal rats. For example, both Moe (1986) and Bernstein and Courtney (1987) found that the youngest animals they tested (3-days-of-age and 5-days-of-age, respectively) contrasted with the others in that they never preferred NaCl solutions to water and avoided them at concentrations that older sucklings preferred. Recall that Hall and Bryan (1981) also found that 3-day-old pups rejected NaCl but they did not report testing older pups to determine whether rejection of NaCl persisted. The appearance at 3–5 days and subsequent disappearance (by 6–10 days) of sensitivity to the aversiveness of concentrated NaCl solutions suggest that studies that look only in the first few days of life may overestimate the maturity of the taste system. In the case of early NaCl rejection, Moe (1986) has speculated that trigeminal mediation might be involved. In any case, it seems likely that different mechanisms may be responsible for NaCl rejection at different ages.

Another problem with the "NaCl insensitivity" hypothesis was encountered when ingestion of ammonium chloride solutions by 10-day-old rats was examined (Bernstein & Courtney, 1987). Significant preference for concentrated ammonium chloride solutions was evident, which contrasts markedly with the adult rats' dislike of ammonium chloride solutions (Smith, 1974). Interestingly, Moe (1986) also found a preference for ammonium chloride (at 12-days-of-age). Ammonium chloride intake is relevant here because of electrophysiological evidence that development of responsiveness to ammonium chloride shows a very different time course from that of NaCl. For example, there are several reports of dramatic age-related increases in sensitivity to NaCl but not ammonium chloride in chorda tympani (Ferrell, Mistretta, & Bradley, 1981; Hill & Almli, 1980; Hill et al., 1982). It was expected that prior to weaning, behavioral responsiveness to ammonium chloride would mirror the relative maturity and sensitivity of the taste system to this salt and that ammonium chloride avoidance would contrast sharply with lack of avoidance of NaCl. Avid ingestion of concentrated ammonium chloride as well as NaCl solutions by 10-day-old rats clearly did not confirm this prediction. Preferential ingestion of concentrated salt solutions at this age was very similar for NaCl and ammonium chloride in spite of the striking differences in the effects of these two salts on the chorda response. Marked preference for ammonium chloride solutions in neonatal rats is particularly surprising since adult rats fail to prefer ammonium chloride solutions to water at any concentration (Smith, 1974). Thus, an insensitive gustatory system which causes concentrated ammonium chloride to be perceived as dilute would clearly be an inadequate explanation for these results since, unlike NaCl, the adult rat does not appear to find even dilute ammonium chloride appealing. These findings challenge the notion that age-related differences in sensitivity alone can account for the young rat's avid ingestion of hypertonic NaCl.

Significant preference for 2% and 4% solutions of NaCl and ammonium chloride in 10 day old rats stands in marked contrast to the findings of Kehoe and Blass (1985) that 2.5% ammonium chloride and 2.7% NaCl disrupted suckling at 10-days-of-age and elicited signs of distaste. This difference would not appear to be due to the latters' use of intraoral infusions, since Moe also infused her solutions into the oral cavity and found salt preference. Because Kehoe and Blass varied both cannula location and mode of fluid delivery, these parameters do not seem likely to be the basis of the difference between avid ingestion of concentrated NaCl and ammonium chloride and avoidance. A critical difference which may account for this striking discrepency is the use of the suckling context and attachment as a dependent measure in assessing taste preference. At this point it remains unclear why this difference should so dramatically reverse the apparent hedonic value of taste solutions.

EARLY EXPERIENCE AND TASTE PREFERENCE

Rats

I begin my discussion of the effects of early experience on taste preference with rat studies simply because it is so much easier to experimentally alter taste exposure in animal studies than it is in humans. Judging from the number of studies that have been done, it would appear that there is wide interest in the subject of "taste imprinting," that is, the question of whether animals develop a lifelong preference for foods they are exposed to as infants. Investigators have approached this question in different ways, using both palatable and unpalatable taste stimuli and different exposure procedures. Rozin, Gruss, and Berk (1979) attempted to induce a preference for an innately unpalatable taste, chili-flavored foods, through exposure during maturation and through gradual introduction of chili powder into the diet. Avoidance of chili-flavored chow persisted essentially unaltered by their various efforts. Wurtman and Wurtman (1979) examined the influence of extensive exposure to an intrinsically palatable taste, sucrose in food, on adult sweetness preference. They found that sweetness preference (as determined by consumption of diets containing different concentrations of sucrose) was similar in adult animals that had received very high concentrations of sucrose in their diet when they were 16–30 days-of-age and in those whose diet had contained no sucrose. Similarly, in my laboratory, we found that early exposure to salt solutions or high salt diets failed to produce lasting changes in adult salt preference (Midkiff & Bernstein, 1983). Thus, extended exposure around the time of weaning to aversive (chili), preferred (sucrose), and neutral (NaCl) taste stimuli failed to significantly alter adult preference for those tastes.

In contrast to these negative findings, some investigators have found that early taste experiences can alter food choice and taste preference. For example, Galef and Henderson (1972) found that rat pups tend to choose the diet that their mothers had been eating during lactation. This pattern was seen even when the mother's diet was less palatable than the alternative. It should be noted, however, that offspring did not continue to choose the less palatable diet throughout life. Rather, their response could be characterized as one that directed the young rat's food choices during the transition from suckling to solid food. Galef and his colleagues (Galef, 1985) have continued to examine the importance of social cues in influencing food selection and avoidance in adult rats as well. Another developmental study that yielded a positive result of early experience was by Capretta and Rawls (1974). They were able to significantly increase the preference for garlic-flavored water in pups whose mothers drank garlic-flavored water (and presumably transferred the garlic taste through their milk to the pups). The latter two studies have been widely cited as evidence that adult flavor preferences can be influenced by experiences during some "critical period" early in life. It should be noted, however, that the changes observed were either short-lived or not very large. Thus, results of animal studies imply that extensive exposure to particular tastes around the time of weaning does not necessarily lead to "imprinting" for those tastes or persistent alterations in food choices. Those studies that found a positive influence of experience involved exposures that occurred prior to the time of weaning and could be characterized as naturalistic, in the sense that taste exposure occurred in a social or nursing context.

Humans

Animal studies, which are able to maintain extensive control over lifelong food exposure and institute random assignment to groups, indicate that lengthy, early exposure to particular tastes does not necessarily alter adult taste preferences. Somehow, these conclusions do not conform to the strong, intuitive notion that, at least in humans, children's early experiences with foods can have dramatic and lasting effects on their food preferences. The popular press frequently admonishes parents against allowing their young children to become overexposed to high levels of sugar and/or salt in their diet lest they be doomed to a lifetime preference for those harmful tastes. Have our intuitive notions about early experience and taste preference simply not kept pace with the empirical evidence or, are there features of childhood taste experiences that have not been adequately modeled in the animal work? A sampling of recent studies with humans provides an interesting perspective on this question.

Beauchamp and Moran (1982) examined sweet preference longitudinally in children who they tested at birth, 6-months-of-age, and 2-years-of-age. At 6 months children were divided into two groups, using diet histories. One group had been regularly fed sweetened water by their parents, while the other group had not. They found that preference for sweetened water at 6-months-of-age was significantly higher in the group regularly exposed to sweetened water than in the group without that experience. While acknowledging that this study is only correlational, the authors suggest that the most likely explanation for group differences is the effect of experience with sweetened water on sweetness preference. Because it is unclear what factors influenced a parent's decision to feed their infants sweetened water, interpretation of these results is difficult. At 2-years-of-age (Beauchamp & Moran, 1984) the group fed sweetened water still had a higher preference for it. However, when sucrose was added to a different vehicle, Kool-Aid, no differences in sweetness preference were noted based on experience with sweetened water. These results suggest that any effects of experience on sweetness preference were narrowly confined to sweetened water and did not represent a generalized preference for sweeter tastes.

In a very different approach to this question, Birch and her colleagues have systematically examined the social context in which foods are eaten and their effects on taste preferences of preschool children. Two studies are particularly instructive, because they are based on feeding practices that are prevalent in our culture (Birch, Birch, Marlin, & Kramer, 1982; Birch, Zimmerman, & Hind, 1980). One study examined the effects on preference of consuming a food instrumentally, that is, in anticipation of a reward. This is analogous to a parent who, out of concern that a child does not eat enough vegetables, rewards the child with ice cream or an opportunity to watch television for eating green beans. In Birch's study (Birch et al., 1982) children drank a fruit juice in order to gain access to a play activity. Subsequent preference testing indicated that the preference for that fruit juice decreased significantly after it had been consumed repeatedly as part of the instrumental contingency. The second study (Birch et al., 1980) examined the effect of repeatedly presenting a particular snack food as a reward for desirable behavior; the analogy to the frequent use of cookies and candy as rewards for good behavior is clear. Twenty presentations of the snack food, contingent on a positive behavior and presented explicitly as a reward, increased preference for that food above its pretraining baseline. No such effects were noted in controls who received comparable snack exposures in a nonsocial context or at snack time. These careful and innovative studies have a number of implications. On the one hand, they indicate that young children's food preferences can be altered by the social context in which these foods are presented. These studies were done in the narrow context of a preschool setting, over a period of weeks. When similar contingencies are instituted by parents over a period of years, it is likely that they exert substantial and durable effects on food preferences. It is also clear that the effect of these contingencies on food selection and consumption is quite different from that which is intended since preference for vegetables is decreased while preference for cookies is enhanced! In contrast to studies where "mere exposure" is manipulated and results are negative or equivocal, social-affective context appears to be an important determinant of food preferences in humans.

Conclusion

The developmental approach has provided fertile ground for examining issues critical to the hedonics of taste. Studies of neonates have indicated fairly clearly that the sweetness preference displayed by most mammalian species does not require experience with the nutritional consequences of ingestion (e.g., Steiner, 1977). Studies examining whether taste preferences change with age, and whether such changes are related to maturational changes in the gustatory system, have yielded more ambiguous results. Some studies point to developmental changes in preference for sweet and salty stimuli, with a preference for higher intensities at younger ages (Beauchamp & Cowart, 1985; Beauchamp, Cowart, & Moran, 1986; Desor, Greene, & Maller, 1975). A direct relationship between such preference changes and maturation of the gustatory system has not been clearly established (Mistretta, 1981). One frustrating feature of the studies on neonatal humans and animals is that significant inconsistencies can emerge when different dependent measures are employed as indicators of taste hedonics (Beauchamp, Cowart, & Moran, 1986; Crook, 1978). When conflicting results are encountered, such as preference *and* aversion for the same tastant at the same age, it is obviously difficult to characterize underlying hedonics (Bernstein & Courtney, 1987; Kehoe & Blass, 1985).

The question of whether early taste experiences play a particularly important role in the determination of adult taste preference has also been considered. Animal studies fail to provide convincing evidence that mere exposure, early in life, leads to lasting alterations in preference for particular tastes. In the case of humans, one encounters the difficulty of experimentally modifying the taste experiences of children in long-term studies. Short-term studies have provided us with some indication of the effects of experience on taste preference. These studies clearly indicate that the social context in which tastes are experienced, particularly in the case of young children, may play a lasting role in molding food preferences (Birch et al., 1980, 1982).

REFERENCES

Beauchamp, G. K., & Cowart, B. J. (1985). Congenital and experiental factors in the development of human flavor preferences. *Appetite, 6,* 357–372.

Beauchamp, G. K., Cowart, B. J., & Moran, M. (1986). Developmental changes in salt acceptability in human infants. *Developmental Psychobiology, 19,* 17–25.

Beauchamp, G. K., & Moran, M. (1982). Dietary experience and sweet taste preferences in human infants. *Appetite, 3,* 139–152.

Beauchamp, G. K., & Moran, M. (1984). Acceptance of sweet and salty tastes in 2-year-old children. *Appetite, 5,* 291–305.

Bernstein, I. L., & Courtney, L. (1987). Salt preference in the preweaning rat. *Developmental Psychobiology, 20,* 443–453.

Birch, L. L., Birch, D., Marlin, D. W., & Kramer, L. (1982). Effects of instrumental consumption on children's food preference. *Appetite, 3,* 125–134.

Birch, L. L., Zimmerman, S. I., & Hind, H. (1980). The influence of social-affective context on the formation of children's food preferences. *Child Development, 51,* 856–861.

Bradley, R. M. (1972). Development of the taste bud and gustatory papillae in human fetuses. In J. F. Bosma (Ed.), *Third Symposium on Oral Sensation and Perception: The Mouth of the Infant* (pp. 137–162). Springfield, IL: Charles C. Thomas.

Bradley, R. M., & Mistretta, C. M. 1975). Fetal sensory receptors. *Physiological Reviews, 55,* 352–382.

Capretta, P. J., & Rawls, L. J. (1974). III. Establishment of a flavor preference in rats: Importance of nursing and weaning experience. *Journal of Comparative and Physiological Psychology, 86,* 670–673.

Cowart, B. (1981). Development of taste perception in humans: sensitivity and preference throughout the life span. *Psychological Bulletin, 90,* 43–73.

Cowart, B. J., & Beauchamp, G. K. (1986). The importance of sensory context in young children's acceptance of salty tastes. *Child Development, 57,* 1034–1039.

Crook, C. K. (1978). Taste perception in the newborn infant. *Infant Behavior and Development, 1,* 52–69.

Davis, M. E., & Potter, E. L. (1946). Intrauterine respiration of the human fetus. *Journal of the American Medical Association, 131*, 1194–1201.

DeSnoo, K. (1937). Das trinkende Kind im Uterus. *Monatasschrift fur Geburtschilfe und Gynaekologie, 105*, 88–97.

Desor, J. A., Greene, L. S., & Maller, O. (1975). Preference for sweet and salty in 9- and 15-year-old and adult humans. *Science, 190*, 686–697.

Desor, J. A., Mallor, O., & Turner, R. (1973). Taste in acceptance of sugars by human infants. *Journal of Comparative and Physiological Psychology, 84*, 496–501.

Farbman, A. I. (1965). Electron microscope study of the developing taste bud in rat fungiform papilla. *Developmental Biology, 11*, 110–135.

Ferrell, M. F., Mistretta, C. M., & Bradley, R. M. (1981). Development of chorda tympani taste responses in rats. *Journal of Comparative Neurology, 198*, 37–44.

Finberg, L., Kiley, J., & Luttrell, C. N. (1963). Mass accidental salt poisoning in infancy. *Journal of the American Medical Association, 184*, 121–124.

Galef, B. G. (1985). Direct and indirect behavioral pathways to the social transmission of food avoidance. In N. S. Braveman & P. Bronstein (Eds.), *Experimental assessments and clinical applications of conditioned food aversions* (pp. 203–215). New York: New York Academy of Sciences.

Galef, B. G., & Henderson, P. W. (1972). Mother's milk: a determinant of the feeding preferences of weanling rat pups. *Journal of Comparative and Physiological Psychology, 78*, 213–219.

Ganchrow, J. R., Steiner, J. E., & Canetto, S. (1986). Behavioral displays to gustatory stimuli in newborn rat pups. *Developmental Psychobiology, 19*, 163–174.

Grill, H. J., & Norgren, R. (1978). The taste reactivity test: II: Mimetic responses to gustatory stimuli in chronic thalamic and chronic decerebrate rats. *Brain Research, 143*, 281–297.

Hall, W. G. (1979). The ontogeny of feeding in rats: I. Ingestive and behavioral responses to oral infusion. *Journal of Comparative and Physiological Psychology, 93*, 977–1000.

Hall, W. G., & Bryan, T. E. (1980). The ontogeny of feeding in rats: II. Independent ingestive behavior. *Journal of Comparative and Physiological Psychology, 94*, 746–756.

Hall, W. G., & Bryan, T. E. (1981). The ontogeny of feeding in rats: IV. Taste development as measured by intake and behavioral responses to oral infusions of sucrose and quinine. *Journal of Comparative and Physiological Psychology, 95*, 240–251.

Hill, D. L., & Almli, C. R. (1980). Ontogeny of chorda tympani nerve responses to gustatory stimuli in the rat. *Brain Research, 197*, 27–38.

Hill, D. L., Mistretta, C. M., & Bradley, R. M. (1982). Developmental changes in taste response characteristics of rat single chorda tympani fibers. *The Journal of Neuroscience, 2*, 782–790.

Jacobs, H. L., Smutz, E. R., & DuBose, C. N. (1977). Comparative observations on the ontogeny of taste preference. In J. M. Weiffenbach (Ed.), *Taste and development: The genesis of sweet preference*. DHEW Publication No. NIH 77-1068. Washington, D.C.: U.S. Government Printing Office.

Kehoe, P., & Blass, E. M. (1985). Gustatory determinants of suckling in albino rats 5–20 days of age. *Developmental Psychobiology, 18*, 67–82.

Lipsitt, L. P. (1977). Taste in human neonates: Its effect on sucking and heart rate. In J. M. Weiffenbach (Ed.), *Taste and development: The genesis of sweet preference*. DHEW Publication No. NIH 77-1068. Washington, D.C.: U.S. Government Printing Office.

Midkiff, E. E., & Bernstein, I. L. (1983). The influence of age and experience on salt preference of the rat. *Developmental Psychobiology, 16*, 385–394.

Mistretta, C. M. (1972). Topographical and histological study of the developing rat tongue, palate, and taste buds. In J. F. Bosma (Ed.), *Third Symposium on Oral Sensation and Perception: The Mouth of the Infant* (pp. 163–187). Springfield, IL: Charles C. Thomas.

Mistretta, C. M. (1981). Neurophysiological and anatomical aspects of taste development. In *Development of perception* (Vol. 1, pp. 433–455). New York: Academic Press.

Mistretta, C. M., & Bradley, R. M. (1983). Neural basis of developing salt taste sensation: Response changes in fetal, postnatal and adult sheep. *Journal of Comparative Neurology, 215,* 199–210.

Moe, K. (1986). The ontogeny of salt preference in rats. *Developmental Psychobiology, 19,* 185–196.

Peterson, F., & Rainey, L. H. (1910). The beginnings of mind in the newborn. *Bulletin of the Lying-In Hospital City of New York, 7,* 99–122.

Rozin, P., Grus, L., & Berk, G. (1979). Reversal of innate aversions: Attempts to induce a preference for chili peppers in rats. *Journal of Comparative and Physiological Psychology, 93,* 1001–1014.

Smith, D. F. (1974). NH_4CL Acceptability in the rat. *Physiology and Behavior, 12,* 513–514.

Steiner, J. E. (1977). Facial expressions of the neonate infant indicating the hedonics of food-related chemical stimuli. In J. M. Weiffenbach (Ed.), *Taste and development: The genesis of sweet preference.* DHEW Publication No. NIH 77-1068. Washington, D.C.: U.S. Government Printing Office.

Wurtman, J. J., & Wurtman, R. J. (1979). Sucrose consumption early in life fails to modify the appetite of adult rats for sweet foods. *Science, 205,* 321–322.

9 Comparative Hedonics of Taste

Gary K. Beauchamp
J. Russell Mason
Monell Chemical Senses Center

Primary knowledge of hedonics comes from introspection. The next best evidence is a verbal report; unless one believes another a liar, it is reasonable to assume that if a taste is described as pleasant, it is indeed pleasant. Comparative studies of hedonics, however, do not have available either of these sources of evidence.

The argument for the existence of hedonics in nonhuman animals is fundamentally that of homology. To the extent that other species are similar to humans they must experience similar feelings including pleasure associated with similar sensory stimulation. This argument is surely generally accepted. However, the species specificity of stimuli that determine hedonic experiences makes it difficult to generalize, even within the primates.

Two sources of indirect evidence are used to inform the argument for nonhuman hedonics. The first is behavioral, examples of which form the body of this chapter. The second is anatomical about which little will be said. Central nervous system structures, which in humans *(Homo sapiens)* are involved in the sensations of pleasure, are activated during certain types of sensory stimulation in nonhuman animals. Recently, there has been considerable interest in the possibility that an endogenous opioid system may modulate some aspects of the pleasure associated with sensory stimulation (Reid, 1985).

OVERVIEW OF THIS CHAPTER

Following a brief discussion of some of the issues involved in comparative chemosensory hedonics, studies of mammals and birds, the authors' respective areas of expertise, are considered. Taste, which is emphasized, is the sensory stimulation detected by taste receptors and transmitted by the 7th, 9th, and 10th cranial nerves. The emphasis is on ingestion and the goal is not to be encyclopedic, but to consider species differences and similarities and how they may reflect ecological factors.

Comparative Hedonics: Behavioral Evidence

If, in an appropriate free choice test, an animal elects to consume one item in preference to another this is proof that it can discriminate between the two items. However, it is also generally assumed that this is evidence that the animal likes the chosen item. This is logically incorrect, as has been noted by Rozin (1979), who argued that only mimetic expression can be taken as evidence for hedonic experience in nonhuman animals. For example, an item could be preferentially selected because it is believed to be beneficial in spite of it providing unpleasant sensory experience (see Booth, 1987, who disputes this point). This distinction may be valid only in verbal humans however (Beauchamp & Cowart, 1987).

In a series of studies, Grill and colleagues (e.g., Berridge, Flynn, Schulkin, & Grill, 1984; Grill & Bernstein, 1988; Grill & Norgren, 1978; Grill & Schulkin & Flynn, 1986) have demonstrated mimetic responses to tastes in rats *(Rattus norvegicus)*. Substances rats find highly palatable in acceptance tests (e.g., sweet solutions, very salty solutions when sodium deficient) elicit facial expressions indicative of acceptance whereas unpalatable tastes (e.g., bitter substances, very salty solutions to nondeficient rats), elicit expressions and behaviors of rejection. Generally speaking, acceptance studies and mimetic evaluation appear to be in accord in rats (although perhaps not in human infants; Cowart, 1981), lending some confidence to the assignment of the categories of pleasant/unpleasant to the results of preference or acceptance tests.

Although it is likely that mimetic responses would be evident in many other mammals were they to be carefully studied, birds may generally not express them. The absence of lips and the presence of a hard elongated beak limits the repertoire of facial expressions shown to oral stimulation (Gentle & Harkin, 1979). While chickens *(Gallus domesticus)* show a characteristic response to aversive oral stimulation typified by persistent tongue and beak movements, head shaking and beak wiping behavior (Gentle, 1973, 1976, 1978), no analogous repertoire has been observed in response to preferred stimuli, and no data have been collected with species other than domestic fowl.

Factors Determining Acceptance/Rejection

As in many facets of animal behavior, the interaction of innate and acquired information must be evaluated. When discussing comparative hedonics, it is assumed that species differences in sensory response somehow reflect species differences in ecological niche. This in turn would be related, for the sense of taste, to food habits. Presumably, differences in sensory systems which permit differences in hedonic sensory experience characterize species with different niches. Hence, an unlearned component to taste hedonics should be widespread. Such is the case.

However, in highly developed forms such as birds and mammals, learning and social factors probably play a prominent interactive role. Aversions to foods may be mediated by conditioned responses (Rozin, 1976; Jacobs, Beauchamp, & Kare, 1978). Evidence for early imprinting-like attachments to odors (e.g., Leon et al., 1987) suggests that positive hedonic responses to chemosensory stimuli may also derive from individual experience, a conclusion consistent with studies of conditioned flavor preferences (e.g., Boakes & Lubart, 1988; Capaldi, Campbell, Sheffer, & Bradford, 1987; Gibson & Booth, 1986; Mehiel & Bolles, 1988; Zellner, Rozin, Aron, & Kulish, 1983). Characteristic species differences could arise from common individual experience as well as common ancestry.

Many avian species feed more efficiently when in flocks (e.g., Feare, 1984). This and other observations support the conclusion that social context may be of greater importance than physical characteristics of the food in some situations. In the laboratory, satiated red-winged blackbirds will consume food at the same rate as deprived conspecifics with whom they are in visual contact (Mason & Reidinger, 1981). Red-wings also prefer novel foods that they have seen presented to demonstrator birds (Mason & Reidinger, 1981). Social facilitation, mediated in part by chemosensation, probably plays a major role in mammalian food selection as well (see below).

Taste and Smell: A Comparison with Respect to Nutrient Intake

In contrast to the sense of taste, smell information in mammals and birds follows a path from olfactory receptors in the airway via cranial nerve 1 to the olfactory bulbs and thence to a variety of limbic and other CNS structures. The olfactory system serves at least two general functions in mammals and perhaps in birds, social (e.g., sex, aggression; other nasal chemosensory organs such as the vomeronasal system are also involved) and nutritive. In contrast, there is no evidence that taste plays any role other than in regulating nutrient intake and utilization. Because taste seems to have this dedicated function, it is reasonable to suppose a primary role in food acceptance. In fact, it has been argued (e.g., Ikeda, 1909; Jacobs et al., 1978; McBurney & Gent, 1979) that taste preferences and presumably taste hedonics evolved to insure adequate consumption of nutrients (calories in particular) and avoidance of poisons (often substances humans label as bitter). Under this argument, the olfactory system would play a more indirect and subtle role in modulating intake/rejection of foods. There is an apparent simplicity to the taste system, dividing as it does into a relatively few "basic" categories (for discussion see McBurney & Gent, 1979; Erickson & Corey, 1980). In contrast, olfaction has no agreed-upon method of categorizing sensations arising from stimulation and it is often assumed that there are many, perhaps an almost infinite number, of qualitatively distinct odors that defy easy classification. This difference in the way stimuli can be categorized in the two chemosensory systems is suggestive of their functional differences. Taste is primitive, often with innately determined hedonic attributes whereas olfaction, at least in so far as food is concerned, may be more plastic, more complex, and more subtle. Animals will work to obtain tastes; in contrast, it has been difficult, although not impossible, to use odors as rewards in learning studies (Long & Tapp, 1967). In fact, while there are a number of publications emphasizing species comparisons of taste (e.g., Bell, 1959; Kare & Beauchamp, 1984), we are aware of no such enterprises for olfaction. It is these considerations that have led us to place our major emphasis on comparative hedonics of taste and to restrict our discussion of olfaction to the last section of this chapter.

TASTE

Substantial species differences in taste preferences and patterns of taste sensitivity exist. Although it is likely that these differences are generally a function of the ecological (food) niche of the different species, this hypothesis is often difficult to verify. Generally speaking, taste seems to be more highly developed in mammals than in birds.

In the following sections, examples are selected that illustrate the presumed fit between taste preference, usually revealed as responses to model aqueous solutions, and presumed food habits. As a matter of organization, this topic is divided by human taste quality; as will be evident, there are substantial problems with this approach.

Sweet Perception

While sugars (and other substances such as amino acids) described by humans as sweet are highly preferred by many species, this preference is not universal nor does it extend to all sweeteners. For example, with the exception of saccharin, most noncarbohydrate sweeteners are not preferred and are often rejected by other species tested (Jackinovich & Sugarman, 1988). An overview of species differences in sweet recognition is presented by Kare and Beauchamp (1984) and is not repeated in detail here.

Some broad differences in response to carbohydrate sweeteners among mammalian species are illustrated in Table 9.1. Cats (*Felis catus*), which are strict carnivores, appear remarkably unresponsive to carbohydrate sweeteners whereas rats and guinea pigs (*Cavia porcellus*), examples of omnivores and herbivores,

TABLE 9.1
Summary of Response of Several Species of Mammals of Aqueous Solutions of Prototypical Taste Substances*

	Species					
	Rat		*Guinea Pig*		*Cat*	
	Wild	*Laboratory*	*Wild*	*Domestic*	*Panthia sp.*	*Felis cattus*
Sweet Stimuli						
glucose/sucrose	+	+	+	+	0	0
saccharin		+	+	+		
L-alanine						0
Salty Stimulus						
NaCl	+	+	+	+		+?0
Sour Stimulus						
citric acid				-		-
Bitter Stimuli						
quinine sulfate		-		0		-
quinine hydrochloride		-		-		-
sucrose octaacetate		-		-		0

+ indicates taste solution preferred to water at at least some concentrations; rejection may occur at high concentrations;
- indicates that rejection is the prominent response; at no concentration was preference evident;
0 indicates indifference (relative to water) at all or nearly all low to moderate concentrations tested; at high concentrations, rejection may occur.
* Adapted from Jacobs, Beauchamp, and Kare (1978).

respectively, avidly consume some sweet substances. Although there is some evidence for carbohydrate preference in cats under very special circumstances (Bartoshuk, Harned, & Parks, 1971; Frings, 1951), the consensus is that cats either lack or have a very poorly developed sweet taste system (Beauchamp, Maller, & Rogers, 1977). However, Boudreau (e.g., 1986) has noted that several of the amino acids to which cats are sensitive are ones humans find sweet; perhaps the cat experiences the sensation of sweet but it occurs in response to amino acids rather than to carbohydrates.

Unfortunately, only cats (domestic and *Panthera* species), among mammalian carnivores have been rigorously investigated for carbohydrate sweet responsiveness. It is unconvincing to use the example of the cat as proof that carnivorous mammals in general lack sweet perception and preference and it would be of considerable value to examine other carnivores. Particularly attractive in this regard are mustilids which include species that are almost strictly meat-eating (e.g., weasels (*Mustela frenata*)), as well as others that are more omnivorous (e.g., skunks (*Mephitis mephitis*)). A comparative study of sweet responsiveness among this group could be most informative.

A further comparative issue needs emphasis when discussing the apparent absence of sweet carbohydrate perception and preference in cats. There is no such thing as *the* cat or *the* dog or *the* rat. Substantial difference among populations and individuals of the same species exist, as is discussed shortly, making it often important to limit generalization (cf. Rowland & Fregley, 1989). Furthermore, most studies of taste are carried out on adult animals with developmental work often focusing on issues of when adult-like responsiveness is first evident (e.g., Hill, 1987; Mistretta & Bradley, 1983). It is conceivable, however, that different sensory capacities and preferences may characterize different developmental stages. For example, for humans it is known that children's sweet preferences are greater than those of adults (Beauchamp & Cowart, 1987; Desor & Beauchamp, 1987), although the physiological basis for this difference remains debatable (Booth, 1987). For cats, it is possible that kittens may differ from adult cats in having a functional sweet preference system, perhaps related to the nursing period. Pfaffmann (1955) reported neurophysiological responses to sucrose in one kitten but the generality of this observation is not known.

It has been argued that the wide-spread existence of a sweet carbohydrate preference in most herbivorous and omnivorous mammals tested reflects a calorie-recognition mechanism (e.g., Jacobs et al., 1978). Apparent species differences in whether sugars are preferred and in which sugars are most preferred (see Kare & Beauchamp, 1984, for examples), are, however, difficult to explain under this hypothesis. This is particularly true for avian species where the pattern of species differences is not easily interpretable.

Nectar-feeding species select flowers with high levels of sucrose, glucose, and fructose (Percival, 1961). Likewise, sugars are preferred by Bobwhite Quail (*Colinus virginianus*), Japanese Quail (*C. japonica*) (Hanrum, 1953; Brindley, 1965; Brindley & Prior, 1968; Harriman & Milner, 1969), Great Tits (*Parus major*) (Warren & Vince, 1963), Rock Doves (*Columba livia*) (Duncan, 1960), Chickens (*Gallus gallus*) (Gunther & Wagner, 1971; Gentle, 1972, 1975), Budgeriars (*Melopsittacus undulatus*) and other parrots, and the broadtailed hummingbird (*Selasphorus platycercus*) (Kare & Rogers, 1976). However, a number of avian species that *should* prefer sugars either reject them or are apparently insensitive to them (e.g., Kare, 1961, 1965; Kare & Mason, 1986; Kare & Medway, 1959). Omnivorous passerines (e.g., European starlings [*Sturnus vulgaris*], red-winged blackbirds [*Agelaius phoeniceus*]) reject sugar solutions in the laboratory (Rogers & Maller, 1973; Espaillat & Mason, 1990, cf. Schuler, 1983) but select *sweet* fruits in the field (e.g., grapes, cherries; Stevens, 1985). Possibly, this rejection of simple (disaccharide) sugar solutions reflects an inability to digest them (Martinez del Rio & Stevens 1989); other factors (e.g., pH) may control the response (Mason, unpublished observations). In addition, many of the species that exhibit preferences for sugars do so only in short-term tests (Gentle, 1975). In long-term trials, preference behaviors dissipate, and are replaced by avoidance (Gentle, 1972).

Recently, it has been argued that there are at least two separate carbohydrate-detecting system in some mammals. One might be labeled the sweet or sugar system whereas the second might be termed a polysaccharide-detecting system. The two systems are presumably mediated by different receptors (Sclafani, 1987). Evidence in favor of such a dichotomy comes mainly from behavioral studies in rats (Sclafani, 1987) although studies in other species have been reported. Among rodents, gerbils (*Meriones unquiculatus*), hamsters (*Mesocricetus auratus*) and spiny mice (*Acomys cahirnus*), all appeared to possess a polysaccharide as well as a sugar system (Feigin, Scalafani, & Sunday, 1987). In contrast to these rodents, cats are, as would be predicted, indifferent to both sugars and polysaccharides (Harrison, Castonguay, Scalafani, & Rogers, 1986, cited in Sclafani, 1987). Amongst primates, humans (Feigin et al., 1987) and squirrel monkeys (*Saimiri sciureus*) appear to lack the polysaccharide system while bonnet macaques (*Macaca radiata*) apparently possess one (Sunderland & Sclafani, 1988). While Sunderland and Sclafani argue that these differences between nonhuman primates are consistent with their natural food preferences, this is speculative; other primate species need to be evaluated to test the fit between dietary behavior and presence or absence of the hypothesized polysaccharide system.

Bitter Perception

As a companion hypothesis to the sweet-calorie association, it has often been suggested that bitter perception exists to protect animals from ingesting poisons, mainly alkaloids, and to protect plants from being eaten. In general, bitter substances are offensive to many species, although as with sweeteners, there are marked interspecific differences.

Quinine hydrochloride is bitter to humans, and rejected by many species; however, the rejection threshold exhibits marked interspecific variation as shown by comparing studies of cats, rats, and guinea pigs (Tables 9.1 and 9.2). While methodological differences could account for some of this variation, Jacobs et al. (1978) suggested that the importance of bitter tastes, and thus sensitivity of the bitter system may depend upon the feeding ecology of the species in question. In particular, the guinea pig is a strict herbivore and as such, is confronted with the problem of consuming sufficient calories from plants, most of which taste bitter to humans. Given this problem, if guinea pigs had a sensitive bitter-rejection mechanism they would have substantial difficulty in finding acceptable foods.

Even more extreme are species differences among birds. Quinine hydrochloride or sulfate are rejected by some species of birds (e.g., pigeons [Duncan,

TABLE 9.2
Relative Sensitivity (in Preference Tests) of Three Domestic Species to a Bitter
Substance, Quinine Hydrochloride

	CAT	RAT		GUINEA PIG	
-6	-5	-4	-3	-2	-1

QHCl CONCENTRATION (10^x)

Note. Rats and, particularly, cats are much more sensitive (several orders of magnitude) to QHCl than guinea pigs. All rejection levels determined in two-choice preference tests with aqueous solutions. For references, see Jacobs, Beauchamp, and Kare (1978).

1960], ducks and chickens [Engelmann, 1934]), and for a few, such as the Black-capped Chickadee (*Parus atricapillus*), these compounds are toxic. However, bread mixed with quinine is readily eaten by some parrots (*Amazona* spp.), and grain dipped in picric acid is readily consumed by seed eaters and titmice (*Parus* spp.) (Heinroth, 1938). Both denatonium saccharide and denatonium benzoate (bitrex) are extremely bitter to humans, but readily accepted by red-winged blackbirds (Mason, 1987). Likewise, sucrose octaacetate at a concentration bitter to humans is readily accepted by the herring gull and the chicken, but rejected by Bobwhite and Japanese Quail (Brindley, 1965). At least for this compound, there are indications of ontogenetic changes in sensitivity. Bobwhite Quail do not respond to sucrose octaacetate as young birds, but gradually develop the ability to detect and avoid it (Cane & Vince, 1968).

If some herbivorous birds and mammals (see Jacobs et al., 1978) have a blunted bitter-rejection system, what is to prevent them from ingesting excessive poisonous compounds? While there apparently is a rough correlation between bitterness and toxicity (Scott & Mark, 1987) this correlation is not perfect. It is suggested that another mechanism to avoid toxins is the formation of conditioned aversions to other flavor components of a toxic plant. If there is no innate bitter-alkaloid-based rejection of plants, the animal is free to sample and, in effect, meter the intake of toxic plants at an acceptable level.

Alternatively, or in addition, herbivorous animals could develop detoxifying mechanisms; this is a common insect strategy. It is probably the plant-insect interactions that have led the way to the bitter-rejection system in vertebrates. In one interesting example of this strategy, Glendinning (1988) has studied mouse (*Peromyscus melanotis, P. aztecus hylocetes, Reithrodontomys sumichrasti* and *Microtus mexicanns*) predation on monarch butterflies (*Danaus plexippus*) at the latters' wintering grounds in Mexico. Of the four species of mice present in the area, only one (*P. melanotis*) makes extensive use of the vast protein store potentially available from these butterflies. Since the butterflies contain toxic cardiac glycosides that are bitter and can cause emesis (e.g., Brower, 1969), how is this ecological challenge met by the mouse species? Experimental studies (Glendinning, 1988) demonstrated that the one species known to prey upon monarchs in the field was the only one which (1) extensively ate monarchs in test situations; (2) gained weight; and (3) selectively ate those parts which were least toxic (for a similar observation with guinea pigs, see Jacobs & Labows, 1979). It is suggested that the predatory species is probably less sensitive (though not completely insensitive) to the taste of cardiac glycosides, a result confirmed in formal taste studies (Glendinning, 1988), is able to withstand ingestion of relatively high levels of toxic compounds and is likely to have well developed behavioral techniques for assessing the nutritive value of food, for example, the ability to form conditioned aversions (Glendinning, 1988). Similar principles may apply in other cases. The skin of salamanders (*Ambystoma tigrinum*) contains toxins that prevent predation. The skin secretions produce primary and conditioned aversions in rats (Mason, Rabin, & Stevens, 1982), yet shrews (*Blarina brericauda*) will eat salamanders (Brodie, Newark, & Harvey, 1979).

The marked species differences in bitter perception suggested by Glendinning's studies are further complicated by the evidence for different types of bitter receptor mechanisms. It is well known that for humans and some other species, an individual's sensitivity to the bitter compound phenylthiocarbamide (PTC) is not strongly predictive of responsiveness to other bitter compounds such as quinine hydrochloride or sucrose octaacetate. The ability to detect PTC at low concentrations is bi- or tri-modally distributed in human populations and is under genetic control (Morton, Cantor, Corey, & Nance, 1981). To the extent that sensitivity to the other bitter substances is also under genetic control, other genes appear to be involved.

Studies of genetic control over bitter perception by inbred strains of mice (*Mus muscullus*) have demonstrated the existence of several genes determining sensitivity to specific bitter substances. Lush (1981, 1982, 1984, 1986; Azen, Lush, & Taylor, 1986) postulates at least four separate genes which have been labeled *Soa, Qui, Rva* and *Cyx,* that control ability to detect specific bitter substances. The presence of these genes has been based on preference studies: Mouse strains which are indifferent to a certain chemical such as sucrose octaacetate (Soa) presented in a two-choice test against water are concluded to be unable to taste Soa. However, because preference tests cannot be used to confirm an absence of sensitivity or ability to detect, the issue remained as to whether these proposed genes were truly involved in sensitivity, perhaps indicating the presence or absence of specific receptor proteins. Recent studies of sucrose octaacetate sensitivity by inbred strains of mice in Whitney's Laboratory (e.g., Harder et al., 1984; Whitney, Harder, Gannon, & Maggio, 1989) have demonstrated that *sensitivity* to Soa is under genetic control. Furthermore, Shingai and Beidler (1985) have shown that the strain differences in behaviorally-determined sensitivity are mirrored in parallel electrophysiological differences, further supporting the idea that the genes are involved in coding for receptor-associated proteins.

These studies lead to the conclusion that bitter perception is not a unitary phenomenon. This is not surprising if one believes that perception and rejection of toxic compounds is the "function" of a bitter taste system. To date, there is no agreed-upon chemical basis for bitterness and this may be because no common molecular configuration exists for this taste. Instead, as plants and perhaps insects (Brower, 1969; Yang & Kare 1968) have evolved substances that are potentially harmful to invertebrates and vertebrates alike, these organisms have evolved means to detect the substances. Specific taste mechanisms have, as a result, developed as a family of different protein-based receptors, all of which are connected to genetic rejection mechanisms and which elicit more or less common sensory experience humans label as bitter and unpleasant. Before this broad scenario is taken very seriously, however, considerably more comparative study is needed, especially studies that attempt, as in the Glendinning work, to correlate sensory capacity with natural food habits.

Salt Perception

The salty taste is probably the most specific of the classic taste qualities reflecting the need to maintain sodium balance (Dethier, 1977). As salt taste is treated in other chapters in this book as well as having been given extensive review in Denton's (1982) monumental work, only a few comparative topics are touched on here.

Two aspects of the behavioral response to salt have been investigated, responses to salt during sodium depletion (often called salt appetite) and response to salt during a period where the animal has sufficient body sodium (often called salt preference). Whereas the same sensory channel is presumably involved in both situations, the mechanisms underlying behavioral responses may be different and species difference could apply in one instance but not another.

Mechanisms of salt appetite have been studied in exquisite detail in rats and sheep (*Ovis aries*), which surprisingly exhibit marked species differences (Denton, 1982; Epstein et al., 1984; Epstein & Sakai, 1987). Particularly relevant to the topic here, depletion appears to induce a hedonic shift in response to high salt concentrations, moving them from unpleasant to pleasant as determined by rat mimetic responses (Berridge et al., 1984). Recent studies, expanding the original work by Contreras and Frank (1979) which demonstrated neurophysiological changes following sodium depletion, now suggest that the neurophysiology of salt taste response becomes more sweet-like during sodium depletion (Jacobs, Mark, & Scott, 1988). However, the interesting question of whether salt tastes sweet to a salt-depleted animal has not yet been adequately evaluated. Perhaps the connection in the literature between sweet and good is more than mere hyperbole: For taste response, the more pleasant may literally be sweeter. This is one of the many interesting issues of sensory effects of salt depletion which could be studied best if it were possible to use modern psychological techniques to deplete human (verbal) subjects (Beauchamp, Bertino, Burke & Engelman, 1990). However, it should be pointed out that the evidence for a salt appetite following acute depletion in adult humans is not strong (Beauchamp, 1987; Beauchamp et al., 1990; Stricker & Verbalis, 1988). Species differences suggest caution in assuming that salt-depleted humans would manifest a salt appetite identical with that observed in sheep or rats. In this regard, the dog, which mainly eats meat and might not experience sodium deficiency in nature without first starving, does not appear to develop a sodium appetite following experimental depletion (Thrasher, personal communication). A chemosensory-connected mechanism to detect depletion of sodium may not exist in carnivorous animals in general (see Table 9.1).

For comparative work, the majority of studies involve salt taste perception in sodium-replete individuals. Under these physiological conditions, some mammalian species exhibit preference for hypotonic and near-isotonic salt solutions relative to water, whereas others do not (Carpenter, 1956). Rensch and Neunzig (1925) assessed sodium chloride sensitivity in 60 avian species. Variability was enormous, ranging from low thresholds for parrots (0.35%) and pigeons (0.5–0.9%) to high thresholds for gray partridge (*Perdix perdix;* 20%) and siskin (*Carduelis*) species (37%). Unlike rodents that avidly select some hypotonic concentrations of sodium chloride, many birds are indifferent up to the threshold concentration for rejection. This threshold is usually the point at which the solutions become hypertonic relative to body fluids (Bartholomew & Cade, 1958; Bartholomew & MacMillian, 1960). Not surprisingly, birds with nasal salt glands will drink seawater, but even these species avoid consumption of saltwater when opportunities arise. Both the Herring Gull (*Larus argentatus*) and the Laughing Gull (*L. atricilla*) will select pure water over salt solutions when given a choice (Harriman, 1967; Harriman & Kare, 1966). Similarly, penguins are said to prefer fresh over seawater after having been at sea for extended periods (Warham, 1971).

It is only among birds without salt glands that preferences for salt are observed. Numerous finches of the family *Cardeulidae* possess notorious appetites for salt, and cross bills can be caught in traps baited with salt alone (Welty, 1975; Willoughby, 1971). Domestic fowl are rather insensitive to sodium chloride (Engelmann, 1934), although if maintained on a low sodium diet they will exhibit a specific appetite and select, in choice situations, the diet or solution that corrects the deficiency (Kare & Rogers, 1976; cf. Hughes & Wood-Gush, 1970).

At least for domestic fowl, there appear to be developmental changes in sensitivity. Engelman (1950) reported that chicks were considerably more sensitive to sodium chloride than adults, and speculated that this might reflect their inability to handle high salt concentrations (Kare & Beily, 1948). Rodents also appear to exhibit developmental changes in sensitivity to salt (Hill, 1987), and recent evidence indicates that there may be critical times during development when the fetal rat must be exposed to salt in order for normal taste responses to emerge. In a series of electrophysiological experiments, Hill and Przekop (1988) have demonstrated that rat pups deprived of salt prior to fetal day 8, via sodium deprivation of their mothers, never develop normal salt sensitivity. These findings are especially intriguing, because the period of deprivation occurs prior to the development of receptor cells. Apparently, changes in the central nervous system are responsible for these observations.

The order of sensitivity of ionic series by birds does not appear to fit into the lyotropic or sensitivity series reported for other animals. No physical or chemical theory has been offered to explain the responses to sodium salts and chlorides, and there is considerable individual variability. Often, the distribution of thresholds is continuous with reactions among birds to a single concentration of one salt varying from preference to rejection. Chemical specificity is involved, because an individual that can taste one salt at either unusually high or low concentrations is likely to respond in an average manner to other salts. It has been possible to select and breed for taste sensitivity to a specific chemical (Kare, 1961).

The inability to predict acceptance of hypotonic saline solutions by avian species is something of an enigma. Jacobs et al. (1978) hypothesized that since free-ranging herbivores tend to experience chronic salt deficiencies (Abraham et al., 1975), then most should exhibit salt preferences, even in the absence of deficiency. This is not generally the case with mammals (Jacobs et al., 1978). Nor, as reviewed here, is it the case with herbivorous (granivorous) birds, who rarely show symptoms of sodium deficiency when kept on a low salt diet (Cade, 1964; Dawson, Shoemaker, Tordoff, & Borut, 1965). Perhaps the discrepancy between prediction and observation is more apparent then real, since for birds no careful attempt has yet been made to examine salt preferences in birds that are given maintenance diets in which sodium levels are controlled.

Does a preference for saline mean that when it occurs, animals *like* or obtain pleasure from the salty-tasting solutions? This is a question that has vexed many investigators and as yet is unresolved. Deutsch and Jones (1960) were among the first to suggest that a salt preference may represent something other than the drive for the pleasant taste of salt. Their hypothesis, put in its most simple form, was that rats consume more salt solution than water because the former is, in effect, dilute water and hence more of it is needed to reach the same hydration level. This hypothesis has aroused considerable controversy (see Denton, 1982) and it is safe to say that the issue remains unsettled. These observations have stimulated a body of work, among the most interesting is the observation that there is some difficulty in inducing rats to work to obtain presumably pleasant salt solutions (see also Mook, 1963; Myer & Van Hemel, 1969; Rabe & Corbit, 1973; Stellar, Hyman, & Samet, 1954), a great contrast with the reinforcing value of sweet stimuli.

Most comparative work has involved salt preference for saline solutions. As is the case for sucrose, there are good reasons for hypothesizing differences in salt taste as a function of the extent to which meat forms a portion of the organism's diet. Meat, in particular blood, is considerably higher in sodium than is the average plant and thus it is likely that omnivores are under considerably more sodium stress than are carnivores. Consistent with this proposal, saline preference in mammals is reported in omnivores and herbivores but generally not in carnivores (see Table 9.1; Denton, 1982). A postnatal maturation of the salt taste system observed in sheep (Mistretta & Bradley, 1983), rats (Hill, 1987), and perhaps in humans (Beauchamp, Cowart & Moran, 1986) also accords well with a hypothesis linking salt taste perception and preference to the possibility of depletion. Presumably, no depletion is possible (before frank starvation) during the nursing period. For precocial chicks, for which *excess* consumption could be a problem, a highly developed sense very early would be important (see above). As with sweet perception, a more focused comparative study of salt taste and diet would be of considerable interest.

One final observation is relevant to the issue of the pleasantness of salt to non-deprived organisms. Recent studies with rats (Beauchamp & Bertino, 1985; Bertino & Beauchamp, 1987) have been unable to demonstrate salt preference in the context of a solid food; instead salty solid foods appear to be rejected relative to the same foods without salt. Since these same rats prefer saline solution to water, the generality of the pleasantness of the salty taste is in question. Although there is little comparative work along these lines, the results of studies with baboons (Barnwell, Dollahite, & Mitchell, 1986) were also consistent with a lack of salt preference in food. In this regard, rats and baboons contrast strongly with humans where salt preferences are almost universally expressed in a food.

Sour Perception

Remarkably little informative work has been conducted on comparative aspects of sour taste perception. Most mammals and avians are sensitive to acids in solution, and exhibit avoidance of them. Rensch and Neunzig (1925) found that most of the 60 bird species they tested showed a narrow tolerance for acetic acid in solution and that rejection thresholds usually were below 1.0%. Engelmann (1934) obtained similar results, reporting that pigeons were more sensitive than either ducks (*Anas platyrhyncous*) or geese (*Anser anser*). Differential sensitivity has also been observed for passerines: starlings are more sensitive than red-winged blackbirds, though both species exhibit rejection (Espaillat & Mason, 1990; cf. Harriman, 1968). For domestic fowl, Engelmann (1950) reported that chicks are more sensitive than adults, suggesting (as for salt) that there might be ontogenetic changes in sensitivity. Analogous developmental changes may be true of European starlings (Stevens, 1985). While most species exhibit rejection of acids, there are exceptions, and some birds exhibit preferences. Thus, Brindley and Prior (1968) reported that Bobwhite Quail prefer 0.05% HCl to water.

The ecological relevance of high sensitivity for acids coupled with low tolerance in unclear, although these characteristics may be useful in food selection (Harriman, 1968). Acids are present in many food items, notably fruits. A high sensitivity for an acidic taste in potential food items could be one clue as to its palatability. Too strong an acidic component could signal unripeness, leading to rejection (hence the low tolerance for acidic solutions). However, while there are likely species differences related to food habits, obvious hypotheses to account for those differences, such as a greater preference among frugivorous species, have not received adequate attention. Even the existence of sour as a fundamental class of taste perception is an enigma since sensitivity to acids apparently occurs at much lower levels than those which could be considered caustic or dangerous.

Other Tastes

Amino acids act as taste stimulants for most species studied. As might be expected, animals that eat foods likely to be identified by free amino acids seem more responsive to their taste. Fish, particularly catfish (*Ictalurus punctatus*), are known to be exquisitely sensitive to a variety of amino acids and this organism has recently become one of the major model species for the investigation of the biochemistry and biophysics of taste reception and transduction (see various papers in Brand, Teeter, Teeter, & Kare, 1989). It is likely that something approaching a full understanding of the biochemical mechanisms of taste will come from studies with this species. Interestingly, the catfish responds to many of the same amino acids with both its olfactory and taste systems.

The available evidence suggests that a variety of avian species are also sensitive to amino acids. Some, such as the European starling (Espaillat & Mason, unpublished observations) and bullfinch (*Pyrrhula pyrrhula;* Greig-Smith, Wilson, Blunden, & Wilson, 1983), exhibit the ability to detect L-alanine and other amino acids at concentrations below those that are generally detectable by mammals (personal observation). At least in part, high sensitivity may help explain foraging responses of these birds in the field. Possibly, the ability to detect low levels of free amino acids may aid starlings in their selection of the high protein fraction of complete diets for livestock (Feare & Wadsworth, 1981). Likewise, foraging by bullfinches on pear flower buds is positively associated with free amino acid concentrations in the buds of various pear cultivars. Suggestively, a variety of shorebirds, including Purple Sandpipers (*Calidris maritima*), Red Knots (*Calidris canutus*), Sanderlings (*Calidris alba*), and Dunlins (*Calidris alpina*), can discriminate between jars filled with sand containing "taste" and "no-taste," where *taste* is derived from worms that had lived in the sand, but had been removed before the experiment (Geritsen & Sevenster, 1985).

It would not be surprising if free amino acids in the skin mucous of the worms was the stimulus detected by the birds.

Among mammals, amino acids may be perceived as similar to other sweet, sour, salty, or bitter stimuli or they may be distinct. As noted earlier, Boudreau (e.g., 1986), has argued that some amino acid-sensitive fibers in cats are identical with sweet-sensitive fibers in other species with the exception that the former do not respond to simple carbohydrates. Similarly, Kasahara, Iwasaki, and Sato (1987) present neurophysiological and conditioned aversion data that mouse preference for D- and L-amino acids is due to their sweetness. Boudreau et al. (1985) have suggested that, relative to carnivores such as the cat and the dog, the rat is insensitive to amino acids.

Humans too tend to describe most amino acids as sweet, bitter, tasteless and less commonly sour and salty (Schiffman, Sennewald, & Gagnon, 1981). However, one qualitatively distinct experience, that labeled "umami," follows stimulation by glutamate (usually the monosodium salt, MSG) often in conjunction with the 5'-ribonucleotides, as well as other amino acids. It has been hypothesized that this flavor is indicative of protein (amino acid) sources and has evolved as a sensory signal for that nutrient in much the same way sweet perception involves calorie regulation (Ikeda, 1909). A rare synergistic interaction between MSG and the 5'-ribonucleotides has been documented (see chapters in Kawamura & Kare, 1987). Interestingly, the flavoring properties of both these substances as well as their synergistic interaction were first discovered and exploited in Japanese cuisine where foods containing MSG (seaweed) and ribonucleotides (mushrooms) were combined long before the chemical nature of the active ingredients was known.

The status of an umami taste remains somewhat controversial but there is no doubting that monosodium glutamate provides a singular sensory experience to humans. Whether such a system exists in other species is controversial (Kawamura & Kare, 1987); Boudreau finds the only similar system from a neurophysiological perspective in the lobster (*Homarus* sp.; Boudreau, 1986; Johnson, Voight, Borroni, & Atema, 1984).

OLFACTION

For many animals, palatability is a function of *flavor,* that is, both taste and volatile characteristics, rather than of taste alone. Thus, for carnivores (e.g., domestic cats) both the duration and the size of meals is increased by perfusing normally preferred meat odors (e.g., cooked rabbit) through the maintenance diet (Mugford, 1977). Even satiated animals can be induced to eat using this method. Similarly, Larue and LeMagnen (1972) report that food odors can enhance feeding by rats. But food odors alone are not the only volatiles that contribute to food selection. Endogenous cues produced by conspecifics are also important. This point is illustrated in a series of recent experiments by Galef and his colleagues. When faced with a choice among several novel foods, naive "observer" rats choose foods eaten by "demonstrator" conspecifics with whom they previously have interacted (Galef & Wigmore, 1983; Posadas-Andrews & Roper, 1983; Strupp & Levitsky, 1984). Social transfer of diet preference is mediated in part by volatile cues (Galef & Stein, 1985).

Important volatile information could be the smell of food that a demonstrator has ingested before interacting with an observer. Alternatively, transmission might require a combination of the smell of ingested diet and some endogenous (demonstrator-derived) cue. In experiments designed to test these possibilities, Galef and Stein (1985) and Galef, Kennett, & Stein (1985) showed that the smell

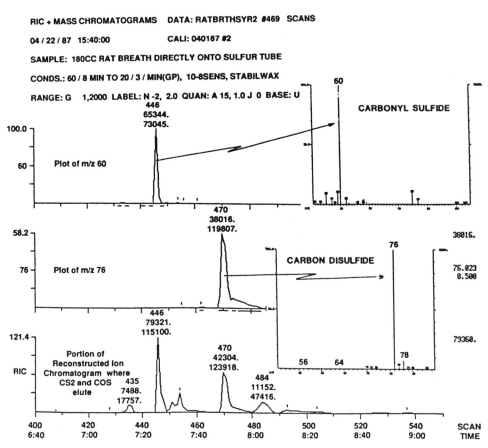

FIG. 9.1.   Reconstructed ion chromatograms of rat breath showing molecular ions for COS and CS_2. The spectrum of CS_2 consists mainly of the molecular ion m/z 76, the sulphur-containing isotope ion at m/z 78, and a small fragment ion at m/z 64. The spectrum of COS consists mainly of its molecular ion at m/z 60 and an isotope at m/z 62. From Galef et al. (1988).

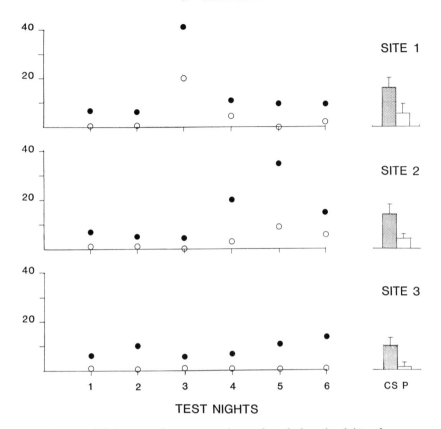

FIG. 9.2. (A) Consumption at several test sites during six nights of bait presentation. Open dots represent consumption (g) of unscented bait. Shaded dots represent consumption of CS_2-scented bait.
(B) Mean consumption at each site, collapsed across tests. Open and striped bars represent consumption (g) of unscented and scented baits respectively. Capped vertical lines show the standard errors of the means. From Mason et al. (1988).

of ingested diet and demonstrator-produced volatile signals provided important information. In a series of gas chromatographic/mass spectroscopic experiments, Galef, Mason, Preti, and Bean (1988) found that carbon disulfide (CS_2) is present on the breath of rats at a concentration of about 1 ppm. (See Fig. 9.1.)

When CS_2 is associated with diet, observer rats subsequently prefer the diet (Galef et al., 1988) and only acquire conditioned taste aversions for it with difficulty. Mice show similar preferences for CS_2, and the effect is stronger for females than it is for males (Bean, Galef, & Mason, 1988). When CS_2 is paired with diet in field tests with wild Norway rats (Mason, Bean, & Galef, 1988), consumption of diet is tripled (Fig. 9.2), and neophobia is significantly reduced.

It is possible that the attractiveness of sulfur compounds is related to the feeding strategies of the animal in question. Sulfurous odors appear to attract meat-eating species. Carbon disulfide is attractive not only to omnivores such as rats and mice, but also to primarily carnivorous species such as dogs and cats. Garlic odor (diallyl disulfide) is a flavor additive to dog foods (D. Passe, personal communication), and since successful coyote lure formulations always contain sulfurous odorants (G. Preti, unpublished), it is likely that sulfurous compounds are attractive to these canids as well.

Unlike carnivores and omnivores, there is both anecdotal information and empirical evidence that sulfur-containing compounds are repellent to herbivores. Grazing ungulates such as mule deer (*Odocoileus hemionus*) and elk (*Cervus canadensis*), as well as herbivorous rodents such as mountain beaver (*Aplodontia rufa*) are repelled by Big Game Repellent (BGR) (Campbell, personal communication), a complex mixture of ingredients (including sulfurous materials). Anecdotal information suggests that BGR may be attractive to coyotes. In the laboratory, CS_2 at 1 ppm (an attractive concentration to rats and mice) is strongly avoided by herbivorous guinea pigs (Mason, unpublished observations). Interestingly, gas chromatographic analyses of guinea pig breath samples indicates that no CS_2 is present, although hydrogen sulfide may be (Preti, unpublished observations).

The omnivore-carnivore/herbivore difference may span across Classes (Aves and Mammalia) as well. Among birds there is evidence that carnivores (e.g., turkey vultures, *Cathartes aura*) not only find food on the basis of sulfur containing volatiles (Houston, 1986; Stager, 1967), but also may reject meat on the basis of sulfurous compounds from carcasses that have rotted (Houston, 1986). Conversely, herbivorous species (e.g., Canada geese, *Branta canadensis)* avoid plants such as wild onion, perhaps because these plants exude sulfur-containing odorants (such as S-propyl propane thiosulfinate).

The origins of sulfur gases on the breath of omnivorous rodents remains unclear, although most likely, these materials are a result of bacterial fermentation (R. O'Connell, personal communication). If fermentation is the source of sulfur attractants, then a variety of intriguing but unaddressed questions arise. Would mice or rats raised without gut bacteria show preferences for foods paired with CS_2? Could preferences be altered by manipulating the kinds of bacteria present in the gut? Could preference for sulfur compounds be induced in herbivores inoculated with appropriate bacterial strains?

CONCLUSIONS

The ecological implications of differences among individual animal strains and species in taste and smell sensitivity and preference are obvious. Differences permit several species to co-exist in the same environment by utilizing different foods. Importantly, intraspecific variability in sensitivity (i.e., individual differences) permits the development of "skill pools" (Giraldeau, 1984), which permit individuals to survive changes in the availability of food types and to rapidly exploit newly available foods.

This generalization, however, is based on remarkably little in the way of rigorous comparative study. Attempts to characterize microadaptation of species' taste behavior and physiology to specific variation in available and exploited food sources are few. The study of monophageous animals could shed considerable light on the relationships between ecological niche and sensory worlds. In this regard, the aardwolf (*Proteles cristatus*) is almost unique (Richardson, 1987a, 1987b) as a carnivorous dog-like mammal which feeds almost exclusively on a single source, the unpalatable harvester termite (*Trinerviternes* sp.). These termites have a defensive sticky noxious terpene-based secretion and are avoided by virtually all other predators, vertebrate and invertebrate alike. In contrast, the aardwolf has evolved a series of anatomical and perhaps sensory adaptations which allow it to overcome the defense system and feed on this source exclusively so that it has been calculated (Richardson, 1987a, 1987b) that an animal consumes over 100 million termites/year. A study of this animal's taste sensitivity and preference would be fascinating and illuminating.

To return to the theme of this volume, it is assumed that sensory stimulation, in this case chemosensory experience, which though evolution has been associated with factors which benefit individual survival, has come to elicit pleasure. If this is so, the senses of taste and smell provide a forum for comparative investigation of hedonics which remains to be fully exploited.

ACKNOWLEDGMENT

Preparation of this manuscript and some of the work described was supported in part by grants NIH HL31736 and DC00882 and cooperative agreement 12-16-74-005 between the Monell Chemical Senses Center and the Animal and Plant Health Investigation Service, USDA.

REFERENCES

Abraham, S., Blaine, E., Denton, D., McKinley, M., Nelson, J., Shulkes, A., Weisinger, R., & Whipp, G. (1975). Phylogenetic emergence of salt taste and appetite. In D. A. Denton & J. P. Coghlan (Eds.), *Olfaction and taste*. New York: Academic Press.

Azen, E. A., Lush, I. E., & Taylor, B. A. (1986). Close linkage of mouse genes for salivary proline-rich proteins (RRPs) and taste. *Trends in Genetics, 2,* 199.

Barnwell, G. M., Dollahite, J., & Mitchell, D. S. (1986). Salt taste preference in baboons. *Physiology and Behavior, 37,* 279–284.

Bartholomew, G. A., & Cade, T. J. (1958). Effects of sodium chloride on the water consumption of house finches. *Physiological Zoology, 31,* 304–309.

Bartholomew, G. A., & MacMillian, R. E. (1960). The water requirements of mourning doves and use of seawater and NaCl solutions. *Physiological Zoology, 33,* 171–176.

Bartoshuk, L. M., Harned, M. A., & Parks, L. H. (1971). Taste of water in the cat: Effects on sucrose preference. *Science, 171,* 699–701.

Bean, N. J., Galef, B. G., & Mason, J. R. (1988). The effect of carbon disulphide on food consumption by house mice. *Journal of Wildlife Management, 52,* 501–507.

Beauchamp, G. K. (1987). The human preference for excess salt. *American Scientist, 75,* 27–33.

Beauchamp, G. K., Bertino, M., Burke, D. & Engelman, K. (1990). Experimental sodium depletion and salt taste in normal human volunteers. *American Journal of Clinical Nutrition, 51,* 881–890.

Beauchamp, G. K., & Bertino, M. (1985). Rats *(Rattus norvegicus)* do not prefer salted solid food. *Journal of Comparative Physiology, 99,* 240–247.

Beauchamp, G. K., & Cowart, B. J. (1987). Development of sweet taste. In J. Dobbing (Ed.), *Sweetness.* London: Springer-Verlag.

Beauchamp, G. K., Cowart, B. J., & Moran, M. (1986). Developmental changes in salt acceptability in human infants. *Developmental Psychobiology, 19,* 17–25.

Beauchamp, G. K., Maller, O., & Rogers, J. G. (1977). Flavor preference in cats *(Felis catus* and *Panthera* sp.). *Journal of Comparative and Physiological Psychology, 91,* 1118–1127.

Bell, F. R. (1959). The sense of taste in domesticated animals. *Veterinary Record, 71,* 1071–1079.

Berridge, K. C., Flynn, F. W., Schulkin, J., & Grill, H. J. (1984). Sodium depletion enhances salt palatability in rats. *Behavioral Neuroscience, 98,* 652–660.

Bertino, M., & Beauchamp, G. K. (1987). Salted food preferences in rats *(Rattus norvegicus)*: Responses to liquid milk products. *Appetite, 8,* 55–66.

Boakes, R. A., & Lubart, T. (1988). Enhanced preference for a flavor following reversed flavor-glucose pairing. *Quarterly Journal of Experimental Psychology, 40B,* 49–62.

Booth, D. A. (1987). Comments. In J. Dobbing (Ed.), *Sweetness.* London: Springer-Verlag.

Boudreau, J. C. (1986). Neurophysiology and human taste sensations. *Journal of Sensory Studies, 1,* 185–202.

Boudreau, J. C., Sivakumar, L., Do, L. T., White, T. D., Oravec, J., & Hoang, N. J. (1985). Neurophysiology of geniculate ganglion (facial nerve) taste systems: Species comparisons. *Chemical Senses, 10,* 89–127.

Brand, J. G., Teeter, J. H., Teeter, R. H., & Kare, M. R. (1989). *Chemical senses: Receptor events and transductions.* New York: Marcel Dekker.

Brindley, L. D. (1965). Taste discrimination in bobwhite and Japanese quail. *Animal Behaviour, 13,* 507–512.

Brindley, L. D., & Prior, S. (1968). Effects of age on taste discrimination in the bobwhite quail. *Animal Behaviour, 16,* 304–307.

Brodie, E. D., Nowak, R. T., & Harvey, W. R. (1979). The effectiveness of anti-predator secretions and behavior of selected salamanders against shrews. *Copeia,* 270–274.

Brower, L. P. (1969). Ecological chemistry. *Scientific American, 220,* 20–29.

Cade, T. J. (1964). Water and salt balance in granivorous birds. In M. J. Wayner (Ed.), *Thirst.* Oxford: Pergamon.

Cane, V. R., & Vince, M. A. (1968). Age and learning in quail. *British Journal of Psychology, 59,* 37–46.

Capaldi, E. D., Campbell, D. H., Sheffer, J. D., & Bradford, J. P. (1987). Conditioned flavor preferences based on delayed caloric consequences. *Journal of Experimental Psychology: Animal Behavior Processes, 13,* 150–155.

Carpenter, J. A. (1956). Species differences in taste preference. *Journal of Comparative and Physiological Psychology, 49,* 139–144.

Contreras, R. J., & Frank, M. E. (1979). Sodium deprivation alters neural responses to gustatory stimuli. *Journal of General Physiology, 73,* 569–594.

Cowart, B. J. (1981). Development of taste perception in humans: Sensitivity and preference throughout the life span. *Psychological Bulletin, 90,* 43–73.

Dawson, W. R., Shoemaker, V. H., Tordoff, H. B., & Borut, A. (1965). Observations on metabolism of sodium chloride in the Red Crossbill. *Auk, 82,* 606–623.

Denton, D. (1982). *The hunger for salt.* Berlin: Springer-Verlag.

Desor, J. A., & Beauchamp, G. K. (1987). Longitudinal changes in sweet preference in humans. *Physiology and Behavior, 39,* 639–641.

Dethier, V. G. (1977). The taste of salt. *American Scientist, 65,* 744–751.

Deutsch, J. A., & Jones, A. D. (1960). Diluted water: An explanation of the rat's preference for saline. *Journal of Comparative and Physiological Psychology, 53,* 122–127.

Duncan, C. J. (1960). The sense of taste in birds. *Annals of Applied Biology, 48,* 409–414.

Engelmann, C. (1934). Versuche uber den Geschmackssinn von Taube, Ente und Huhn. *Zeitschrift Verleichende Physiologie, 20,* 626–645.

Engelmann, C. (1950). Uber den Geschmackssinn des Huhnes, IX. *Zeitschrift Tierpsychologie, 7,* 84–111.

Epstein, A. N., Zhang, D. M., Schultz, J. Rosenberg, M., Kupsha, P., & Stellar, E. (1984). The failure of ventricular sodium to control sodium appetite in the rat. *Physiology and Behavior, 32,* 683–686.

Epstein, A. N., & Sakai, R. R. (1987). Angiotensin-aldosterone synergy and salt intake. In J. P. Buckley & C. Ferrario (Eds.), *Brain peptides and catecholamines in cardiovascular regulation in normal and disease states.* New York: Raven Press.

Erickson, R. P., & Corey, E. (1980). On the singularity of taste sensations: What is a taste primary? *Physiology and Behavior, 25,* 527–533.

Espaillat, J. E. and Mason, J. R. (1990). Differences in taste preference between red-winged blackbirds and European starlings. *Wilson Bulletin, 102,* 292–299.

Feare, C. (1984). *The starling.* Oxford: Oxford University Press.

Feare, C., & Wadsworth, J. T. (1981). Starling damage on farms using the complete diet system of feeding dairy cows. *Animal Production, 32,* 179–183.

Feigin, M. B., Sclafani, A., & Sunday, S. R. (1987). Species difference in polysaccharide and sugar taste preferences. *Neuroscience and Biobehavioral Review, 11,* 231–240.

Frings, H. (1951). Sweet taste in the cat and the taste spectrum. *Experientia, 7,* 424–426.

Galef, B. G., Kennett, D. J., & Stein, M. (1985). Demonstration influence on observer diet preference: Effects of simple exposure and the presence of a demonstrator. *Animal Learning and Behavior, 13,* 25–30.

Galef, B. G., Mason, J. R., Preti, G., & Bean, N. J. (1988). Carbon disulphide: A semiochemical mediating socially-induced diet choice in rat. *Physiology and Behavior, 42,* 119–124.

Galef, B. G., & Stein, M. (1985). Demonstration influence on observer diet preference: Analysis of critical social interactions and olfactory signals. *Animal Learning and Behavior, 13,* 31–38.

Galef, B. G., & Wigmore, S. W. (1983). Transfer of information concerning distant foods: A laboratory investigation of the "information-centre hypothesis". *Animal Behavior, 31,* 748–758.

Gentle, M. J. (1972). Taste preference in the chicken, *Gallus domesticus. British Poultry Science, 13,* 141–155.

Gentle, M. J. (1973). Diencephalic stimulation and mouth movement in the chicken. *British Poultry Science, 14,* 167–171.

Gentle, M. J. (1975). Gustatory behavior of the chicken and other birds. In P. Wright, P. G. Caryl, & D. M. Vowles (Eds.), *Neural and endocrine aspects of behavior in birds.* Amsterdam: Elvesier.

Gentle, M. J. (1976). Quinine hydrochloride acceptability after water deprivation in *Gallus domesticus. Chemical Senses, 2,* 121–128.

Gentle, M. J. (1978). Extralingual chemoreceptors in the chicken (*Gallus domesticus*). *Chemical Senses and Flavor, 3,* 325–329.

Gentle, M. J., & Harkin, C. (1979). The effect of sweet stimuli on oral behavior in the chicken. *Chemical Senses and Flavor, 4,* 183–190.

Geritsen, A. F. C., & Sevenster, J. G. (1985). Foraging behavior and bill anatomy in sandpipers. *Fortschritte de Zoologie, 30*, 237–239.

Gibson, E. L., & Booth, D. A. (1986). Acquired protein appetite in rats: Dependence on a protein-specific need state. *Experientia, 42*, 1003–1004.

Giraldeau, L. A. (1984). Group foraging: The skill pool effect and frequency-dependent learning. *American Naturalist, 124*, 72–79.

Glendinning, J. I. (1988). Overwintering monarch butterflies as food for mice (*Peromyscus melanotis, P. aztecus hylocetes, Reithrodontomys sumichrasti* and *Microtus mexicanus*) in Mexico. In *Biology and conservation of the monarch butterfly*, in press.

Greig-Smith, P. W., Wilson, M. F., Blunden, C. A., & Wilson, G. M. (1983). Budeating by bullfinches, *Pyrrhula pyrrhula*, in relation to the chemical constituents of two pear cultivars. *Annals of Applied Biology, 103*, 335–343.

Grill, H. J., & Bernstein, I. L. (1988). Strain differences in taste reactivity to NaCl. *American Journal of Physiology, 255*, R424–R430.

Grill, H. J., & Norgren, R. (1978). The taste reactivity test, I: Mimetic responses to gustatory stimuli in neurologically normal rats. *Brain Research, 143*, 263–279.

Grill, H. J., Schulkin, J., & Flynn, F. W. (1986). Sodium homeostasis in chronic decerebrate rats. *Behavioral Neuroscience, 100*, 536–543.

Gunther, W. C., & Wagner, M. W. (1971). Preferences for natural and artificial sweeteners in heat-stressed chicks of different ages. *Proceedings of the Indiana Academy of Sciences, 81*, 401–409.

Hanrum, C. L. (1953). Experiments on the sense of taste and smell in the bobwhite quail (*Colinus virginianus virginianus*). *American Midland Naturalist, 49*, 872–877.

Harder, D. B., Whitney, G. Frye, P., Smith, J. C., & Rashotte, M. E. (1984). Strain differences among mice in taste psychophysics of sucrose octaacetate. *Chemical Senses, 9*, 311–323.

Harriman, A. E. (1967). Laughing gull offered saline in preference and survival tests. *Physiological Zoology, 40*, 273–279.

Harriman, A. E. (1968). Rejection thresholds for critic acid solutions in cowbirds, starlings and red-winged blackbirds. *American Midland Naturalist, 79*, 240–242.

Harriman, A. E., & Kare, M. R. (1966). Aversion to saline solutions in starlings, purple grackles and herring gulls. *Physiological zoology, 39*, 123–126.

Harriman, A. E., & Milner, J. S. (1969). Preference for sucrose solution by Japanese quail (*Coturnix coturnix japonica*) in two-bottle drinking tests. *American Midland Naturalist, 81*, 575–578.

Harrison, J., Castonguay, T. W., Sclafani, A., & Rogers, Q. R. (1986). *Carbohydrate solution intake in young male cats.* Paper presented at the International Conference on the Physiology of Food and Fluid Intake, Seattle.

Heinroth, O. (1938). *Aus dem Leben der Vogel.* Berlin: Springer-Verlag.

Hill, D. L. (1987). Development of taste responses in the rat parabrachial nucleus. *Journal of Neurophysiology, 57*, 481–195.

Hill, D. L., & Przekop, P. R. (1988). Influences of dietary sodium on functional taste receptor development: A sensitive period. *Science, 241*, 1826–1828.

Houston, D. C. (1986). Scavenging efficiency of turkey vultures in tropical forests. *Condor, 88*, 310–323.

Hughes, B. O., & Wood-Gush, D. G. M. (1970). Investigations into specific appetites for sodium and thiamine in domestic fowls. *Physiology and Behavior, 6*, 331–339.

Ikeda, K. (1909). On a new seasoner. *Journal of the Tokyo Chemical Society, 30*, 820–836.

Jackinovich, W., & Sugarman, D. (1988). Sugar taste reception in mammals. *Chemical Senses, 13*, 13–31.

Jacobs, K. M., Mark, G. P., & Scott, T. R. (1988). The influence of sodium depletion on taste responses in the NTS of the rat. *Journal of Physiology, 406*, 393–410.

Jacobs, W. W., Beauchamp, G. K., & Kare, M. R. (1978). Progress in animal flavor research. In

R. W. Bullard (Ed.), *Flavor chemistry of animal foods*. Washington: American Chemical Society.

Jacobs, W. W., & Labows, J. N. (1979). Conditioned aversion, bitter taste, and the avoidance of natural toxicants in wild guinea pigs. *Physiology and Behavior, 22*, 173–178.

Johnson, B. R., Voight, R., Borroni, R., & Atema, J. (1984). Response properties of lobster chemoreceptors: Tuning of primary taste neurons in walking legs. *Journal of Comparative Physiology, 155*, 593–607.

Kare, M. R. (1961). Comparative aspects of taste. In M. R. Kare & B. P. Halpern (Eds.), *Physiological and behavioural aspects of taste*. Chicago: University of Chicago Press.

Kare, M. R. (1965). The special senses. In P. D. Sturkie (Ed.), *Avian physiology*. London: Bailliere, Tindall and Cassell.

Kare, M. R., & Beauchamp, G. K. (1984). Taste, smell and hearing. In M. J. Swenson (Ed.), *Duke's physiology of domestic animals* (10th ed.). Ithaca, NY: Cornell University Press.

Kare, M. R., & Beily, J. (1948). The toxicity of sodium chloride and its relation to water intake in baby chicks. *Poultry Science, 27*, 751–758.

Kare, M. R., & Mason, J. R. (1986). The chemical senses in birds. In P. D. Sturkie (Ed.), *Avian physiology*. New York: Springer-Verlag.

Kare, M. R., & Medway, W. (1959). Discrimination between carbohydrates by the fowl. *Poultry Science, 38*, 1119–1127.

Kare, M. R., & Rogers, J. G. (1976). Sense organs. In P. D. Sturkie (Ed.), *Avian physiology*. New York: Springer-Verlag.

Kasahara, T., Iwasaki, K., & Sato, M. (1987). Taste effectiveness of some D- and L-amino acids in mice. *Physiology and Behavior, 39*, 619–624.

Kawamura, Y., & Kare, M. R. (1987). *Umami: A basic taste*. New York: Marcel Dekker.

Larue, C. G., & LeMagnen, J. (1972). The olfactory control of meal pattern in rats. *Physiology and Behavior, 7*, 817–821.

Leon, M., Coopersmith, R., Lee, S., Sullivan, M. R., Wilson, D. A., & Woo, C. C. (1987). Neural and behavioral plasticity induced by early olfactory learning. In N. A. Krasnegor, E. M. Blass, M. A. Hofer, & W. P. Smotherman (Eds.), *Perinatal development, a psychobiological approach*. New York: Academic Press.

Long, C. J., & Tapp, J. T. (1967). Reinforcing properties of odors for the albino rat. *Psychonomic Science, 7*, 17–18.

Lush, I. E. (1981). The genetics of tasting in mice. I. Sucrose otaacetate. *Genetics Research* (Cambridge), *38*, 93–95.

Lush, I. E. (1982). The genetics of tasting in mice, II. Strychnine. *Chemical Senses, 7*, 93–98.

Lush, I. E. (1984). The genetics of tasting in mice, III. Quinine. *Genetical Research, 4*, 151–160.

Lush, I. E. (1986). The genetics of tasting in mice. II. The acetates of raffinose, galactose and β-galactose. *Genetic Research* (Cambridge), *47*, 117–123.

McBurney, D. H., & Gent, J. F. (1979). On the nature of taste qualities. *Psychological Bulletin, 86*, 151–167.

Martinez del Rio, C. and B. R. Stevens. (1989). Physiological constraint on feeding behavior: intestinal membrane disaccharides of the Starling. *Science, 243*, 794–795.

Mason, J. R. (1987). Ro-Pel efficacy: Evaluation of active ingredients under optimum conditions with red-winged blackbirds (*Angelaius phoeniceus*). Denver Wildlife Research Center Bird Damage Research Report No. 384.

Mason, J. R., Bean, N. J., & Galef, B. G. (1988). Attractiveness of carbon disulphide to wild Norway rats. *Proceedings of the Vertebrate Pest Conference*, 13:95-97.

Mason, J. R., Rabin, M. D., & Stevens, D. A. (1982). Conditioned taste aversions: Skin secretions used for defense by tiger salamander, (*Ambystoma tigrinum*), *Copeia*, 270–274.

Mason, J. R., & Reidinger, R. F. (1981). Effects of social facilitation and observational learning on behavior of the red-winged blackbird (*Agelaius phoeniceus*). *Auk, 98*, 778–784.

182   BEAUCHAMP AND MASON

Mehiel, R., & Bolles, R. C. (1988). Hedonic shift learning based on calories. *Bulletin of the Psychonomic Society, 26*, 459–462.

Mistretta, C. M., & Bradley, R. M. (1983). Neural basis of developing salt taste sensation: Response changes in fetal, postnatal and adult sheep. *Journal of Comparative Neurology, 215*, 199–210.

Mook, D. G. (1963). Oral and postingestal determinants of the intake of various solutions in rats with esophageal fistulas. *Journal of Comparative and Physiological Psychology, 56*, 645–659.

Morton, C. C., Cantor, R. M., Corey, L. A., & Nance, W. E. (1981). A genetic analysis of taste thresholds for phenylthiocarbamide. *Acta Genetic Medicine, 30*, 51–57.

Mugford, R. A. (1977). External influences upon the feeding of carnivores. In M. R. Kare & O. Maller (Eds.), *The chemical senses and nutrition II*. New York: Academic Press.

Myer, J. S., & Van Hemel, P. E. (1969). Saline as a reinforcer of barpressing by thirsty rats. *Journal of Comparative and Physiological Psychology, 68*, 455–460.

Percival, M. S. (1961). Types of nectar in angiosperms. *New Phytology, 60*, 235–281.

Pfaffmann, C. (1955). Gustatory nerve impulses in rat, cat and rabbit. *Journal of Neurophysiology, 18*, 429–440.

Posadas-Andrews, A., & Roper, T. J. (1983). Social transmission of food preferences in adult rats. *Animal Behavior, 31*, 748–758.

Rabe, E. F., & Corbit, J. D. (1973). Postingestinal control of sodium chloride solution drinking in the rat. *Journal of Comparative and Physiological Psychology, 84*, 268–274.

Reid, L. D. (1985). Endogenous opioid peptides and regulation of drinking and feeding. *American Journal of Clinical Nutrition, 42*, 1099–1132.

Rensch, B., & Neunzig, R. (1925). Experimentelle Untensuchungen uber den Geschmackssinn der Vogel II. *Journal of Ornithology, 73*, 633–646.

Richardson, P. R. K. (1987a). Food consumption and seasonal variations in the diet of the aardwolf (*Proteles cristatus*) in southern africa. *Zeitschrift der Sauetierkunde, 52*, 307–325.

Richardson, P. R. K. (1987b). The most specialized myrmecophagous mammal? *South African Journal of Science, 83*, 643–646.

Rogers, J. G., & Maller, O. (1973). Effects of salt on the response of birds to sucrose. *Physiological Psychology, 1*, 199–200.

Rowland, N. E., & Fregley, M. E. (1990). Sodium appetite: Species and strain differences and role of renin-angiotensin-aldosterone system. *Appetite*, in press.

Rozin, P. (1976). The selection of foods by rats, humans and other animals. *Advances in the Study of Behavior, 6*, 21–76.

Rozin, P. (1979). Preferences and affects in food selection. In J. H. A. Kroeze (Ed.), *Preference behavior and chemoreception*. London: Information Retrieval.

Schiffman, S. S., Sennewald, K. & Gagnon, J. (1981). Comparison of taste qualities and thresholds for D- and L-amino acids. *Physiology and Behavior, 27*, 51–59.

Schuler, W. (1983). Responses to sugars and their behavioral mechanisms in the starling (*Sturnus vulgaris*). *Behavioral Ecology and Sociobiology, 13*, 243–251.

Sclafani, A. (1987). Carbohydrate, taste, appetite, and obesity: An overview. *Neuroscience and Biobehavioral Review, 11*, 131–153.

Scott, T. R., & Mark, G. P. (1987). The taste system encodes stimulus toxicity. *Brain Research, 414*, 197–203.

Shingai, T., & Beidler, L. M. (1985). Interstrain differences in bitter taste responses in mice. *Chemical Senses, 10*, 51–55.

Stager, K. E. (1967). Avian olfaction. *American Zoologist, 7*, 415–419.

Stellar, E., Hyman, R., & Samet, S. (1954). Gastric factors controlling water and salt-solution drinking. *Journal of Comparative and Physiological Psychology, 47*, 220–226.

Stevens, J. (1985). Foraging success of adult and juvenile starlings (*Sturnus vulgaris*): A tentative explanation for the preference of juveniles for cherries. *Ibis, 127*, 341–347.

Stricker, E. M., & Verbalis, J. G. (1988). Hormones and behavior: The biology of thirst and sodium appetite. *American Scientist, 76,* 261–267.

Strupp, B. J., & Levitsky, D. A. (1984). Social transmission of food preferences in adult hooded rats. (*R. norvegicus*). *Journal of Comparative and Physiological Psychology, 98,* 257–266.

Sunderland, G., & Sclafani, A. (1988). Taste preferences of squirrel monkeys and bonnet macaques for polycose, maltose and sucrose. *Physiology and Behavior, 43,* 685–690.

Warham, J. (1971). Aspects of the breeding behaviors in the Royal Penguin (*Endyptes chrysolophus schlegeli*). *Notornis, 18,* 91–94.

Warren, R. P., & Vince, M. A. (1963). Taste discrimination in the Great Tit (*Parus major*). *Journal of Comparative and Physiological Psychology, 56,* 910–913.

Welty, J. C. (1975). *The life of birds.* Philadelphia: Saunders.

Whitney, G., Harder, D. B., Gannon, K. S., & Maggio, J. C. (1990). Congenic lines differing in ability to taste sucrose octaacetate. In C. J. Wysocki & M. R. Kare (Eds.), *Chemical senses: Genetics of perception and communication.* New York: Marcel Dekker.

Willoughby, E. J. (1971). Drinking responses of the red-crossbill (*Loxia curvirostra*) to solutions of NaCl, MgCl$_2$ and CaCl$_2$, *88,* 828–838.

Yang, R. S. H., & Kare, M. R. (1968). Taste response of a bird to constituents of arthopod defense secretions. *Annals of the Entomological Society of America, 61,* 781–782.

Zellner, D. A., Rozin, P., Aron, M., & Kulish, C. (1983). Conditioned enhancement of human's liking for flavor by pairing with sweetness. *Learning and Motivation, 14,* 338–350.

10 Taste Hedonics in Anorexia Nervosa and Bulimia Nervosa

Suzanne R. Sunday
Katherine A. Halmi
Cornell University Medical College

Anorexia nervosa and bulimia nervosa are disorders that involve abnormal feeding behavior. We know that taste hedonics affect food consumption in either positive (preferences) or negative (aversions) directions in nonhuman (e.g., Sclafani, 1987) as well as human (e.g., Kissileff, 1986) subjects. It is therefore reasonable to assume that differing hedonic judgments may underlie some of the abnormal eating patterns found in persons with eating disorders, and that patterns of taste perception and preference may be reflected in the actual food choice of these subjects.

Anorectics severely restrict their food intake, and clinical observations have suggested that many are exclusive vegetarians, who avoid sweet, fatty, and calorically dense foods, and hoard sweet, carbohydrate-rich candies. Several researchers have examined these anecdotal reports empirically; however, there is no agreement on the eating patterns of anorectics. Anorectics were reported to dislike and avoid sweets and other carbohydrates by researchers such as Crisp (1967) and Russell (1967). Drewnowski, Pierce, and Halmi (1988) have shown that anorectics have an aversion to fats and Beumont, Chambers, Rouse, and Abraham (1981) reported lower intakes of fats. VanBinsbergen, Hulshof, Wedel, Odink, and Coelingh Bennink (1988) found anorectic subjects to have an aversion to many sweets and starchy foods as well as some high fat foods, such as meat. Huse and Lucas (1984) found no "typical" macronutrient composition of meals in anorectic patients.

Several researchers have studied the eating behavior of persons with bulimia nervosa. Bulimics display recurring episodes of bingeing and purging and it has been assumed that binges consist largely of dessert foods that are high in calories, fat and sweetness. A few studies have been conducted in which the composition of binges has been examined. Rosen, Leitenberg, Fisher, and Khazam

(1986), using a self-report diary method over a 2-week period, found binges to contain a higher proportion of snack and dessert foods than nonbinge meals. Similar findings were reported by Mitchell and Laine (1985) in a hospital setting where food intake was monitored directly. Kissileff, Walsh, Kral, and Cassidy (1986) did not find differences in the macronutrient composition of binge and nonbinge meals of bulimics in a series of laboratory meal tests.

Although the findings concerning the macronutrient composition of meals and/or binges of eating disorder subjects are not clear, there is a strong indication that levels of fat and/or sweetness are involved. An exploration of the hedonic and sensory responses to fat and sugar in taste tests may elucidate the nature of the relationship in these subjects.

A number of studies have examined the relationship between body weight and hedonic responses to sweetness (e.g., Drewnowski, Brunzell, Sande, Iverius, & Greenwood, 1985). Most of these experiments have focused on obese subjects; only a few have explored reactions to sweetness among subjects with anorexia or bulimia. Garfinkel and his colleagues (Garfinkel, Moldofsky, Garner, Stancer, & Coscina, 1978; Garfinkel, Moldofsky, and Garner, 1979) found a lack of sucrose aversion following a glucose load (using Cabanac's procedure) in anorectic subjects shortly after diagnosis and after weight recovery. Drewnowski, Bellisle, Aimez, and Remy (1987) examined hedonic responses of bulimics to semisolid mixtures of fat and sugar and found that bulimics preferred higher levels of sugar and lower levels of fat than did controls. Drewnowski, Halmi, Pierce, Gibbs, and Smith (1987) using a slightly different methodology (see Drewnowski, 1984), reported that anorectics preferred sweet solutions and disliked high fat solutions and that bulimics preferred sweet solutions. The number of eating disorder subjects examined in this study was rather small (12 anorectics, 7 bulimics, and 13 anorectic-bulimics) and there was fairly large individual variation. We have continued collecting these taste test data on eating disorder subjects and now have sufficient numbers to examine more precisely differences between control and eating disorder subjects and across eating disorder subdiagnoses.

This study examines the sensory and hedonic ratings of solutions that vary in fat and sucrose concentration in anorectic, anorectic-bulimic, bulimic, and control subjects. Subjects were tested before and after weight restoration for the anorectics and before and after cessation of bingeing and purging for the bulimics to assess whether sensory responses, preferences, and/or aversions are related to the current physiological status of the individual (e.g., body weight) or are stable, trait characteristics of eating disorders.

METHOD

Twenty four subjects meeting the DSM-IIIR criteria for anorexia nervosa (AN-R), 26 subjects meeting the criteria for both anorexia nervosa and bulimia nervosa (AN-B), 17 normal-weight subjects meeting the criteria for bulimia nervosa (NW-B), and 15 normal-weight control subjects with no history of an eating disorder were tested. All eating disorder persons were receiving inpatient treatment for their eating disorder and were tested twice, once within the first week of hospital admission and once before hospital discharge. At the second test all subjects had been at a normal body weight and were free of bingeing and purging for at least 6 weeks. Controls were tested twice at similar intervals. All subjects were tested after fasting from 11 PM the preceding day.

Twenty solutions of varying levels of sugar and fat were used: four concentrations of sugar (0%, 5%, 10%, and 20% wt/wt) and five concentrations of fat (skim milk–.1% fat wt/wt, whole milk–3.5%, half and half–10.5%, heavy cream–37.6%, and a mixture of heavy cream and 15% safflower oil–52.6%). All solutions were served at 5°C in 10 ml paper cups. Subjects followed a standard sip and spit procedure and rinsed their mouths with water between each solution. Solutions were presented in random order.

Subjects rated each solution for pleasantness, sweetness, and fattiness. Hedonic ratings were made on a 9-point Likert scale which ranged from dislike extremely to like extremely with 5 being neutral. The two perceptual scales were unipolar 9-point Likert scales ranging from absent to extreme.

The data were analyzed using multivariant analyses of variance (MANOVA) for repeated measures, followed by specific univariant ANOVAs. Separate analyses were conducted for pleasantness, sweetness, and fattiness. All results reported were significant at the .05 level and all pairwise contrasts had alpha levels corrected using the Bonferroni procedure. Detailed statistical results of this and other related data appear in Sunday and Halmi (1990). Additional log-linear chi squares were conducted.

RESULTS AND DISCUSSION

The pre and posttreatment sweetness ratings appear in Figs. 10.1 and 10.2, respectively. Perception of sweetness was strongly influenced by sugar content of the solution with increasing levels being perceived as sweeter. This was true across all five levels of fat although the perception of sweetness was slightly modified by the fat content. For all groups, increasing fat concentrations slightly reduced the perception of sweetness. The only effect of diagnosis was that AN-B differed from controls in that their sweetness ratings declined for the highest fat solutions (52.6%) as compared with the 0% fat solutions. There was a slight effect of treatment. AN-R differed from controls in that their posttreatment ratings for the 5%, 10%, and 20% sucrose solutions were slightly lower, especially at moderate levels of fat.

Figures 10.3 and 10.4 depict fattiness ratings pre and posttreatment. The actual level of fat in the solution did affect subjects' perception of fat; higher fat solutions were perceived as being fattier. The perception of fat was, however,

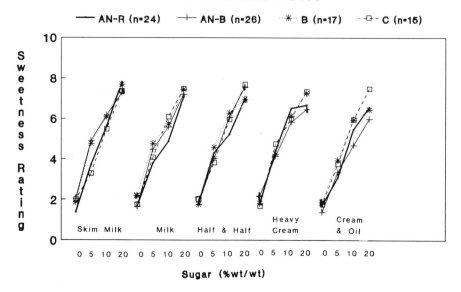

FIG. 10.1. Mean estimates of sweetness intensity as a function of sucrose concentration for each type of dairy product before treatment for eating disorder subjects and at first testing for controls.

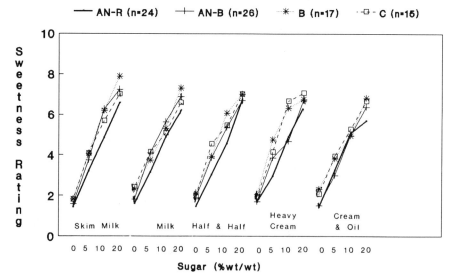

FIG. 10.2. Mean estimates of sweetness intensity as a function of sucrose concentration for each type of dairy product following treatment for eating disorder subjects and at second testing for controls.

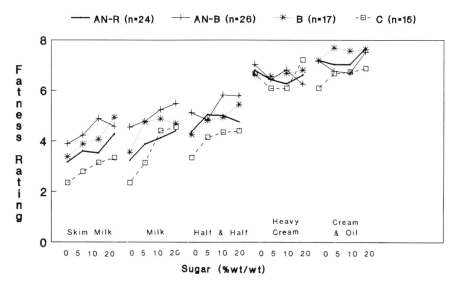

FIG. 10.3. Mean estimates of fat intensity as a function of sucrose concentration for each type of dairy product before treatment for eating disorder subjects and at first testing for controls.

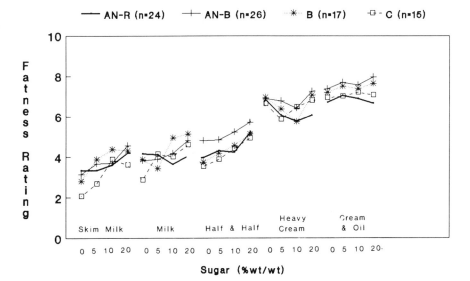

FIG. 10.4. Mean estimates of fat intensity as a function of sucrose concentration for each type of dairy product following treatment for eating disorder subjects and at second testing for controls.

more difficult than the perception of sweetness. Whereas the difference in intensity ratings between the four successive concentrations of sucrose was between 1.5 and 2 intensity units, the differences between the five successive levels of fat were .43, .57, 1.67, and .63 intensity units, respectively. Subjects were able to distinguish the high levels of fat (37.6% and 52.6%) from the other levels but finer discriminations were difficult.

The level of sugar in the solution also affected the perception of fattiness. At 0%, 3.5%, and 10.5% fat, increasing sucrose led subjects to rate solutions as being more fatty. Curves at 37.6% and 52.6% fat were fairly flat across increasing sucrose. There was no effect of treatment.

Pretreatment hedonic ratings appear in Fig. 10.5 and posttreatment ratings appear in Fig. 10.6. There was an overall effect of diagnosis, with AN-R giving lower ratings than controls. AN-R were also different from controls for sugar level; they showed a pronounced aversion to solutions which contained no sugar. AN-B were different from controls in that they showed an aversion to the high fat solutions, those containing 52.6% fat.

The relationship between hedonic ratings and fat concentration (with no sugar

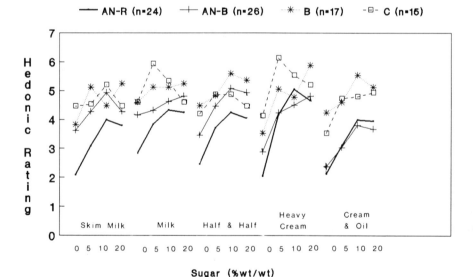

FIG. 10.5. Mean hedonic ratings as a function of sucrose concentration for each type of dairy product before treatment for eating disorder subjects and at first testing for controls.

Hedonic Preference Ratings
Posttreatment

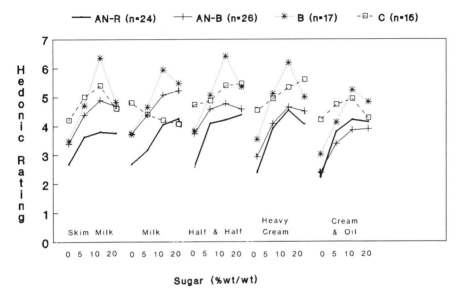

FIG. 10.6. Mean hedonic ratings as a function of sucrose concentration for each type of dairy product following treatment for eating disorder subjects and at second testing for controls.

added) in control subjects was very similar to that found by Mela (1988). Pleasantness ratings remained at the neutral point (approximately 5 on the 9-point scale) across all levels of fat. These results are somewhat different from those reported by Drewnowski. For example, Drewnowski, Shrager, Lipsky, Stellar, & Greenwood (1989) found that normal-weight subjects rated solutions with no sugar added as less pleasant with increasing fat concentration.

There were no differences across treatment for either anorectic group or for controls. There was a difference between NW-B and controls across treatment by level of sugar; after treatment, NW-B rated solutions containing 10% sugar higher than did controls. Posttreatment, NW-B showed an enhanced preference for the 10% sugar solution over the 0% and 20% solutions.

Bulimic patients did not differ from controls in their hedonic responses prior to treatment. This differs markedly from recent findings of Drewnowski, Bellisle, et al. (1987). Using slightly different stimuli (soft white cheeses with varying added levels of sugar), they found that normal-weight bulimics preferred sweeter and lower fat mixtures than did the controls. They did not specify past eating disorder histories of their bulimic subjects; it is possible that many of their subjects had a past history of anorexia which may have altered their hedonic responses. The different results also may have reflected stimuli-specific hedonic ratings. The usage of semisolid stimuli (Drewnowski, Bellisle, et al., 1987) or solid stimuli (Drewnowski et al. 1989) seemed to alter subjects' hedonic responses; therefore, it may be impossible to compare findings when different taste test stimuli are used. Bulimics may not differ from controls in their pleasantness ratings of liquid stimuli, however, when given more *normal* solid foods they may show a fat aversion.

We were curious whether the hedonic differences we found in our analyses reflected differences across our diagnostic groups in the usage of very negative hedonic ratings or very positive hedonic ratings. We therefore, decided to supplement our previous analyses with frequency analyses of low (ratings of 1, 2, or 3), moderate (ratings of 4, 5, or 6), and high (ratings of 7, 8, or 9) hedonic ratings across diagnosis and treatment for sugar and for fat using log-linear chi-squares.

The overall chi-square on sugar concentration was significant and there were a number of significant chi-squares for single degrees of freedom. Before and after treatment, both anorectic groups used more low and fewer high ratings for the 0% sucrose solutions. NW-B used fewer low and more high ratings for 10% sugar solutions, posttreatment.

The frequency analysis across fat concentration also yielded a significant overall chi-square. Pretreatment, AN-R were more likely to use low ratings at .1%, 10.5%, and 52.6% fat and showed the same tendency at 3.5% and 37.6% fat. Posttreatment, they were more likely to use low ratings at .1%, 3.5%, and 52.6% fat and showed the same tendency at 10.5% and 37.6% fat. Before treatment AN-B were more likely to use low ratings and less likely to use high ratings for the 52.6% fat solutions; after treatment they were more likely to use low ratings for those solutions. NW-B were less likely to use low ratings for the solutions containing the three lowest levels of fat after treatment.

Several researchers (e.g., Thompson, Moskowitz, & Campbell, 1976; Witherly, Pangborn, & Stern, 1980) have analyzed hedonic responses to sweetness by categorizing the shape of each subject's preference curve. We attempted a similar analysis by collapsing across fat level and examining individual hedonic patterns to sucrose level and collapsing across sucrose level and examining individual hedonic patterns to fat level. All individual curves were classified as either: (1) increasing (monotonic increase or a monotonic increase followed by a plateau), (2) decreasing (monotonic decrease or monotonic increase followed by a monotonic decrease), or (3) no clear pattern.

For the analysis across sugar level, very few subjects (ranging from 0 to 3 in each diagnosis) were placed in the no pattern group, therefore, the chi-square analysis excluded that group. Although the overall chi-square analysis was not significant, the majority of eating disorder subjects tended to show an increasing pattern for sweetness before treatment whereas the majority of controls tended to show a decreasing pattern for sweetness. Thompson et al. (1976) found lean and obese subjects displaying decreasing responses differed from those displaying increasing responses in hedonic ratings in that only subjects in the former group showed a decline in hedonic ratings following caloric loads. It is possible that our eating disorder subjects who showed an increasing pattern may differ from those showing a decreasing pattern in their responses to foods. We are currently exploring this hypothesis by examining hunger and satiety responses in subjects with increasing and decreasing hedonic patterns for sugar concentration.

Considerably more subjects showed a lack of pattern across fat level (ranging from 2 to 11 across diagnosis), therefore, that group was included in the chi-square analysis. The chi-square was not significant nor were there any differences between diagnoses. Most subjects showed a decreasing pattern both before and after treatment.

This study has shown that patients with eating disorders have no deficits in sensory perception of increasing sweetness or fatness of dairy solutions. There were, however, differences in preferences. Taste hedonics in anorectic patients were distinctly different from controls and did not change appreciably with weight restoration. These findings are consistent with those of Garfinkel et al. (1979); unlike controls, their anorectic subjects failed to demonstrate a satiety aversion to sucrose following a glucose load when tested in an emaciated state and when tested one year later at a normal weight. Anorectics demonstrated a pronounced aversion to solutions containing no sugar while anorectic-bulimics showed an aversion to high fat solutions. These taste preferences seem to be a stable trait characteristic of anorectics and of anorectic-bulimics and may be useful as prospective markers to identify persons at risk for these disorders. Normal-weight bulimics were the only eating disorder patients to show a treatment effect on taste hedonics. Their increased liking for the 10% sugar solutions is puzzling. This enhanced preference, however, did not reflect a change in perception since their intensity ratings for sweetness did not change with treatment.

There was little change in fat preference across the different fat concentrations. Unlike sweetness, which is most likely a "hard-wired" taste, fat is not a specific taste. Intensity of fattiness is most likely determined by response to texture (Mela, 1988), and is more difficult to discern, which may explain the small variation in fat hedonics. It is questionnable whether the level of fat is important for hedonic judgments. Anorectic-bulimics were the only subjects who showed any fat-related alteration in hedonic ratings and this was evident only at the highest fat concentration. The types of solutions used in this and similar experiments may not be best for examining perceptual and preference differences in eating disorder subjects. It is also likely that fat preference in eating disorder subjects may reflect a cognitive rather than a sensory process. If this is true, these subjects' attitudes toward foods may well reflect their assessment of the level of fat in the foods. We have begun a questionnaire study to assess this relationship and present some of the preliminary findings here.

Eating disorder subjects (12 AN-R, 7 AN-B, 13 bulimics with a past history of anorexia nervosa (B-AN), and 7 bulimics with no history of anorexia (B)) and control subjects (16 nondieters or so-called unrestrained eaters (U - those scoring in the lower third on the DEBQ (vanStrien, Frijters, vanStraveren, Defares, & Deurenberg, 1986)) and 19 dieters or so-called restrained eaters (R—those scoring in the upper third on the DEBQ)) were given a series of questionnaires. Subjects were asked, in part, to rate each of 38 common foods varying in fat, carbohydrate, and caloric levels on 9-point Likert scales for preference, how guilty or guilt-free the foods made them feel, and what they believed was the fat content of each food. The analyses of preference and guilt were conducted based on each individual subject's perceived fat content of the foods.

The preference ratings across perceived fat categories appear in Fig. 10.7. For all eating disorder groups and for the dieters, foods that were perceived as lower in fat were more highly preferred; that was not the case for the nondieting

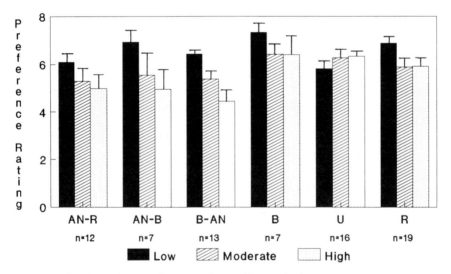

FIG. 10.7. Mean preference ratings with standard errors across low, moderate, and high levels of perceived fat for 38 common foods for eating disorder subjects and unrestrained and restrained controls. A rating of 1 indicates dislike extremely, 5 is neutral, and 9 indicates like extremely.

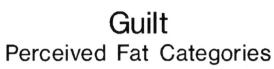

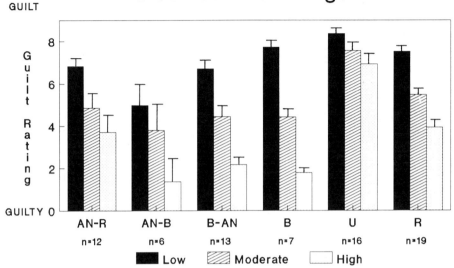

FIG. 10.8.   Mean guilt ratings with standard errors across low, moderate, and high levels of perceived fat for 38 common foods for eating disorder subjects and unrestrained and restrained controls. A rating of 1 indicates extremely guilty, 5 is neutral, and 9 indicates extremely guilt-free.

controls. This is consistent with findings of Drewnowski, Pierce, and Halmi (1988) in which their eating disorder patients were found to dislike high fat foods using a multidimensional scaling procedure. Figure 10.8 presents guilt ratings for perceived fat categories. Although nondieters (U) associated slightly more guilt with high fat than low fat foods, they associated significantly less guilt with all foods (particularly those perceived as containing moderate or high levels of fat) than did the other groups. The eating disorder subjects and the dieters associated more guilt with moderate fat than low fat foods and with high fat than moderate fat foods. All three groups of bulimics (AN–B, B–AN, and B) associated more feelings of guilt with foods they perceived as being high in fat than did AN–R or R. Ruggiero, Williamson, Davis, Schlundt, and Carey (1988) reported that subjects who binged and purged associated stronger negative emotions with moderate and high calorie foods (foods that were generally higher in fat) than did obese and control subjects. Although the findings of our food attitude study are preliminary due to the small n, they are suggestive that food preferences and feelings of guilt are strongly related to what eating disorder subjects perceived the fat content of the food to be.

It is interesting to note that bulimic subjects showed an aversion to food perceived as high in fat in this context but not toward the high fat taste test solutions. This may again reflect the lack of generalizability from the liquid sip-and-spit taste test stimuli to actual responses to solid foods. Lucas and Bellisle (1987) reported differences in subjects' preferences in a sip-and-spit taste test and in consumption tests with identical yogurt stimuli. We are currently testing our eating disorder patients utilizing a similar procedure to explore the relationship between taste and consumption.

In summary, anorectic subjects differed from controls in their hedonic ratings but not in their sensory ratings of fatness and sweetness of dairy and sugar solutions. Further, these responses did not change over time or with weight restoration, and may therefore reflect a trait difference in these subjects which may account, in part, for their food choices. These differences may have important implications for nutritional counseling of anorectic patients. Normal-weight subjects who were bingeing and purging did not differ from controls in sensory or hedonic ratings of the solutions. If bulimics do display differing food choices from control subjects, it would seem unlikely that those differences reflect different sensory or hedonic judgments.

ACKNOWLEDGMENT

This research was supported by NIMH grant MH43314 and NIH grant MH00516 and a grant from General Foods, all to K. A. H. The authors thank Beverly Pierce for help collecting the data.

REFERENCES

Beumont, P. J. V., Chambers, T. L., Rouse, L., & Abraham, S. F. (1981). The diet composition and nutritional knowledge of patients with anorexia nervosa. *Journal of Human Nutrition, 35,* 265–273.

Crisp, A. H. (1967). The possible significance of some behavioral correlates of weight and carbohydrate intake. *Journal of Psychosomatic Research, 11,* 117–131.

Drewnowski, A. (1984). New techniques: Multidimensional analyses of taste responsiveness. *International Journal of Obesity, 8,* 599–607.

Drewnowski, A., Bellisle, F., Aimez, P., & Remy, B. (1987). Taste and bulimia. *Physiology & Behavior, 41,* 621–626.

Drewnowski, A., Brunzell, J. D., Sande, K., Iverius, P. H., & Greenwood, M. R. C. (1985). Sweet tooth reconsidered: Taste responsiveness in human obesity. *Physiology & Behavior, 35,* 617–622.

Drewnowski, A., Halmi, K. A., Pierce, B., Gibbs, J., & Smith, G. (1987). Taste and eating disorders. *American Journal of Clinical Nutrition, 46,* 442–450.

Drewnowski, A., Pierce, B., & Halmi, K. A. (1988). Fat aversion in eating disorders. *Appetite, 10,* 119–131.

Drewnowski, A., Shrager, E. E., Lipsky, C., Stellar, E., & Greenwood, M. R. C. (1989). Sugar and fat: Sensory and hedonic evaluation of liquid and solid foods. *Physiology & Behavior, 45,* 177–183.

Garfinkel, P. E., Moldofsky, H., & Garner, D. M. (1979). The stability of perceptual disturbances in anorexia nervosa. *Psychological Medicine, 9,* 703–708.

Garfinkel, P. E., Moldofsky, H., Garner, D. M., Stancer, H. C., & Coscina, D. (1978). Body awareness in anorexia nervosa: Disturbances in "body image" and "satiety." *Psychosomatic Medicine, 40,* 487–498.

Huse, D. M., & Lucas, A. R. (1984). Dietary patterns in anorexia nervosa. *American Journal of Clinical Nutrition, 40,* 251–254.

Kissileff, H. R. (1986). Quantitative relationship between palatability and food intake in man. In: *Interaction of the Chemical Senses with Nutrition* (pp. 293–317). New York: Academic Press.

Kissileff, H. R., Walsh, B. T., Kral, J. G., & Cassidy, S. M. (1986). Laboratory studies of eating behavior in women with bulimia. *Physiology & Behavior, 38,* 563–570.

Lucas, F., & Bellisle, F. (1987). The measurement of food preferences in humans: Do taste-and-spit tests predict consumption? *Physiology & Behavior, 39,* 739–743.

Mela, D. J. (1988). Sensory assessment of fat content in fluid dairy products. *Appetite, 10,* 37–44.

Mitchell, J. E., & Laine, D. C. (1985). Monitored binge-eating behavior in patients with bulimia. *International Journal of Eating Disorders, 4,* 177–184.

Rosen, J. C., Leitenberg, H., Fisher, C., & Khazam, C. (1986) Binge-eating episodes of eating behavior in bulimia nervosa. *International Journal of Eating Disorders, 5,* 255–267.

Ruggiero, L., Williamson, D., Davis, C. J., Schlundt, D. G., & Carey, M. P. (1988). Forbidden food survey: Measure of bulimic's anticipated emotional reactions to specific foods. *Addictive Behaviors, 13,* 267–274.

Russell, G. F. M. (1967). The nutritional deficit of anorexia nervosa. *Journal of Psychosomatic Research, 11,* 141–149.

Sclafani, A. (1987). Carbohydrate taste, appetite, and obesity: An overview. *Neuroscience & Biobehavioral Reviews, 11,* 131–153.

Sunday, S. R., & Halmi, K. A. (1990). Taste perceptions and hedonics in eating disorders. *Physiology and Behavior,* in press.

Thompson, D. A., Moskowitz, H. R., & Campbell, R. G. (1976). Effects of body weight and food intake on pleasantness ratings for a sweet stimulus. *Journal of Applied Psychology, 41,* 77–83.

vanBinsbergen, C. J. M., Hulshof, K. F. A. M., Wedel, M., Odink, J., & Coelingh Bennink, H. J. T. (1988). Food preferences and aversions and dietary pattern in anorexia nervosa patients. *European Journal of Clinical Nutrition, 42,* 671–678.

vanStrien, T., Frijters, J. E. R., vanStaveren, W. A., Defares, P. B., & Deurenberg, P. (1986). The predictive validity of the Dutch Restrained Eating scale. *International Journal of Eating Disorders, 5,* 747–755.

Witherly, S. A., Pangborn, R. M., & Stern, J. S. (1980). Gustatory responses and eating duration of obese and lean adults. *Appetite, 1,* 53–63.

11 How Foods Get to be Liked: Some General Mechanisms and Some Special Cases

Debra A. Zellner
Shippensburg University

Humans are omnivores and as such ingest a wide variety of foods. Each individual likes or dislikes, to varying degrees, many of the foods that are available. These likes and dislikes are not static. They can change over the lifetime of an individual due to a number of factors. This paper is concerned with understanding hedonic shifts from negative to positive, i.e., how disliked foods become liked.

In particular, coffee and chili pepper are discussed because the most pronounced shifts in liking from negative to positive occur with these substances. They are initially rejected (often strongly) because of their bitter or "burning" properties but are often later liked. In fact, liking of these initially disliked foods often develops to such a degree that people become connoisseurs of them. They become aware of subtle differences in the flavor of various instances of these substances and may expend extra time, money, and effort to acquire their favorite coffee beans and chili peppers.

Coffee and chili pepper are initially disliked for different reasons. Coffee contains a number of bitter constituents including caffeine, and bitter substances appear to be innately rejected by humans (Steiner, 1973). Although the degree of initial aversion to coffee may be related to genetic factors which cause some people to be less sensitive than others to bitterness (Davis, 1978; Hall, Bartoshuk, Cain, & Stevens, 1975), liking for coffee still appears to be mostly an acquired taste.

Chili peppers are not initially aversive because of their taste in the technical sense, but because of the presence in them of capsaicin, an irritant. When eaten they cause a burning sensation in the mouth accompanied by lacrimation which many people, at least initially, find unpleasant.

Although the origins of the initial aversions for coffee and chili pepper are different, the development of liking for these substances may occur via some similar mechanisms. Some mechanisms may be the same as those that result in positive hedonic shifts for other, initially less aversive foods such as broccoli. Others may be more specific to bitters or irritants.

This paper tries to explain how such a large increase in liking occurs to substances that in the beginning are so aversive. Many other foods that are initially only slightly aversive (e.g., many vegetables such as broccoli) never become as liked as do chili pepper and coffee, even though the size of the hedonic shift needed to make them as liked is often smaller. What makes foods such as coffee and chili pepper special? In order to answer that question this paper discusses mechanisms by which hedonic shifts to foods may occur and addresses the possible contribution of these mechanisms to the development of liking for coffee, chili pepper, and broccoli.

LIKING VERSUS PREFERENCE

In discussing the mechanisms by which positive hedonic shifts occur I refer to research on both animals and humans. Much of the research deals with preference (differential intake) data rather than direct measures of liking for the flavors involved. A preference does not necessarily reflect a hedonic comparison. For example, an individual who consumes a salad rather than a hamburger may not like the flavor of the salad more than the flavor of the hamburger but rather may desire to lose weight or avoid red meat. Such people, when asked how much they like the flavor of the salad and hamburger might rate the hamburger as more hedonically positive. In such a case, therefore, preference does not reflect liking.

In the animal literature, preference data is difficult to avoid since it is almost impossible to have a rat provide a hedonic rating for a flavor. The only technique that produces something close to a liking rating in rats is the taste reactivity test (Grill & Berridge, 1984; Grill & Norgren, 1978), which measures positive and negative facial and bodily responses to infusions of solutions into the rat's mouth.

Although preferences do not inevitably reflect hedonic comparisons the two can coincide. I will often discuss preference changes as reflecting hedonic changes since, according to Rozin (1979), one can weakly infer that preference changes reflect hedonic changes if: (1) there is no reason to believe there is an instrumental basis for the preference and/or (2) the demonstration of the preference does not appear to depend on the physiological state of the organism. These factors should be kept in mind when examining the following data.

FACTORS THAT CHANGE LIKING

Mere Exposure

Increases in liking for items, including foods, appear to develop over repeated exposure to them (Zajonc, 1968). This has been found with liking for Chinese characters and pictures of men (Zajonc, 1968) as well as with food items. Pliner (1982) found that undergraduates' liking for unfamiliar tropical fruit juices increased with repeated tastings. Liking for novel cheeses and fruits in 2-year-olds has also been found to increase with frequency of tasting (Birch & Marlin, 1982).

These findings are supported by multidimensional scaling studies which found that familiarity accounted for the greatest proportion of the variance of food preferences in preschool children (Birch, 1979a, 1979b). Those foods that are more familiar are liked better.

Liking for coffee and chili pepper may also develop via this mechanism. Usually liking for these substances increases with repeated exposure to them (see Schweid, 1980, for a self-report for chili pepper). For example, chimpanzees exposed to increasingly piquant crackers eventually preferred them to plain crackers (Rozin & Kennel, 1983). This increase in liking with increased exposure to a food may be the result of familiarity alone. As Titchener (1921) suggested, familiar objects may be liked more than unfamiliar objects because they result in subjective feelings of recognition which are positive. Familiar objects cause an individual to experience a "glow of warmth, a sense of ownership, a feeling of intimacy" (p. 408), all of which are hedonically positive. However, Rozin (Rozin, 1984; Rozin & Kennel, 1983) points out that other mechanisms such as social factors may be at work during exposure. This view of the effect of repeated exposures was also taken by Thorndike (1935). He suggested that the increased liking of cod-liver oil reported by his subjects following repeated exposure "may be and usually [is] influenced by factors other than the mere repetition of the same situation" (p. 208).

This view is supported by the animal literature. When exposure is really "mere," rats do not show increased liking for chili and other irritants (e.g., black pepper) (Hilker et al., 1967; Rozin, Gruss, & Berk, 1979). Such exposure may also not increase liking for foods in humans. Eating flavored rat chow in a wire mesh cage must be the equivalent of getting your first taste of something in solitary confinement. I believe few people would come to like a food in this situation, even with hundreds of exposures. This isolation would certainly allow no social factors to work. When social factors are active as with chimpanzees and dogs who have a close social relationships with humans, preferences do develop for foods given to them by those humans (Rozin & Kennel, 1983). Even social contact with other animals while eating increases liking for foods in rats. Duncan, Buxbaum, and Tordoff (1987) found that rats prefer a food previously eaten in the presence of another rat to a food previously eaten in isolation.

Not only may social factors be at work during repeated exposure to coffee and chili pepper in humans but so may a number of additional factors which are discussed in this paper. For example, conditioning could be a factor (see Rozin & Zellner, 1985, for a review). Both coffee and chili pepper are usually consumed with other foods, allowing for flavor–flavor and flavor–calorie conditioning to occur. Coffee has potent pharmacological effects and repeated exposure to it may cause increases in liking through pairing with these effects.

Although it is well known that conditioning effects can be strengthened with repeated pairing, it may also be true that other mechanisms discussed in this chapter (benign masochism and opponent-process) may also benefit from repeated exposure. Repeated exposure to a food is therefore important for the development of liking for a food, whether or not mere exposure is itself a contributor.

Social Factors

Social factors could influence liking for foods in at least three ways (see Rozin, 1988, for a review). First, a person's family and cultural group could provide multiple exposures to a certain food, thereby causing liking for that food to develop. Second, liking for particular foods may develop through modeling others' behavior. Third, liking for foods may develop through conditioning if they are consumed in a pleasant social situation or if social reinforcement occurs as a consequence of eating the foods.

Many of the studies investigating the effect of social factors in liking for foods examine the relationship between the preferences of parents and their children. Because children eat most meals with their parents it seems likely that children's preferences would be similar to those of their parents. Children should have more exposure to the foods their parents like and therefore also like them. In addition, if modeling of others is a factor in getting to like a food, children's preferences should be similar to their parents' as the parents should be the primary role models.

However, studies looking at parent-child similarities find low correlations between parents' and children's food preferences (Birch, 1980a; Rozin, Fallon, & Mandell, 1984). Birch (1980a) found that preschoolers' food preferences are as similar to those of unrelated adults in the same subcultural group as they are to their parents'. Pliner and Pelchat (1986) also found that children's food preferences are similar to those of unrelated individuals. Both studies suggest that the similarities in liking of foods between children and their parents are due to cultural processes rather than familial ones. The foods the parents eat and thus expose their children to, are the same foods that others in their subculture eat frequently. However this does not explain the low correlations between parents and children. If children eat the same foods as others in their subculture, the correlations should be higher. Clearly, the mere exposure effect from the culture and family is only a minor factor in determining liking for foods.

Greater similarities in food preferences were seen between siblings than between parents and children (Pliner & Pelchat, 1986). This effect could be caused by the smaller range of foods accepted by children than by adults. This factor might also explain the low parent-child correlations. However, Rozin et al. (1984) also found low correlations between young adults' and their parents' hedonic ratings of foods (mean r = .152).

It is possible that children are more influenced in their food liking by what other children eat than by adult eating behavior because other children are better role models. Children may model the eating behaviors of other children because they are more like themselves. This phenomenon was demonstrated by Dunker (1938). Children's choices of foods were influenced by other children but not by a familiar adult. The tendency for children to come to like foods eaten by their peers has also been demonstrated by Birch (1980b). In her study, a target child was seated at a lunch table with a group of children, all of whom preferred the target child's least preferred vegetable. After 4 days of this procedure, the target child was choosing and consuming the originally least preferred vegetable. This shift in preference persisted even in the absence of the peer group. This shift may have been the consequence of modeling the behavior of a peer group, or of mere exposure. It could be that peer pressure caused the child to eat the disliked vegetable for 4 days and this amount of exposure itself resulted in a shift in preference.

In addition to allowing for exposure and providing models to imitate, social factors also can be used to condition shifts in liking for foods. Pairing foods with adult attention and pairing foods with praise for performing a behavior both causes increases in preference for the paired foods (Birch, Zimmerman, & Hind, 1980). Thus, foods paired with interaction with a pleasant adult increases liking for the foods through conditioning.

In fact, many of the shifts in preference demonstrated using social factors can be explained as conditioning effects. Marinho (1942) found that producing changes in children's food preferences was most effective when the peer models choosing a subject's less preferred food were liked by the subject. She concluded that, "In many cases not only kindness but a personal relation of friendship between the two children is necessary in order to obtain positive results" (p. 466). Likewise, people are more likely to purchase products paired with a celebrity they find attractive than one they find unattractive (Kahle & Homer, 1985). In both of these cases an item is being paired with a person who has positive hedonic value.

These three social factors (exposure, modeling, and conditioning) may contribute to the development of liking for coffee and chili pepper. People might come to like coffee or chili pepper because their family and/or culture eats them frequently and they have thus had much exposure to them (exposure), because their peer group consumes them (modeling), or because they have eaten them in a pleasant social situation with somebody they like, admire, or find attractive (conditioning).

Coffee and chili are consumed more frequently and liked to a greater extent by more people in some cultures than in others. Thus, exposure to and liking for these items seems to be correlated, at least cross culturally. For example, in one Mexican village Rozin and Schiller (1980) found that virtually all residents over the age of 5 or 6 ate chili pepper every day at all three meals. Americans surveyed in the United States ate chili pepper once or twice a week. Given the differences in numbers of exposures it is not surprising that 88% of the Mexicans they polled liked chili pepper as opposed to 68% of the Americans. In addition, 16% of Americans and only 4% of the Mexicans disliked it. Mere exposure could currently be working in the American culture at large to cause an increase in liking for chili pepper (especially in urban areas) since Tex-Mex, Cajun, and other ethnic cuisines using chili are becoming more readily available.

Although no analogous data exist for cultural differences in liking for coffee, Rozin and Cines (1982) collected some data in Philadelphia that are suggestive. Italian-Americans generally come from families having more coffee drinkers than do other ethnic groups (e.g., White North-Central Europeans). For Italian-Americans, social factors were the most commonly reported reasons for drinking coffee (versus taste, to wake up, etc.). This group also drank more coffee than many other ethnic groups and therefore had more exposure. Although the percentage of drinkers in the various ethnic groups is not available, other evidence points to the effect that this social exposure to coffee had on liking. The Italian-Americans in Rozin and Cines' (1982) study became regular coffee drinkers younger (by about 4 years) than did members of the other ethnic groups. In addition, the Italian-Americans gave hot coffee a higher (though not significantly) liking rating than did the other ethnic groups.

Modeling and other peer influence may be a significant factor in the development of liking for coffee and chili pepper. Rozin and Schiller (1980) found that among Mexicans, 77% said there was some pressure from friends or siblings to consume chili pepper. This suggests that social acceptance may reinforce eating of chilies, which may increase liking. That modeling peers and social acceptance may be a factor in chili pepper eating in the American culture is supported by anecdotal evidence. While in graduate school an acquaintance of mine had friends from the South-western United States who would frequent a Tex-Mex restaurant and have contests to see who could consume food containing the most hot sauce (available ad lib in a bottle on the table). Although this individual had never consumed chili pepper before, she added the hot sauce to her food (at first in small doses) because of the behavior of her peers and eventually could also take part in the contests (she became a member of the club). She also soon found herself developing a liking for the initially aversive substance.

Although there is no direct evidence that peer modeling is involved with coffee consumption it is not unlikely that it is. In addition, both coffee and chili pepper (at least in Mexico) might be consumed initially because of the desire to eat an adult food. Neither coffee nor chili is pushed on children (Rozin & Cines, 1982; Rozin & Schiller, 1980) but both *are* commonly consumed by adults. Adolescents may initially ingest these foods to appear more adult.

Again peer modeling and the desire to eat adult foods only explain why one would start consuming a food, not how one would get to like it, other than by mere exposure. However, if social acceptance is a consequence of eating chilies, the increase in liking may be the result of conditioning.

Eating the food in a family setting or in other social situations may result in the pairing of the substance with not only social acceptance, but also a number of other hedonically positive stimuli such as family, friends, or just a pleasant social situation. Pairing with these stimuli may result in a conditioned increase in liking for the foods. That such conditioning may occur is suggested by Rozin and Cines (1982). Fifty-six percent of the Italian-Americans in their study reported that they drank coffee for social reasons. Drinking coffee in our culture has typically been part of many social events (e.g., coffee breaks, coffee klatsches, and "going out for coffee"). Coffee is therefore frequently paired with good friends and conversation.

Chili pepper, is also eaten in the social context of the meal and is therefore paired with that social event as well as the food it is contained in (which is discussed in the next section). For my graduate student acquaintance it was paired with friends and a much needed night out from the lab.

Conditioning (Flavor–flavor Associations)

Hedonic shifts as a result of classical conditioning have been demonstrated for a wide variety of stimuli (see Martin & Levey, 1978, for a review) such as paintings, slogans, and potential sexual partners. For example, Razran (1940) found increases in liking for sociopolitical slogans when they were paired with the consumption of a free lunch.

Hedonic shifts for foods have also been demonstrated in both rats (Fanselow & Birk, 1982; Holman, 1975) and humans (Zellner, Rozin, Aron, & Kulish, 1983) as a consequence of pairing a food with a flavor of negative or positive hedonic value. Since such flavor–flavor pairings occur frequently over the course of a meal, they may be an important source of hedonic shifts for foods.

Rats decrease their preference for flavors previously paired with quinine and increase their preference for flavors previously paired with saccharin compared to flavors sampled the same number of times without pairing with quinine or saccharin (a control for mere exposure) (Fanselow & Birk, 1982; Holman, 1975). Inasmuch as saccharin has a hedonically positive taste but has no nutritive value, the increased preference is the result of flavor–flavor associations rather than an association of a flavor with postingestional consequences (see next section).

Hedonic shifts in both directions have also been reported in early studies on humans. A negative shift was found by Moss (1924). In his study, one subject (a child named Billie), had orange juice squirted into his mouth followed by, on occasion, a squirt of vinegar. The result was a decreased liking for oranges as evidenced by the following quote: "Before the experiment he [Billie] was very fond of oranges, but subsequently he lost all his relish for oranges and very much preferred apples" (p. 477). Positive shifts were reported by Gauger (1929). In her study, eating a small piece of chocolate after tasting an aversive flavor (salt solutions and vinegar) increased liking for the aversive substance. Unfortunately there was no control for a mere exposure effect so one cannot be sure that the results are due to a learned association between the two flavors.

That hedonic enhancement due to flavor–flavor associations occurs in humans over and above mere exposure effects has been demonstrated by Zellner et al. (1983). Subjects in this study consumed 24 samples of each of two beverages (herbal teas) during the conditioning phase. Throughout this phase, one of the teas was always sweetened with sugar while the other was always unsweetened. In the testing phase subjects were presented with samples of both teas, each of them sometimes sweetened and sometimes unsweetened, and asked for hedonic ratings. Higher hedonic ratings were given to teas that had been paired with sugar during conditioning (in both their sweetened and unsweetened versions) both on the day of exposure and 1 week later. Since subjects had an equal number of exposures to both the sweetened and unsweetened teas during conditioning, mere exposure can be ruled out as a cause of the effect. Because exposures to the two teas were randomly intermixed, the nutritive consequences of ingesting the sugar can also be ruled out as a possible UCS since those effects would have occurred following ingestion of both flavors.

These findings bear directly on the question of how people get to like the taste of coffee. Like the beverages used by Zellner et al. (1983), coffee is frequently consumed with sugar and/or cream added (Rozin & Cines, 1982). Both sugar and cream are hedonically positive to humans (Drewnowski & Greenwood, 1983). Thus, pairing coffee with one or both of these hedonically positive flavors may result in an increase in liking for the initially aversive coffee. In fact, a history of this pairing should result in people's eventually liking the flavor without cream or sugar.

Liking for chili pepper may also be influenced by pairing with other hedonically positive flavors since it is usually consumed as a flavorant in other foods. However, in the case of chili pepper, the foods it is added to are varied and are not as obviously hedonically positive as are cream and sugar in the case of coffee.

Conditioning (Postingestional Consequences: Calories)

An extensive literature demonstrates that rats easily associate the flavor of a food with negative postingestional consequences and subsequently avoid and dislike the flavor (Pelchat, Grill, Rozin, & Jacobs, 1983; see Riley & Tuck, 1985, for a bibliography of the conditioned taste aversion literature).

That negative postingestional consequences can cause a flavor aversion suggests that positive postingestional consequences might cause an increase in liking for a flavor. The usual consequences of eating a food include satiety or some nutritional outcome from the intake of calories. Pairing a flavor with calories increases rats' preferences for that flavor over others tasted equally often but not paired with calories (Booth, 1972; Fedorchak & Bolles, 1987; Mehiel & Bolles, 1984). For example, Mehiel and Bolles (1984) demonstrated that when one flavor is paired with sucrose and another with ethanol (both containing calories), the flavor paired with the solution with the caloric advantage was preferred. If the two flavors were given in isocaloric solutions no preference was seen. Such preferences conditioned by associating a flavor with calories are enhanced if rats are tested while hungry. Enhancement of the preference by hunger does not occur in flavor–flavor association-produced taste preferences (Fedorchak & Bolles, 1987). This result could mean that the flavor–calorie induced preference does not reflect a hedonic change but an instrumental response. That is, the rats consume more of the calorie-rich flavor when hungry for the nutritive consequences rather than because the flavor has become hedonically positive.

However, results with humans suggest that there may, in fact, be a hedonic shift. Booth, Mather, & Fuller (1982) found that associating a flavor with satiety causes an increase in liking for that flavor relative to a flavor presented an equal number of times but with low caloric content. Subjects showed an increase in hedonic ratings to starch-paired flavors they ate when hungry relative to flavors not paired with extra starch. The increase in hedonic ratings of starch-paired flavors did not occur if pairing occurred while the subjects were not hungry. In fact, a decrease in pleasantness of the starch-paired flavor was reported by subjects conditioned and tested while replete.

Both coffee and chili pepper might come to be liked through flavor–calorie associations. Chili pepper is usually consumed as an additive to food during a meal (usually eaten when the individual is hungry). Thus the chili pepper flavor could be associated with the consequences of ingesting the calories during the meal. An association of the taste of chili pepper with the consequences of ingesting calories should be extremely robust in cultures where chili pepper is used as a flavorant in almost all foods consumed, such as in Mexico (Rozin & Schiller, 1980). Under such circumstances chili pepper always signals calories. In the United States calories are signalled by many flavors and only rarely by chili pepper. Therefore, if flavor–calorie associations increase liking for chili pepper, chili-liking should be more common in cultures using it as a predominant flavoring, and it is (Rozin & Schiller, 1980).

Some evidence exists that in rats at least one postingestional consequence, recovery from thiamine deficiency, may increase preferences for foods containing chili pepper (Rozin et al., 1979). Seven pairings of a flavored diet containing chili pepper with recovery from thiamine deficiency resulted in a preference for this diet over a differently flavored safe diet. Also, although no preference was seen for chili pepper in a preference test between the recovery diet with and without chili pepper added, an attenuation of the initial chili aversion did occur. This effect was stronger when the animal was tested in the deficient state. Because recovery from thiamine deficiency is probably a more positive postingestional consequence than is recovery from hunger, the fact that the pairing only attenuated the aversion for chili pepper is not impressive. However, seven pairings are few compared to the number of exposures most chili-likers have had to chili pepper and even with only seven pairings a true preference for chili pepper was seen in one rat.

The case for positive postingestive effects' increasing liking is less convincing for coffee than for chili pepper. Although coffee is often consumed with sugar and cream, containing calories, it is also often consumed with nonnutritive sweeteners or alone. It is possible that liking for coffee develops more rapidly in people who initially drink coffee with sugar rather than a nonnutritive sweetener; however no data exist on this subject. The likelihood of seeing a difference in liking for coffee between nutritive and nonnutritive sweetener users is slim since coffee is consumed both during states of hunger (the first cup in the morning) and satiety (with dessert after a meal). When one consumes coffee when sated the additional calories from the sugar and cream should not be especially positive. The fact that coffee is consumed under various levels of food deprivation also argues against a strong influence of flavor–calorie associations on liking as coffee is not consistently paired with recovery from hunger.

Conditioning (Postingestional Consequences: Pharmacological)

In addition to providing calories and causing satiation, many foods have other, pharmacological, postingestional consequences. The pharmacological effects of the food itself and/or relief from withdrawal symptoms caused by addiction to the pharmacological effects of the food have been found to increase liking for the flavors associated with them in rats.

Zellner, Berridge, Grill, and Ternes (1985) found an increase in rats' liking for the taste of morphine, a bitter substance usually avoided by rats, following weeks of exposure to oral morphine which resulted in addiction. Using the taste reactivity test they found that the rats consuming morphine showed predominantly positive facial responses to infusions of morphine into their oral cavity while rats raised on water showed predominantly negative facial responses to morphine infusions. Long-term exposure to quinine did not result in similar appetitive facial responses to infusions of that bitter substance. This demonstrates a hedonic shift for the flavor of the morphine solution following experience with drinking it that is not simply the result of mere exposure. The effect is most likely due to association of the flavor of morphine with its pharmacological effects or relief from withdrawal.

However, in a study using human opiate addicts as subjects, the results were quite different. Pliner, Rozin, Cooper, and Woody (1985) found no difference in hedonic ratings of Tang or Tang with quinine between opiate addicts who had gotten an average of 1800 doses of methadone in Tang and control subjects who were not former heroin addicts. Even subjects who reported having nausea prior to ingesting the Tang with methadone and a relief of this symptom following ingestion evinced no increased liking for Tang.

Further investigation of the acquisition of liking for the taste of medicines revealed that although the flavors of some medicines can shift from the negative to the positive side of the hedonic scale, liking for initially aversive *foods* is much more common (Pliner et al., 1985).

One reason for the discrepancy between the findings with rats and humans may be that some cognitive factor occurs in humans but not rats that interferes with conditioning of likings to substances considered medicines (e.g., methadone–Tang). It is possible, for example, that humans attribute their consumption of medicines to some extrinsic reward (''I'm eating this so I'll feel better, not because I like the taste.''). This attribution may prevent increases in liking due to postingestional effects. This sort of phenomenon has been shown in a study in which children were given rewards (access to play activities) for drinking beverages. Liking for those beverages decreased (Birch, Birch, Marlin, & Kramer, 1982).

If consuming a substance for its medicinal effects interferes with the formation of an association between the taste and the postingestional effects, liking for the taste of coffee should not occur among those people who drink it for its pharmacological effect (e.g., alertness). Although this has not been directly studied, the data of Rozin and Cines (1982) hint at such a pattern. The two ethnic groups (Blacks and White North-central Europeans) containing many subjects who gave ''wake-up'' and ''other caffeine effects'' as their primary reasons for drinking coffee also had fewer subjects who said they drank it for its taste. Therefore, association of the taste with the pharmacological effects of coffee may be a more potent factor in getting to like the flavor of coffee only if one does not start drinking it specifically for its pharmacological effects.

The role of pharmacological effects in getting to like chili pepper is less clear than for coffee. Chili pepper is not eaten specifically for its pharmacological consequences. Most people report that they eat it because they like its taste, its burn, or the flavor it imparts to the foods it is added to (Rozin & Schiller, 1980).

Although chilies are rich in capsaicin which produces many pharmacologic effects (Buck & Burks, 1986), most people are unaware of any pleasant pharmacologic effects. Chilies are also rich in vitamins A and C, however the consequences of eating these vitamins are not as immediate or obvious as the pharmacological effect of coffee. As a result, even though purposefully eating chili pepper for its postingestional consequences will not interfere with conditioning, the fact that the postingestional effects are not very noticeable probably prevents them from contributing much to the development of chili pepper liking.

Other Conditioning Factors

In addition to association with liked others (see section on Social factors), good flavors, calories or satiety, and pharmacological effects, foods may come to be liked through association with other positive stimuli. For example, foods may come to be liked if they are consumed in pleasant surroundings, are served on attractive plates or in attractive cups, or sold in attractive containers. Through advertising, foods can also be associated with a multitude of attractive, hedonically positive stimuli. Some increase in liking for coffee and chili pepper could occur via these mechanisms.

Benign Masochism

When chili pepper likers are asked why they like chili pepper one of the most commonly given responses (79% of American and 85% of Mexicans) is that they like the burning sensation (Rozin & Schiller, 1980). This has led Rozin and his colleagues (Rozin, 1979; Rozin & Schiller, 1980) to suggest that people get to like chili pepper *because* of its irritant effects, not in spite of them. According to this theory eating chili pepper is similar to riding a roller coaster. Both cause unpleasant feelings initially but after one discovers that they don't (or rarely) lead to negative consequences (permanent damage) they become liked. Engaging in an activity which only appears to be dangerous is what causes the enjoyment of these initially negative sensations.

Evidence for this idea comes from a study by Logue and Smith (1986) showing a small positive correlation between liking for spicy foods and scores on Zuckerman's Sensation Seeking Scale (Zuckerman, 1979). The Sensation Seeking Scale tests for a personality trait that includes thrill seeking, experience seeking, susceptibility to boredom and other related characteristics. The correlation between these traits and liking chili suggests that some people may come to like the irritant effects because of the idea that they are flirting with danger.

Opponent-Process

The opponent-process theory of motivation holds that hedonically negative events result in a central nervous system response which opposes the negative feelings (Solomon, 1980). This opponent response increases in strength with repeated exposure to the negative event, reducing its aversiveness. In addition, the hedonically positive opponent is slower to decay than the negative feelings caused by the event, resulting in a positive feeling following termination of the unpleasant event. This theory has been used to explain the "high" following jogging and parachuting.

The opponent-process theory has also been entertained as an explanation of how people come to like the burn of chili pepper (Rozin, Ebert, & Schull, 1982; Rozin & Vollmecke, 1986). The painful burn caused by chili pepper in the mouth may result in the release of endogenous opiates in the brain to counteract the painful burn. Following multiple experiences with chili pepper, larger and larger amounts of these endogenous opiates may be released resulting in an affectively neutral response initially, followed by a hedonically positive response.

That endogenous opiates play a role in liking for foods is supported by data showing that humans given the opiate antagonist, naltrexone, decrease their liking for sucrose and food odors but not for nonfood odors (Fantino, Hosotte, & Apfelbaum, 1986). In addition, the presence of stress-producing stimuli (loud noise and music) has been found to increase hedonic ratings for sucrose (Ferber & Cabanac, 1987). As chili pepper causes an aversive effect on its own it is possible that it also causes increased release of endogenous opiates above baseline levels. According to the opponent-process theory, this release increases with the number of exposures resulting in eventual liking for the chili pepper.

A similar mechanism could possibly work for coffee, however, the effect should be weaker since the bitterness of coffee should not result in a stress response as large as that to the burn of chili pepper.

Expectations

Initial hedonically negative expectations about a food may actually play a role in the formation of a preference. If people expect a food to be worse than it actually is when they taste it they are pleasantly surprised and like it more than they would if they did not hold these negative expectations. This mechanism has been used to explain people's satisfaction with hospital food (Feldman, 1962). People generally hold the belief that hospital food is terrible and when it proves not to be as bad as they expected they rate it as satisfactory. That same food would not, however, be rated as satisfactory if eaten at an expensive restaurant where expectations would be higher.

Although one can imagine how violations of a negative expectation could enhance the hedonic rating of a substance, one study suggests that any violation of expectations is negative. Carlsmith and Aronson (1963) found saccharin and quinine solutions to be judged as more unpleasant on trials where subjects' expectations concerning what they were going to consume were violated. The quinine was rated as more bitter and the sugar was rated as less sweet than on trials where the subject had no expectation of which solution was to follow.

Violations of expectations concerning foods usually do result in a negative hedonic shift either because violations are inherently negative or because we are expecting a certain liked flavor and instead experience a different flavor which is not as good or as familiar. The result is that the unfamiliar flavor is liked less than it would be had we been expecting a novel flavor. Carlson (1930) relates a poignant instance of this phenomenon.

> I had never eaten fresh tomatoes until I was fifteen years old—I had never seen them. . . . The first time I saw a ripe red tomato I thought it was some new kind of apple. I was fond of apples, so I got one and bit into it, and the disgusting, disagreeable effect on me of that fluid, insipid, warm mass that filled my mouth was something very striking, and I have not forgotten it in forty years. (p. 89)

Nevertheless, although there is little support for the idea that expecting the worst of a food may increase its hedonic rating, it remains a possibility. If it is a factor, it most certainly should work in increasing the hedonic ratings of both chili pepper and coffee. Coffee has the reputation of being very bitter. Chili pepper has the reputation for *burning* your mouth which is probably strengthened in some people by watching others eat it and seeing the results (e.g., runny eyes and nose, and gasping). The actual experience of consuming either of these two items may be much less aversive than their reputations lead a person to expect.

DISCUSSION

Obviously there are many factors that can be at work in increasing liking for a food. I have discussed some of them and there may be more. However, the question of how such a large shift to the positive occurs to initially aversive substances such as coffee and chili pepper still remains. Large affective shifts should be more difficult to produce than small ones yet the number of people in the world who like coffee and chili pepper and cannot imagine living without them is enormous. Why is the hedonic shift that occurs for these substances so extreme compared to that for, say, broccoli? Broccoli is generally not as initially as aversive as coffee or chili pepper but rarely comes to be liked as much as either of them.

I suggest that the reason coffee and chili pepper become so hedonically positive is that they engage more of the above mechanisms to a greater degree than do other foods which are less initially aversive such as broccoli. (See Table 11.1). Although exposure to a food may not itself cause an increase in liking for that food it allows other processes to work. Exposure is therefore the most important mechanism. Not only may it increase liking on its own, but the more

TABLE 11.1
Mechanisms' Contibutions to Liking[a]

Mechanism	Coffee	Chili	Broccoli
Mere exposure	2	2	1
Social factors (exposure and modeling)	2	2	0
Social conditioning	2	1	1
Flavor-flavor conditioning	2	1	1
Flavor-calorie conditioning	1	2	1
Flavor-pharmacological conditioning	2	0	0
Benign Masochism	0	2	0
Opponent-process	1	2	1
Violation of expectations	1	1	0
Total	13	13	5

a(0) - none, (1) - some, (2) - a lot.

exposure one has to a food the more chance there is for liking to develop through other mechanisms. Exposure to coffee and chili pepper is generally greater than to other foods which may be initially less disliked (e.g., broccoli). The reason for the greater exposure has to do with social factors. Coffee and chili pepper are in many cultures an important part of the cuisine. Therefore a child is frequently exposed to these items because they are constantly around. They are not as easy to avoid as is broccoli.

Also, there is generally social modeling of peers in consumption of coffee and chili pepper which is made even stronger because these items are thought to be ''adult'' foods or because, in the case of chili pepper, it is perceived to be risky.

Eating coffee and chili pepper is often met with more reinforcing social consequences than is eating broccoli. In adolescence, peers are much more likely to be impressed if one drinks coffee or eats chili pepper than if one eats broccoli. Similar social reinforcement occurs with some adults in the United States now that chili-rich cuisines such as Cajun and Thai are becoming fashionable. Other positive events are also more likely to be associated with coffee and chili pepper than with broccoli. Coffee is more often associated with social events, as is chili (since it is often eaten in restaurants—unless you are from an ethnic group that consumes it avidly or you are a good cook) than is broccoli. In addition, positive flavor–flavor conditioning through pairing with hedonically positive sugar and cream occurs more frequently with coffee than it does with most other foods, especially when one initially begins drinking it. Coffee, unlike most other food items, is also associated with a strong pharmacological postingestional effect (unless ones drinks decaf). The increase in alertness following coffee drinking is a positive effect that few other foods produce.

Chili pepper is probably also more strongly associated with positive postingestional consequences (calories) than are other foods. Because chili pepper is generally a flavoring (usually the most salient) in the food considered the main part of the meal it is more frequently associated with satiety and calories than are other foods, especially in cultures using it as a predominant flavoring (e.g., Mexican).

Chili pepper may also get to be liked because it is one of the few food substances that produces a thrill. This safe thrill by itself may increase liking of chili pepper in thrill-seeking individuals or it may cause a release of endogenous opiates (or some similar positive physiological response) which dominates the aversive burn after a number of exposures via an opponent-process.

Clearly, coffee and chili pepper have properties that allow several mechanisms to work that are known to cause positive hedonic shifts. The large numbers of exposures that some people have to these two substances should increase the effect of these mechanisms. Multiple mechanisms all serving to increase liking, repeated a large of number of times, may be enough to make even a very aversive substance liked more than most foods. (See Table 11.1). However, it could be that the initial exposure to these substances is not as negative as we think. Having extremely bad expectations concerning the taste of chili pepper and coffee might make them better than they would be if one had positive or no expectations. This factor could decrease the distance they have to move to reach the top of the hedonic scale where they often wind up.

ACKNOWLEDGMENTS

Thanks to Scott Parker and Paul Rozin for their helpful comments on earlier drafts of this manuscript.

Preparation of this manuscript was supported by a Shippensburg University Summer Stipend.

REFERENCES

Birch, L. L. (1979a). Dimensions of preschool children's food preferences. *Journal of Nutrition Education, 11,* 77–80.

Birch, L. L. (1979b). Preschool children's food preferences and consumption patterns. *Journal of Nutrition Education, 11,* 189–192.

Birch, L. L. (1980a). The relationship between children's food preferences and those of their parents. *Journal of Nutrition Education, 12,* 14–18.

Birch, L. L. (1980b). Effects of peer models' food choices and eating behaviors on preschoolers' food preferences. *Child Development, 51,* 489–496.

Birch, L. L., Birch, D., Marlin, D., & Kramer, L. (1982). Effects of instrumental eating on children's food preferences. *Appetite, 2,* 125–134.

Birch, L. L., & Marlin, D. W. (1982). I don't like it; I never tried it: Effects of exposure on two-year-old children's food preferences. *Appetite, 3,* 353–360.

Birch, L. L., Zimmerman, S. I., & Hind, H. (1980). The influence of social-affective context on the formation of children's food preferences. *Child Development, 51,* 856–861.

Booth, D. A. (1972). Conditioned satiety in the rat. *Journal of Comparative and Physiological Psychology, 81*, 457–471.

Booth, D. A., Mather, P., & Fuller, J. (1982). Starch content of ordinary foods associatively conditions human appetite and satiation, indexed by intake and eating pleasantness of starch-paired flavours. *Appetite, 3*, 163–184.

Buck, S. H., & Burks, T. F. (1986). The neuropharmacology of capsaicin: Review of some recent observations. *Pharmacological Reviews, 38*, 179–226.

Carlsmith, J. M., & Aronson, E. (1963). Some hedonic consequences of the confirmation and disconfirmation of expectancies. *Journal of Abnormal and Social Psychology, 66*, 151–156.

Carlson, A. J. (1930). Physiology of hunger and appetite in relation to the emotional life of the child. In *The Child's Emotions: Proceedings of the Mid-West Conference on Character Development* (pp. 81–90). Chicago: The University of Chicago Press.

Davis, R. G. (1978). Increased bitter taste detection thresholds in Yucatan inhabitants related to coffee as a dietary source of niacin. *Chemical Senses and Flavour, 3*, 423–429.

Drewnowski, A., & Greenwood, M R C (1983). Cream and sugar: Human preferences for high-fat foods. *Physiology and Behavior, 30*, 629–633.

Duncan, H. J., Buxbaum, A., & Tordoff, M. G. (1987). Rats eating together prefer the taste of their food. In S. D. Roper & J. Atema (Eds.), *Olfaction and taste IX, Annals of the New York Academy of Sciences, 510*, 263–264.

Dunker, K. (1938). Experimental modification of children's food preferences through social suggestion. *Journal of Abnormal and Social Psychology, 33*, 489–507.

Fanselow, M., & Birk, J. (1982). Flavor–flavor associations induce hedonic shifts in taste preference. *Animal Learning and Behavior, 10*, 223–228.

Fantino, M., Hosotte, J., & Apfelbaum, M. (1986). An opioid antagonist, naltrexone, reduces the preference for sucrose in man. *American Journal of Physiology, 251*, R91–R96.

Fedorchak, P. M., & Bolles, R. C. (1987). Hunger enhances the expression of calorie- but not taste-mediated conditioned flavor preferences. *Journal of Experimental Psychology: Animal Behavior Processes, 13*, 73–79.

Feldman, J. J. (1962). Patients' opinions of hospital food. *Journal of the American Dietetic Association, 40*, 325–329.

Ferber, C., & Cabanac, M. (1987). Influence of noise on gustatory affective ratings and preferences for sweet or salt. *Appetite, 8*, 229–235.

Gauger, M. (1929). The modifiability of response to taste stimuli in the preschool child. In *Contributions to Education*, No. 348. New York: Bureau of Publications, Teacher's College, Columbia University.

Grill, H. J., & Berridge, K. C. (1984). Taste reactivity as a measure of the neural control of palatability. In J. M. Sprague & A. N. Epstein (Eds.), *Progress in Psychobiology and Physiological Psychology*. New York: Academic Press.

Grill, H. J., & Norgren, R. (1978). The taste reactivity test: I. Mimetic responses to gustatory stimuli in neurologically normal rats. *Brain Research, 143*, 263–279.

Hall, M. J., Bartoshuk, L. M., Cain, W. S., & Stevens, J. C. (1975). PTC taste blindness and the taste of caffeine. *Nature, 253*, 442–443.

Hilker, D. M., Hee, J., Higashi, J., Ikehara, S., & Paulsen, E. (1967). Free choice consumption of spiced diets by rats. *Journal of Nutrition, 91*, 129–131.

Holman, E. (1975). Immediate and delayed reinforcers for flavor preferences in rats. *Learning and Motivation, 6*, 91–100.

Kahle, L. R., & Homer, P. M. (1985). Physical attractiveness of the celebrity endorser: A social adaptation perspective. *Journal of Consumer Research, 11*, 954–961.

Logue, A. W., & Smith, M. E. (1986). Predictors of food preferences in adult humans. *Appetite, 7*, 109–125.

Marinho, H. (1942). Social influence in the formation of enduring preferences. *Journal of Abnormal and Social Psychology, 37,* 448–468.

Martin, I., & Levey, A. (1978). Evaluative conditioning. *Advances in Behavior Research and Therapy, 1,* 57–102.

Mehiel, R., & Bolles, R. C. (1984). Learned flavor preferences based on caloric outcome. *Animal Learning and Behavior, 12,* 421–427.

Moss, F. A. (1924). Note on building likes and dislikes in children. *Journal of Experimental Psychology, 7,* 475–478.

Pelchat, M., Grill, H., Rozin, P., & Jacobs, J. (1983). Quality of acquired responses to tastes depends on type of associated discomfort. *Journal of Comparative Psychology, 97,* 140–153.

Pliner, P. (1982). The effects of mere exposure on liking for edible substances. *Appetite, 3,* 283–290.

Pliner, P., & Pelchat, M. L. (1986). Similarities in food preferences between children and their siblings and parents. *Appetite, 7,* 333–342.

Pliner, P., Rozin, P., Cooper, M., & Woody, G. (1985). Role of specific postingestional effects and medicinal context in the acquisition of liking for tastes. *Appetite, 6,* 243–252.

Razran, G. (1940). Conditioned response changes in rating and appraising sociopolitical slogans. *Psychological Bulletin, 37,* 481. (Abstract)

Riley, A. L., & Tuck, D. L. (1985). Conditioned taste aversions: A bibliography. In N. S. Braveman & P. Bronstein (Eds.), *Experimental assessments and clinical applications of conditioned food aversions, Annals of the New York Academy of Sciences, 443,* 381–436.

Rozin, P. (1979). Preference and affect in food selection. In J. H. A. Kroeze (Ed.), *Preference behavior and chemoreception* (pp. 289–302). London: Information Retrieval.

Rozin, P. (1984). The acquisition of food habits and preferences. In J. D. Matarazzo, S. M. Weiss, J. A. Herd, N. E. Miller, & S. M. Weiss (Eds.), *Behavioral health: A handbook of health enhancement and disease prevention,* (pp. 590–607). New York: Wiley.

Rozin, P. (1988). Social learning about food by humans. In T. R. Zentall & B. G. Galef, Jr. (Eds.), *Social learning: Psychological and biological perspectives,* (pp. 165–187). Hillsdale, NJ: Lawrence Erlbaum Associates.

Rozin, P., & Cines, B. M. (1982). Ethnic differences in coffee use and attitudes to coffee. *Ecology of food and nutrition, 12,* 79–88.

Rozin, P., Ebert, L., & Schull, J. (1982). Some like it hot: A temporal analysis of hedonic responses to chili pepper. *Appetite, 3,* 13–22.

Rozin, P., Fallon, A., & Mandell, R. (1984). Family resemblance in attitudes to foods. *Developmental Psychology, 20,* 309–314.

Rozin, P., Gruss, L., & Berk, G. (1979). Reversal of innate aversions: Attempts to induce a preference for chili peppers in rats. *Journal of Comparative and Physiological Psychology, 93,* 1001–1014.

Rozin, P., & Kennel, K. (1983). Acquired preferences for piquant foods by chimpanzees. *Appetite, 4,* 69–77.

Rozin, P., & Schiller, D. (1980). The nature and acquisition of a preference for chili pepper by humans. *Motivation and Emotion, 4,* 77–101.

Rozin, P., & Vollmecke, T. A. (1986). Food likes and dislikes. *Annual Review of Nutrition, 6,* 433–456.

Rozin, P., & Zellner, D. A. (1985). The role of Pavlovian conditioning in the acquisition of food likes and dislikes. In N. S. Braveman & P. Bronstein (Eds.), *Experimental assessments and clinical applications of conditioned food aversions, Annals of the New York Academy of Sciences, 443,* 189–202.

Schweid, R. (1980). *Hot peppers: Cajuns and capsicum in New Iberia, Louisiana.* Seattle, WA: Madrona Publishers.

Solomon, R. L. (1980). The opponent-process theory of acquired motivation: The costs of pleasure and the benefit of pain. *American Psychologist, 35,* 691–712.

Steiner, J. E. (1973). The human gustofacial response. In J. F. Bosma (Ed.), *Fourth symposium on oral sensation and perception: Development in the fetus and infant* [DHEW Publication No. (NIH) 73-546, pp. 254–278). Bethesda, MD: U.S. Department of Health, Education, and Welfare, National Institute of Health.

Thorndike, E. (1935). *The psychology of wants, interests, and attitudes.* New York: Appleton-Century.

Titchener, E. B. (1921). *A text-book of psychology.* New York: Macmillan.

Zajonc, R. (1968). Attitudinal effects of mere exposure. *Journal of Personality and Social Psychology, 9,* 1–27.

Zellner, D. A., Berridge, K. C., Grill, H. J., & Ternes, J. W. (1985). Rats learn to like the taste of morphine. *Behavioral Neuroscience, 99,* 290–300.

Zellner, D. A., Rozin, P., Aron, M. & Kulish, C. (1983). Conditioned enhancement of human's liking for flavor by pairing with sweetness. *Learning and Motivation, 14,* 338–350.

Zuckerman, M. (1979). *Sensation seeking: Beyond the optimal level of arousal.* Hillsdale: NJ: Lawrence Erlbaum Associates.

Author Index

A

Abelson, M. L., 101, 102
Abraham, S. F., 170, 177, 185, 196
Adair, E. R., 22, 26
Adam, W. R., 93, 101
Adler, N. T., 92, 104
Adolph, E. F., 127, 141
Aguilar-Baturoni, H. U., 118, 124
Aimez, P., 186, 191, 196
Alheid, G. F., 101, 102
Allan, R. W., 92, 102
Almli, C. R., 147, 151, 156
Ambrose, F. G., 119, 124
Anderson, N. H., 42, 52
Antonucci, R. F., 64, 71, 83
Apfelbaum, M., 211, 215
Arbour, K. J., 33, 52
Archer, T., 40, 57
Arent, H., 91, 102
Arnell, P., 93, 97, 104
Aron, M., 21, 28, 107, 126, 161, 183, 205, 206, 217
Aronson, E., 211, 215
Ashby, F., 42, 52
Atema, J., 173, 181
Autry, W. L., 119, 124
Azen, E. A., 167, 177

B

Baile, C. A., 119, 124
Bailey, C., 2, 12

Bain, A., 4, 12
Baker, B. J., 32, 34, 36, 38, 41, 48, 52, 54
Banks, W. A., 118, 126
Barbaz, 119, 124
Bare, J. K., 91, 101
Barnwell, G. M., 171, 177
Barone, F. C., 118, 124
Bartholomew, G. A., 169, 177
Bartoshuk, L. M., 16, 17, 18, 19, 20, 23, 24, 25, 26, 27, 28, 93, 101, 163, 178, 195, 215
Bean, N. J., 175, 178, 179, 181
Beauchamp, G. K., 21, 22, 26, 28, 96, 101, 147, 150, 153, 154, 155, 160, 161, 162, 163, 164, 165, 166, 169, 170, 171, 178, 179, 180, 181
Beumont, P. J. V., 185, 196
Bedard, M., 70, 73, 74, 82
Beebe-Center, J. G., 10, 12
Beidler, L. M., 23, 26, 63, 82, 167, 182
Beily, J., 169, 181
Bellisle, F., 186, 191, 196, 197
Bell, F. G., 162, 178
Beltramino, C. A., 101, 102
Bentham, J., 4, 12
Berk, G., 152, 157, 201, 208, 216
Berkun, M. M., 73, 82
Bermudez-Rattoni, F., 43, 56
Bernstein, I. L., 22, 26, 150, 151, 152, 155, 156, 160, 180

219

Subject Index